TO LISA
& PAUL.

The
Reluctant
Refugee

Are lingering memories worth retaining?

The Reluctant Refugee

George M. Decsy

Buccaneer Books

ISBN printed book: 979-8-69601-923-9

Cover design by Danzig Decsy
Internal design by Nonon Tech & Design

PROLOGUE:

If you asked me where I'm from my answer would be England. This is the land that welcomed, nurtured and educated me. I am grateful for that.

Yet there is a part of me that will always be the refugee, the 'other', the onlooker, the outsider, the stranger.

Is the place we call 'home' a mere accident of birth or where one finds comfortable refuge? Is 'father' the unwitting sperm donor or the man who is there to catch you when you fall, shows the way when lost, tucks you in, reads you to sleep?

To seek answers to these pressing questions I make plans to take my family on a journey back to Hungary.

In my eagerness to belong, to settle in my new home, I have purposefully remained ignorant of the land of my birth.

Now, driven by recent events I am keen to take the measure of the land and its people.

To connect with my childhood friend Laci and above all to find this mythical man, this ghost, this legend, my father.

Does he know of me, who I am, where or how I live?

Probably knows no more of me than I know of him.

We are adrift in time separated by space, I am determined to close the gap.

CHAPTER 1

Tooting Bec, London 1989

Panting, her tongue lolling, Jessie stood waiting patiently as I fiddled with the keys. Removing the padlocks, I squatted, gripped the shutters with both hands and in an Olympic-style snatch, jerked them past the bent bit. The Brixton Riots a few years ago had stimulated some local activity, and a half-arsed attempt to breach the outer defences had left a bit of a kink in the mechanism. The 'emporium' was open for business.

Jessie pushed past me, making straight for her mat behind the counter and flopped with a grunt to snooze.

A fine example of her breed, and a well-loved family pet, but a reluctant deterrent.

When her doggie suspicions were aroused the shiny canines behind snarl-curled lips were indiscriminately bared at all customers including, often, regulars bearing treats.

She was reliably inconsistent.

In spite of me nudging her gently with my feet under the counter she managed to slumber through two strong-arm robberies in the last 7 years. I loved that dog.

I hardly had time to turn the lights on before the first of my Friday visitors edged up to the window. I hesitate to call them customers as they rarely bought anything.

Except for 'Radio Man'. He was the first to arrive. Cupping his hands to shade his eyes from the reflected morning sun, he peered at the dusty, haphazardly displayed merchandise on offer.

Satisfied all was well, he straightened up, leaving a greasy smudge on the glass. No matter, this is the day a man claiming to be a window cleaner was due to smear a dirty rag around the window.

'Radio Man' was unpredictable but could be relied upon to spend a good deal of his weekly allowance on cheap transistor radios. Opening the door he shouted, "Hello... I am here!" Jessie just twitched an ear.

Stumbling over the threshold, his slight frame burdened by many more layers of clothing than the August temperatures warranted, he shuffled menacingly towards me, a clear indication of the effects of his medication, Thorazine.

In his outstretched right hand was a jumble of multi-coloured wires bursting out of an orange plastic box.

Jessie snoozed on.

"It doesn't work." Clutched in his grubby hands was what once had been a small, orange plastic transistor radio.

He squinted at me through thick lenses of skewed glasses astride his thin, pointy nose.

The whole effect was of a rather confused weasel with a roll-up seemingly glued to his bottom lip.

"What have you done now?" I chided him gently, annoyed that he was so early.

"Let me see it."

Somewhat reluctantly he handed it over. At a glance I saw that since his last visit the previous Friday, for reasons known only to him and perhaps his minders, he had rewired the internal circuitry of the radio with predictable results.

It was what we in the trade referred to as 'beyond repair'. I threw it in the bin and reached up for a replacement.

"I'm out of orange, I have blue, red, grey and white." He settled for red. I prised the cover off of the battery compartment, inserted two fresh double As, and turned it on. Tinny music emanated from the washer-sized speaker. Retailing at £6.95 it was not what one would call high fidelity.

I pressed him. "Why do you keep fiddling around with it? If you move even one wire it will stop working."

Scanning the shop left and right, satisfied that we were alone, he leaned in conspiratorially. "I am talking to Mars." It was a slow morning and my curiosity was aroused.

"What do you talk about?"

He opened his gap-toothed mouth to speak but was suddenly distracted by the contents of the large, brown ceramic ashtray lurking behind the Duracell rack.

Yesterday it had taken Mrs. White ten minutes of idle chit-chat and two king-sized Marlboros to ask me to sub her a tenner until she could get down to the P.O. to pick up her pension. The maroon smudges on the filters hinted at a much younger, sexier woman.

Radio Man pointed to the ashtray. "Can I have those?"

"Help yourself, mate...take whatever you want." Without hesitation he fished the fag ends out of the tray and put them on the counter.

Reaching deep, he unburdened the pockets of his heavy overcoat, laying the contents next to the dog-ends.

In no particular order: Two grubby, snot-encrusted handkerchiefs; a cast metal double-decker London bus; Golden Virginia tobacco pouch; orange plastic BiC lighter; a small notebook with an elastic band around it; a handful of coins; and finally a jumbo-sized box of matches with no lucifers but housing a rather large and shiny cockroach-like beetle. As the creature made no attempt to escape I assumed it was dead. He added Mrs. White's leavings to the collection.

"What about those?" He pointed to the empty ashtray. "What about what?"

"Those!"

"WHAT!?"

This could go on.

There was nothing in the ashtray apart from a few dead matches.

"Why do you want them?"

Without answering, he scooped up the dead matches. Selecting the one which must have failed to ignite and was merely blackened at the phosphor end, he inserted it in his left ear (alarmingly deep for my liking). Enraptured, he manipulated the stick even deeper into his lughole.

"Stop that! What the fuck are you doing?" Removing his glasses he looked at me with childlike intensity.

"I'm talking to my people...on Mars." Without pause he added, "I could kill you if I wanted to."

"If you did where would you get your weekly radio fix from?" That was good.

I waited to see what was coming next but he just stared at me. We stood inches apart as he inserted a second match into his other ear, rolling the sticks between his thumbs and index fingers apparently fine-tuning the messages beamed to him from the red planet.

It was my lucky day. My life was to be spared.

As if they had spent their potential, he removed the sticks from his ears and threw them back in the ashtray. Turning without a word he left the shop, the red transistor pressed against his ear, faint distorted sounds of what might have been 'Space Oddity' leaking past his right ear.

He would be one of many today.

Close proximity to Tooting Bec Psychiatric Hospital had its challenges.

Normally, Friday was the day that the socially adept were allowed out to irritate local shopkeepers: some even had special outfits for the occasion.

There was the Milkman. I think it was the cap that he was fond of wearing which prompted his name. He usually popped in to pass the time. Unduly fond of snuff, brown rivulets dribbled out of his nostrils as he snorted his way through a series of questions/ statements directed at a stack of used amps. Failing to get a response, he twiddled some of the knobs before turning to face me with further inquiries. I looked at him evenly as he continued to ramble on, knowing that any response from me would only prolong the episode.

Having made his opening statements he gestured wildly, spun on his glossy, black, eight-eye DMs and headed for the door. As he stepped into the street he looked back at me with undisguised pity to remind me that there were prisons without bars.

I rang up another 'No Sale'.

From behind me, in the workshop I could hear the kettle being filled.

Then this Jock breezed in flogging fire extinguishers.

"Hey, Kev!" I shouted over my shoulder. "Come and see this."

"What is it?"

"Just come upfront for a minute, you might want one of these for your van."

I could barely follow what Jocky was all about but sensing mild interest on my part he was keen to demo the sleek, red contraption.

"Have ye got a wee bit o' pepper?" he gushed in anticipation.

"What do you need pepper for?" Kev and I looked at each other, then Jocky.

"No, no, I mean like an old newspaper." This delivered in heavy Glaswegian.

I found an old *Exchange & Mart* under the counter, tore out some pages and crumpled them, building a neat pyre on the carpet.

Jocky had the extinguisher in hand. "Ready?" He thumbed the wheel on his Zippo. As the flames rose Kev and I took a step back. Jocky, relishing the moment, waited a little longer than may have been prudent before he finally pointed the nozzle at the base of the fire and pulled the trigger.

Nothing happened. He squeezed again, harder this time with an additional little jiggle of the trigger mechanism. Ashen cheeks turned rosy and tiny beads of sweat appeared on his forehead.

Perhaps it was from the infrared generated by the rapidly rising flames. Hard to tell as the plastic carpet was now starting to melt and a noxious cloud obscured much of the view. Spluttering, cursing colourfully, Jocky made a dash for the door, abandoning extinguisher and demo.

Laughing hysterically Kevin and I did a fair imitation of a Scottish sword dance on the smouldering carpet. Our efforts only managed to spread the flames and it was getting out of control when our shouts brought Paul, armed with the large extinguisher, from the workshop.

"Insurance job, is it? You could have fucking warned us!"

It took a while to convince him that Jocky was not a figment… even with the extinguisher as evidence.

It was shaping up to be just another Friday in Tooting.

Then the phone rang.

Normally I would answer, "TV Centre!" But today I just said, "Hello."

What I heard would change my life.

"Darlink…I just gotta letta from Ilona. Your fava is very sick and vil die soon!"

Even though my mother Gita was not known for her subtlety, this offhand statement came as a bit of a shock.

I had never met this man, my father. He existed in legend and played no part in my childhood or formative years, yet he somehow persisted in my thoughts; I even carried a small, crinkle-cut black and white photo of him in my wallet. From time to time I wondered who he was and what might have been but shied away from deeper speculation.

"I'll come round and read the letter after work." She was a slave to drama and the mouthpiece on her phone, strapped with layers of Sellotape to prevent germs from hiding in the holes, did nothing to promote clear communications.

I hung up.

"That was my mother. She says my father is on his last legs…I need to talk to Billy about some jeans."

Kev looked puzzled. "You told me you didn't have a father… why do you need jeans?"

"I'll explain later…give Billy a call." Also… "I may need a bit of help…Do you think you could look after Jesso for a few days?"

If he agreed I could easily stretch those few days to a couple of weeks.

"Of course, mate!" Kev did not hesitate. "Just have to OK it with her indoors."

Before Kevin could pick up the phone Billy staggered in with a huge, 27" Sony Trinitron.

His fondness for single malt and Marlboros did little to prepare him for the ever-larger, heavier TV sets. Panting with the effort; a bead of sweat dripped from his nose onto the charred carpet.

I waited as he lowered the giant screen to the floor and caught his breath.

"Need a lot of jeans, Billy…can you have a word with Charlie?"

I never knew my father but I did know of him. Gita had nothing but glowing praise for this man.

I had learned to take the tales of her previous life with a very large pinch of salt. The misty-eyed accounts of moonlight on the Danube, as they strolled arm-in-arm across the Chain Bridge from Buda to Pest left me unconvinced.

If they were so besotted with each other how could he abandon her knowing she was carrying his child? Maybe he did not know. I found that notion a little hard to believe but gave him the benefit of the doubt.

Should I be angry, resentful?

Perhaps…but mostly I was curious.

Life was full of distraction; it was easy to find excuses to put aside thoughts of my father. But now the news of his illness had forced my hand and I felt I had to go and find him. There were questions that only he could answer.

I needed to look into my father's eyes.

The possibility of meeting him suddenly became real and I was overwhelmed by a deep wave of sadness.

I started to make preparations to go back to Hungary.

"Have you got your keys? Can you lock up for me if I leave early?"

"No worries, mate!" Kevin said in a poor imitation of Crocodile Dundee.

"Why are you doing Paul Hogan today?"

Kevin shrugged. "Got bored with Scotty." He rattled his keys at me, I threw some mail into my briefcase and clicked it shut.

Jessie immediately perked up, coming over and wagging her tail.

"Sit!" Patting her head I clipped the leash to her collar and headed out of the door. Eager to leave, she pulled me around the corner to the parked car, and settled herself on the back seat as I headed for Streatham.

My mother's street, tucked behind the ice rink, was typical of the area.

The semi-detached Edwardian houses, inhabited by the aspiring working classes, vied for distinction. This eternal internal struggle was manifest in the upgrades visible to the casual observer.

These 'improvements' often included the replacement of the original leaded glass doors with sharp-edged mahogany. Imported Chinese brass fittings completed the 'upgrade'.

On some of the houses the windows were replaced with eye-popping Arctic-white double-glazed units. For those swayed by the sales patter and easy terms offered the red London brick was clad in precast stone-like panels, transforming the modest dwelling into an ersatz castle.

Gita greatly admired the customising efforts of her neighbours but thankfully lacked the necessary funds to make any spectacular changes. Nevertheless, her house was easily distinguished by its dilapidation.

At some point the previous occupants had made their mark on the property. The house was now shedding its pebble-dash, shrugging off its roof tiles, the paint peeling. Paving stones leading up to her front door lay unevenly, ready to twist the ankles of the unwary visitor.

Ever practical, she had replaced the missing panes of stained glass with cereal box-quality cardboard reinforced with sticky tape.

The wildly exuberant privet hedge obscured the rubbish tip which could have been her small front garden. A rotting wooden gate sagged on its hinges and had to be lifted to swing.

Here lived a woman unable to leave unmolested a screw blissfully rusting in a puddle. The elastic band dropped by a careless postman would be scooped up and added to her hoard.

The bell had not worked for years.

Over time she had almost imperceptibly slipped from being that jolly old lady with the red hair and funny accent to her present state of disconnection. Hard to say when the behaviours went from odd to eccentric. What had reduced this proud, funny, independent woman to the queen of junk?

Rejecting the world, she erected a bulwark behind which she spent her days in slow decline. Her only companions were a collection of cats and a doleful-looking dog named Lulu. Isolated by the ever-increasing piles of clutter, she sank into despair. Seeing her so diminished was profoundly saddening to me, making the yearning to seek out my father all the more compelling.

So with a sigh I lifted the heavy metal knocker and brought it down hard, hammering until the loose screws on the strike plate were threatening to jump out of their holes. Muffled barking from somewhere deep inside indicated that she must be home.

I stood waiting; perhaps she was busy rearranging the rusting heaps of junk in the back garden or taking a nap.

Just as I was about to turn to leave – "Who is it?"

"It's me!"

She made cooing noises as the sturdy bolts were drawn.

As ever she welcomed me with hugs and kisses before backing up slightly to let me in. There was some dried cat shit on the threadbare rug.

Turning, she flicked it off the carpet onto the floorboards with the side of her foot.

I had to accept that she was beyond any help her children could practically offer. The very idea that she should seek professional help was met with derision and hostility.

She would become agitated at the mere suggestion that there may be something unconventional about her lifestyle. "I do not want strangers poking their noses into my business."

Possessed by the demon of accumulation, she was incapable of letting go of any item that may, by the remotest of chances, at some vague future date be just the thing she needed.

"That knob you want for your kitchen door, I have one, I just don't know where it is!"

Nothing was without value. Nothing was past utility. Whatever was needed she had at least one of them. But where could it be found?

The usable strip of the hallway was so narrowed by the accumulation of stuff that she had to barge her way back in. I followed, turning sideways to avoid being smeared by unknown contaminants.

Sensing my silent condemnation, she said, "I will move this stuff next time."

I had been hearing that for years.

The piles of boxes, bundles of clothes and unidentifiable objects so dear to her hoarder's heart crowded the hall, leaving just enough of a gap to squeeze through to the first door on the left. I followed her into the space the estate agent had optimistically labelled as the 'drawing' room.

This was not for the faint of heart.

"How are you, darling? You too thin! Wanna cuppa tea? Biscuit?" It is hard to talk while holding one's breath.

"No thanks, Mum...I just ate." Oblivious to the smell she chatted on cheerily.

Taking advantage of a pause, I got to the point; "Could I see the letter you told me about on the phone?" She looked confused, as if it had already slipped her mind.

"The letter from Ilona about my father."

"Oh yes, it's around here somewhere".

She looked around then abruptly left the room.

I stood waiting.

Many minutes later, with a big smile she returned.

"I found it!"

I took it from her and looked at the page.

It was in Hungarian.

"Can you read it to me please?"

There was a lot of chit-chat but the crux of the matter was that my father was gravely ill and was not expected to be around much longer.

My mind was made up.

"I am going to Hungary to find him. Where should I start?"

Suddenly silent she looked around for somewhere to sit.

I moved a huge bundle of mildewing fabric off an armchair. She sat heavily, raised her head as I stood waiting, a little closer than I would normally consider a proper distance.

"I will tell you everything I know."

As it turned out this was not much.

"Do you have a phone number or address for him?"

"Ay, Istenem, Istenem. No, I do not have phone number or address, I will give you my sister Ilona address she maybe has it." Gita had a tendency to mash her languages when stressed.

I had no memory of ever having met her, but Ilona's name had come up from time to time. Gita had shown me photos but was never able to fully explain how they looked nothing like each other and there did not seem to be any evidence which would indicate sisterhood.

As if forewarned she uncurled her fingers to show a crumpled piece of paper with some wobbly words scratched on it.

"Here is her address, maybe Ilona can help you." I took it from her, smoothed it out with the heel of my hand. It was just about legible.

"Are they still into denim over there?"

"Ah yes yes…You can easy sell all you take, take big size, many fat bottoms over there."

She chuckled, her round face lit up. "Look, my forehead, no lines. Do not frown it make you look grumpy and wrinkly."

As ever she was full of helpful pointers to improve my life.

The trafficking advice, however, did turn out to be sound. Back in 1976 Gita had driven her temperamental old Hillman Minx to Hungary, financing the whole affair with a boot full of pre-shrunk 501s in popular sizes.

To her delight and my surprise she sold the lot in a couple of days. This was good news.

Although still under Communist rule, the government, sensing a whiff of change, practised a much less oppressive stance on petty capitalism and a more relaxed travel policy than the other members of the Warsaw Pact.

Emboldened by the protection offered by her brand new British passport she felt safe enough to start making plans. It was impossible not to admire her cheerful optimism in spite of all indicators pointing to an unequivocal thumbs-down from the Examiner.

What to most would be a hurdle worthy of Aintree was to her a mere trifle, the driver's licence.

Like a beacon for distressed mariners, orange/red hair plainly visible against the lush green grass of the 'Common', she wandered aimlessly, dragging her reluctant dog which, having done its business, just wanted to go home.

As if in silent prayer, her lips moved involuntarily as she periodically glanced down at the thin booklet.

In her head the dream of driving back to the land of her birth. In her hand a copy of the Highway Code.

As an instructor I was a complete and utter failure, at least as far as my mother was concerned. Her lack of co-ordination, wilful ignorance of the basic functions of mechanical transportation and a complete disregard for the rules of motoring made her a rolling menace.

What to the average driver would have been easily avoidable fender benders were for her a fairly frequent fact of motoring life. These minor knocks often happened when she momentarily took her attention away from the road and onto the plastic flowers (courtesy Lever Bros Industries) crammed into a jam jar affixed to the dash with home-made glue.

This paste was of her own devising; the full list of ingredients were known only to her, but to my certain knowledge included flour, milk and eggs. I am unsure if this was a last resort food source in case of nuclear war (she was convinced it was imminent) as she also routinely kept a small pantry-full of emergency rations in her glovebox.

In any case she used this 'glue' whenever or wherever adhesion was called for.

So effective was this recipe that the jar remained fast in all weathers while the flower arrangement routinely needed rearrangement mainly due to her reckless cornering which, she insisted, was 'sporty' motoring.

In spite of the erratic driving her copybook remained unblotted, never troubled by parking tickets, and was the proud holder of a clean provisional licence.

I abandoned her to professional instruction.

Many lessons and instructors followed, some of whom did not last long enough to get out of the driveway before experiencing life-changing events and others, forewarned through the local grapevine, simply failed to show at the appointed time.

One particular unfortunate sent her a full refund of prepaid monies and along with the cheque offered the strongly worded suggestion that she continue to use the excellent public transport available.

To avoid all further contact he followed this with a cryptic note written on St George's Hospital headed paper, informing her that he had been voluntarily admitted and was under indefinite observation.

Sometime later, much to everybody's astonishment, by a combination of luck and artifice, she passed her driving test.

Coming from a culture where bribery and backhanders were the norm and the test a much more casual affair, she sweetened the pot by 'gifting' her examiner a cigar.

Designed to impress and to facilitate a favourable outcome, the rolled leaf had to have the appearance of outstanding quality. Through her connections in what we now call the 'hospitality industry' she acquired a selection of aluminium cigar tubes and the 'rings' of renowned brands harvested from the ashtrays of fancy restaurants.

With a small investment, little fuss and crafty fingers the cheap and nasty were transformed.

The lucky recipient, unacquainted with the genuine article, showed appropriate appreciation.

Though I admired the enterprise and the pioneering counterfeiting effort I still strongly disapproved of the practice and was embarrassed for her.

Fluttering her hands, she waved me aside. "Darlink…that is how the world goes round!"

The deed done, the ink barely dry on her new licence, she began preparations to drive herself to Hungary.

In the days before charity shops abutted Chicken Shacks and Kebab Joints were considered too exotic for the high street she trawled the markets for quality used clothing, carefully selecting and combining complete outfits for her intended recipients. The packages were then wrapped in brown paper tied with string and labelled. Neatly arranged on top of the stash of Levi's crammed into every corner of the boot the custom packages intended for specific individuals could, with luck and her ability to obfuscate, help to conceal the contraband.

Unaccustomed to such abuse, the leaf springs on the old Minx straightened alarmingly, manfully exceeding the engineers' wildest calculations.

The car was also customised to meet her needs; the black rubber floor covering was overlaid by beige shag pile carpet, tastefully complemented by hand-sewn custom-fitted patchwork quilt seat covers throughout with small, round fabric-covered centre-button scatter cushions in lime green, arranged, sofa- like, on the back seat.

To facilitate steering accuracy and to make it easier for her chubby fingers to grip, the wheel was sheathed in the carpet remnants.

Nothing was left unmodified.

Additional ashtrays made from the heavy tinfoil saved from individual steak and kidney pies were hung from the tops of the front windows.

Thin wire coat hangers were painstakingly fashioned into brackets to hold jam jars for the plastic flowers and, as at this time she was still under her own God delusion, a small, hand-painted papier mâché Virgin Mary was glued to the top of the dash.

Interior decorations complete, she turned her attention to provisioning.

Assorted cutlery, salt, pepper, toilet paper and a vicious-looking carving knife the size of a small scimitar were stored in the glovebox.

Wire fittings were fastened to one of the back windows upon which conjoined-twin jumbo salamis were hung. Gradually succumbing to Newton's law they tugged towards the earth's molten core, preventing the window from being fully wound shut. Running out of usable storage space, the passenger seat was rendered immovable due to the jars of gherkins and pickled red peppers wedged therein and below.

With fuel expenses calculated to the penny there was nothing left for hotels, or indeed for restaurant meals; she intended to supplement the salamis with shop-bought bread and salad items, stopping at the side of a suitable road to bed down on the back seat.

The fact that both she and the car would smell like a well-established Soho deli frequented by chain-smoking bohemians was of little interest to her – it was a small price to pay for economy and independence.

Finally, a detailed Michelin map of Europe was spread on the kitchen floor. Pointing excitedly, her finger traced the intended route.

"Darlink… Let's have a cuppa!"

Although wily enough to flee the tentacled embrace of the Communist regime, she had not escaped the particularly British compulsion to soothe her troubled mind with a nice cup of Rosie Lee.

In the end Gita only managed a few days in Budapest, long enough to unload the denim and do the legwork to visit some of her friends. She made no attempt to find my father, the oft-proclaimed love of her life. Returning with fingernails unmolested she told me that, although she had managed to find some of her old friends, the relatives proved more elusive. How would my father and his wife have reacted to her showing up? I suspected she was afraid of what she would have found.

"How could you leave without trying to find him?" She shrugged.

Two days before she was due to start driving back to London she learned that my father was alive but for reasons unknown confined to a wheelchair.

"I had no time, what could I do? No address, no phone – nothing!"

It seemed a pretty flimsy excuse. I felt she did not try very hard; cherished memories will not stand close scrutiny.

I would not give up so easily.

My mother was always somewhat of a mystery to me. I could never get a solid explanation from her as to where exactly she was born and under what circumstances. As the years took their toll she slipped further into fantasy, and stories relating to her earlier life in Budapest became increasingly implausible. Seeing her so diminished had a dramatic effect on all her children, but was especially hard on my younger brother Akos, who, as if by contagion, had also become obsessive.

While vital and fully engaged in life, she was a short, round, Hungarian lady of indefatigable spirit who spoke like Zsa Zsa

Gabor and drove like Attila the Hun rampaging through the leafy lanes of Clapham.

Parking her car was never a problem: she simply abandoned her vehicle wherever the fancy took her without regard to road markings, signage or indeed pedestrians.

Somehow, she had a way of confusing the police and parking wardens with a combination of unintelligible excuses and the projected image of an amiable yet potentially dangerous eccentric. This was exactly what she was.

Until the grave news landed in Gita's letter box I had never really felt compelled to return to Hungary. News of my father's condition and imminent demise spurred me to action and now I had an urgent need to find this man before it was too late.

Not only had I detached from my father but had also lost touch with my best friend and constant childhood companion, Laci.

In truth, I made no effort to keep in touch. Trying hard to be in my new life, I wanted to leave the old world behind. Yet at times his open, smiling face still popped into my consciousness. Even after all these years some of the antics we used to get up to bring a smile to my face.

We watched hours of newsreels and feature films. One of our favourite games was 'Runner'.

Our flats were in a three-storey, eclectically styled building formed around a square central courtyard; on one corner was a cinema to which I had unfettered access without riffling my mother's purse.

Through simple observation I had figured out an easy way of getting in without paying. This piece of intelligence was shared freely with Laci, my main co-conspirator, and any number of my mates.

The rear exit opened up into our courtyard and had a 'push bar'-type of lock on the inside. Throughout the day a steady trickle of people would use this door to leave and I would be ready to slip in and take a seat if one was available. As the cost of entry was relatively cheap more often than not there was standing room only at the sides and back of the auditorium with some people sitting on the floor in the aisles. Cinema, as with all other forms of media, was an organ of state propaganda; theatres were everywhere, and attendance was strongly encouraged.

Eventually, when the number of gatecrashers became impossible to ignore, the management would station an usher by the door.

Plan 'B' was a little more involved and needed an accomplice; Laci was always ready to go.

When the door was pushed open, one kid (the Runner) would rush past the aged attendant (the largely sedentary nature of this job made it a 'special occupation' which was generally reserved for the older workforce in this Communist nirvana); instinctively he/she would creakily chase after the kid with little chance of actually catching the nimble scamp, leaving the door unguarded and making it easy for any number of us to slip in unhindered.

Being egalitarians and good Young Communists we took turns at being the 'Runner'. It was a low-risk high-reward business; at worst, we had an ear tweaked, some mild rebuke followed by ejection.

As with just about everything else the movie house was state-owned and the employees had little incentive to enforce rules. We saw every show on offer at least once; weekends, Laci and I wasted many hours watching films over and over again, especially if it was a good war film. The heroic Red Army beating the snot out of the Nazis was a favourite recurring theme.

I could only hope that Laci was still at the same address. It would be fantastic to see him. No way to make contact so it would just have to be a surprise visit. I could hardly wait to see the look on his face when he found me at his door.

Seeing him was, in many ways, just as important to me as a meeting with my enigmatic father.

While making preparations I was, at times, very conflicted about the visit. I desperately wanted to preserve my mother's image of this mythical man. The feeling that I was walking into an emotional quagmire was never far from my mind.

When Gita's mind took her back to her youth and happier times, she told me. "He was such an interesting, wonderfully romantikus man, we were so in love. I still have a hole in my heart that only his shoes could fill."

I knew what she meant and stayed my lips.

Combining a family holiday with sleuth work seemed like a good solution and appealed to my inner Sherlock.

Technically 'stateless' I was still using a travel document issued by the Home Office to get around on. It took over three weeks to get the Hungarian visa organised and almost as long for Billy to unleash Charlie, who in turn came up with the jeans in appropriate sizes and quantities. Charlie (not his real name) was one of the local villains specialising in men's apparel.

Tooting had a fair cohort of sole trader entrepreneurs who could somehow come up with very affordable goods of excellent quality if given time.

The denim started to pile up in the back of the shop.

I often take rumours for reliable information but I was not entirely convinced and did not fully trust my mother's account of her foray into the black market for blue jeans.

Nevertheless, I invested heavily, ready to take advantage of the market if Mr. Levi's fashionably cut, double-stitched, copper-riveted products were still in high demand.

Some would be given away as gifts, bartered or sold, and at a pinch (or to avoid a pinch) could come in handy to bribe low-level officials, Customs, traffic cops and such.

The process of transitioning from Communism to some form of free market commercialism hopefully still held the Magyars in a state of transitional-capitalist torpor.

CHAPTER 2

GETTING READY

It was all coming together. Travel plans were firmed up. Arrangements for Jessie to stay at Kevin's finalised. As our departure date approached my trepidation about the whole enterprise increased dramatically. What were my motives?

What would I learn from him? What skeletons would rattle out of the family closet? Maybe I should just change direction and head south to the sun-drenched Côte d'Azur! In spite of the internal conflict I pressed on.

I raised my eyes from the chessboard and looked across at my daughter.

"Are you excited about driving to Hungary?"

Hesitantly Petra fingered the bishop and met my gaze.

How did Phoebe and I manage to produce such a beautiful, clever child? She knew all the moves, but at six years old she was still learning strategy and I could see that she was about to make a fatal move.

"Y-es…I am…but a little bit scared, too." That was exactly how I felt but I wanted to allay her fears.

"It's not like it used to be when I was a kid: they welcome tourists now."

Phoebe, my partner, was thumbing the remote for something to watch on the box. We had 'cohabited' for some 10 years, most of which were happy or at least with some measure of contentment. More recently, indications were that we were dragging our anchor onto a lee shore.

Perhaps this journey would bring us fair winds.

Jessie was lying on her bed next to the fireplace, gnawing happily on a rawhide chewy. Ears pricked up momentarily as the phone rang.

"Having a few people over for dinner Saturday, can you make it?"

I placed my hand over the mouthpiece and turned to Phoebe. "Fancy dinner at the 'Mansions' on Saturday?"

"What... with that nutty friend of yours? What's his name? Harry, Larry, Gary?"

"His name is Barry and he's an actor!" So he claims, I thought to myself.

"No! No! At Zoe's place."

Phoebe hesitated a long second. "You go...I have to get ready for the trip."

Her flat was a lively gathering spot for the neighbourhood and a refuge for an eclectic bunch of characters. Zoe always had a pot of coffee or a bottle of wine on the go. She had a sympathetic ear and a knack of putting people together.

Need a plumber? She knew a good one.

Marriage on the rocks? She would reach for her Filofax.

She and I had lived together a few years before and, even though she chucked me out, we stayed very good friends.

Her regular, well-attended dinner parties often ended in a jolly, alcohol and hashish-induced haze.

It was all good, clean fun.

Around the kitchen table were arranged the usual suspects.

Directly across from me sat Colin: rotund, gold wire-rimmed glasses, he covered his highly reflective head, in keeping with his calling as an artist, with a black beret. Inexplicably, he somehow managed to combined his love for WWII-era militaria with the life of a bohemian. The walls of his house were heavily arrayed with his speciality, erotic art. To his left, wife Noli perched delicately on the edge of her chair. She was a rather shrill diminutive Filipino lady with a fondness for slim, well-chiselled younger men. Colin, immersed in his artistic life, appeared to pay no heed to her infidelities.

On the other side of Colin, appealingly arranged, sat Elliot, a great raconteur and ladies' man. I suspected he had shagged just about every eligible woman in the 'Mansions', and arguably much further afield. He lived in the flat directly above Zoe, and when not lecturing in French at a London college he tinkled on his piano and recited poetry as part of a larger effort to seduce the current object of his desire. I admired his sophisticated wit, easy laugh and roguish charm.

Ahmed, Zoe's brother, uncorked his bottles. A connoisseur of wine and indeed the founder of Oddbins, the first warehouse-style vintners in the UK, he nevertheless enjoyed hearing our totally unqualified opinions of the wines he was generous enough to bring to the party.

Flitting from stove to table with steaming dishes of food was Julie, Zoe's lodger from New Zealand. At times she was known to hide under the very same kitchen table in an effort to avoid the unwanted attentions of would-be suitors!

Warren was quiet, a bit on the moody side, as befitted a musician.

Q: What do you call those people that hang around musicians? Groupies, I hear you say. A: Drummers.

Warren was the drummer in a band called Tiger Lily (later Ultravox) which meant nothing to any of us at the time.

Trying to engage Warren was Darren, Zoe's flouncy hairdresser.

"Show me how you hold your sticks." He handed Warren the wooden salad spoon and fork in what I thought to be a highly suggestive way. With a raised eyebrow he said, "Do you prefer the traditional or matched grip?"

The heavy slash of mascara darkening Warren's lids combined with the jet black nail polish sent a confusing message. Looking at Darren evenly he said, "Many blokes have made the mistake of assuming that I'm gay, the most persistent of which have had to acquire a liking for hospital food." Darren inexplicably lost interest and turned his attentions to Young Steve. With a tug at his Ali Baba-style trousers, he said, "Why do you use string to keep them up?"

"To stop them from falling down, besides, it is not string, it's twine." The pedantic bohemian Steve was the only true hippy at the table. To say that he was sartorially challenged would be a gross understatement. He paid no attention to his appearance, preferring to spend his money on King Crimson and Zappa albums. Said very little but rolled the best joints for miles around.

I was a part of all this yet still apart. The feeling that somehow I was an impostor, a fraud and did not belong followed me everywhere, and to this day I have never experienced a real sense of belonging.

Gita had been over visiting a friend in the 'Mansions' and was on her way back to her car. Her current canine companion Sally, tugging at the leash, eager to get home

Through the kitchen window Zoe spotted her returning from a walk in the garden. The raucous laughter and artificial light seeping into the courtyard attracted Gita and she strayed too close.

The back door flew open. "Come and have a glass of wine with us, Gita!"

With gentle cajoling and the offer of chocolate cake she deigned to join the company.

The dinner was over and the party well underway... wine was drunk, lies were told, spliffs were rolled and chillums puffed.

Although not a drinker she was persuaded to stay and have a glass of chilled Blue Nun.

We seated her near the open door, the dog settled under the dining table. Still, she complained loudly about the clouds of smoke and the low quality of my 'prolly' friends.

Curling her lip and eyeing the somewhat stupefied gathering with distaste, she muttered under her breath, but loud enough for all to hear, "Fuy! Disgusting!"

Two small glasses of wine were enough to fully realise her potential (not to mention the second-hand smoke).

Sitting back, visibly relaxing, and with a captive audience she launched into her favourite topic – the beauty and charm of Budapest and her place in the life of the city.

Among her many boasts she claimed to have rowed the Danube – when pressed to qualify the statement (length or breadth) she deftly changed the subject.

She told of her many suitors and admirers...

"Darling, when I was in Budapest, young, slim and beautiful I have many men of quality and knocking my doors... doctors, professors, earls, barons, cunts."

"She means COUNTS," I added hastily to the slightly shocked gathering, thinking – no, knowing – without reservation that she was right in her pronunciation of those morally suspect aristocrats.

She looked around the room wistfully, eyes momentarily resting on the framed print of Ganesh hanging above Elliot's head.

"Why does that man have the head of an elephant?" Without waiting for an answer she launched into her story.

Her eyes grew moist as she transported herself back to Budapest 1944–5, struggling to convey her depth of feeling for this man... my father... Janos Strohmeyer.

It occurred to me for the first time that this man, whose surname had, until recently, not been mentioned, may well be Jewish. This was puzzling to me as Gita was a self-professed, unapologetic racial bigot having scant regard for Jews, Gypsies, Negroes or Russians.

In many ways her political views neatly coincided with those of Herr Hitler.

The Germans were gentlemen, always respectful and polite even as they packed her neighbours into cattle wagons.

Black people were outside her direct experience but her prejudices were readily reinforced by the images as depicted on the silver screen. As a result she considered them savages, little better than semi-articulate chimps, and indeed would cross the road to avoid getting too close, fearing she would be assaulted.

"Darling, you can't tell what they are thinking!"

No amount of zigzagging down the street would put enough of a bubble around her to make her feel safe. To my knowledge she had never met a 'person of colour' until we landed in England, so where did this fear come from? To my shame and regret, until I ended up in an English RC school and made my first black friend, I held similar beliefs.

Ironically, my mother's prejudices were abruptly challenged one fateful afternoon.

Her lover, Victor, not inclined to accurate measurement, especially when in his cups, had been instructed to install a peephole in the front door of our flat (increasingly popular with wary city dwellers) set just slightly off-centre and at a height that she would have to stand on tiptoe to see out of.

From this relatively lofty vantage point it was easier to spot the rent collector or the milkman wanting his money.

Before we children had our own set of keys a prearranged sequence of rings or knocks would let her know that it was one of 'us'. The peephole was fitted too late to avoid the following event.

I stood behind her as Gita cracked open the front door. Two black ladies stood at the threshold.

"Have you found Jesus?"

Even she could not just shut the door on them.

"Where is He?" Gita asked.

"No…do you know Him?" asked the taller lady.

"Of course I know 'of' Him, but have not seen Him. Do you know where He is?"

This simple, everyday encounter would change her life. "

Yes…we know Him and He knows and loves us!" They smiled radiantly.

"Oh, would you like a cup of tea?" Gita opened her door and her heart.

This is how Peggy, Susan and Jesus became part of her life.

I resented this missionary assault on our newfound domestic bliss but said nothing.

At this disjointed time in her life she was vulnerable to daft ideas.

Although her decline was gradual one manifestation was her increased interest in the supernatural. She had flirted with spiritualism and attended sessions in a darkened room in Chelsea presided over by a 'mystic' named Olga, an accomplished charlatan with many customers eager to contact dead relatives.

With the arrival of Jesus, a divine bolt of light incinerated Olga.

The knocking under the table was replaced by regular uncontrived knocking on our front door by Peggy and Susan.

The two ladies wore her down with promises of worldly riches and heavenly rewards. All you needed was to accept the Lord Jesus as your saviour and swallow a large dose of this mysterious commodity called 'faith'.

The pile of unread 'The Watchtower' magazines grew on her bedside table in direct proportion to her belief in the Kingdom of Jesus and its imminent manifestation.

Peggy in particular would visit often. Over cups of tea and chunks of yellow cake she turned Gita into a non-smoking Witness of Jehovah.

I had a deep aversion to these marauding missionaries with their smug, smiley faces and easy convictions.

How dare they interrupt us just as we settled down to watch the wrestling!

"Why do you listen to that stupid woman?"

"Darling, she is a kind lady…we will, she and me, meet in Heaven!" She stroked the well-thumbed Bible left by the itinerant evangelist, which may just as well have been in Aramaic, as Gita struggled to read the directions on a can of beans.

"Can't you see what a lot of kaka all this is?" I could not make a dent in her armour, at least not until Peggy asked for a loan.

Another ethnicity she had little time for was Gypsies. Bereft of humanity, filthy thieves and brigands. She attributed all manner of diabolical atrocities to the Romany, including abducting and trading in children.

"They cannot be trusted…never turn your back on them, they will steal your eyes."

Her prejudices I readily accepted; there was no instruction as such, just a steady drip of offhand references and sly digs. Slowly, as if by osmosis, I became convinced by her words. Without evidence I came to believe and fully agreed that Gypsies were cut-throats, swindlers, conmen and common thieves. These myths we handed down from lips to ears over generations. She was programmed to educate me in the ways of the world as it appeared to her.

For years she kept her thoughts on Russians to herself and in my presence had only praise for the Soviets. With time and distance she had no qualms about unleashing her true feelings. "Scum of the earth…they are drunken animals." Wide-eyed, her mouth snarling, she held nothing back. "They are not human… ignorant peasants with guns."

The Soviets bore the full potency of her not inconsiderable venom, face distorted in disgust as she spat the word 'Vörös' – which is Hungarian for 'Reds'.

"Those Russians are pigs…worse than rats in the toilet."

I had seen a rat here and there in cellars and war-damaged buildings mainly. Do I have to worry about rats in the toilet now? The very idea that one would pop its head up as I sat uneasily on the porcelain was enough for me to want to go back to using the potty!

Gita had turned the soil before I could walk; irrigating my unformed mind with her own insecurities, she made sure that her fears took root in me. Young minds are fertile ground for sowing the seeds of prejudice.

Around the table, the assembled company sat in silence while she launched into a story that I was very familiar with.

"I will tell you something." She waited until she had everybody's attention, faces turned towards this strange little lady I called my mother.

"The Germans were running away. My beautiful city was in ruins."

"The Russian pigs were everywhere... so drunk that they fell on their faces. Thieving everything, robbin' and rapin' even the grandmothers!" She covered her eyes with the palms of both hands as if to stop the visions.

"We hear them outside our building and so me and my friend Gabi we lock the door and tried our best place to hide. She go under the bed and I go in the cupboard under a pile of cloths. They shouting and we hear the boots coming closer. They try to open the door and we terrified hiding! The pigs kick down the door and find poor Gabi straight away...well you can imagine what happened, I be very hush and pray to 'eaven. Ay, Istenem... they rape so many times." Her voice trailed to a whisper, eyes distant for a long moment. Took a big breath, raised her head, looked around the room. The party around the table sat quietly, leaning in eager to hear what she had to say. She reached for a tissue and dabbed her eyes. I picked up where she left off.

Gabi was subjected to the brutal sexual abuse the second échelon Red Army was notorious for. The spearhead combat troops, having taken the city, moved on. The second wave, safe from all but the occasional booby trap or fanatically suicidal defender, were able to loot at leisure, taking revenge in the form of indiscriminate random acts of violence, rape and pillage.

The invading Soviets spared no female. If young girls and women were hard to find an aged babushka would have to do; the primitive need to humiliate the vanquished, exercise power and satisfy their sexual cravings would not be denied.

With the tacit approval of their officers and indeed Stalin himself they feared no repercussions.

Gita cowered in the wardrobe, stifled whimpers unheard feet away from the soiled mattress on which Gabi was brutally raped by an unknown number of Soviet troops.

Severely torn, she was left lying in a pool of blood, the swarm moved on to feed on fresh shoots elsewhere.

Taking a huge gulp of air Gita raised her hands to signal she was ready to continue. "I stay quiet an' wait until the filthy bastards are finished an' they leave. I wait a long time before I come out to make sure they not trick me. When I think they gone, I come out to see an 'elp Gabi. Poor, poor darlink. I think she dead but then she make noise like a cat. Nothing for me to do. I must get doctor."

Her eyes welled up again and she reached for another tissue. Blowing her nose loudly she shook her head and could not continue.

The gathering looked to me to finish the story.

It was dangerous out on the streets but Gabi was losing a lot of blood and needed urgent care. At great risk from bullets and rapists, Gita made her way to a doctor she knew living nearby and managed to cajole and shame the reluctant medic into coming back with her to treat Gabi. As Gita stood lookout, Doctor Boris (both cursing the 'Soviet barbarians' colourfully) worked on staunching the bleeding and stitching Gabi back up.

As a precaution, he left the tools of his trade in the apartment, said he would come back after dark to check on Gabi and pick up his bag.

He did not return that night or the next. His sister found the body, yards from the apartment they shared, bullet hole in the back of his head, pockets empty, no watch or shoes. Dr. Boris – died of a good deed, a reluctant hero.

I know my mother never really got over this horror. Gabi seemed to be better able to put this trauma behind her, at least for a while; she made a convincing show of being 'normal' until later in life when her demons gained the upper hand. She spent years in and out of mental hospitals.

Both women blamed themselves for the death of Dr. Boris. She and Gabi lost touch after our walk to the West in 1956. Understandably, my mother's hatred for all things Russian knew no bounds.

I looked over at Gita, her wild eyes now dull as slate, the grand theatrical gestures stilled.

The gathering around the table had listened quietly, somewhat awestruck by the tragic story of this odd little lady with the strange accent.

Suddenly she jolted back to the present and stood to leave. Normally a very private person, in spite of her abrasive ways and brash personality, and feeling that she had told too much to people she did not know, quietly gathered up her things, dragged the reluctant dog from under the table and left. I followed her out of the door and took her hand. She started to sob. We stood in the courtyard. I held her tight as she rained tears on my shoulder.

Even though the narrative was not new to me it still had a profound effect and I walked her to her car, wanting to stay with her a while.

"You go back, Babili, I need to be alone."

She shut the car door with a clunk. Her shoulders seemed to shudder as she rolled out of the drive. I sat on the stairs. What should I do? I went back to the party to find the gathering somewhat subdued as they digested the full weight of the story that they had just heard.

I turned my thoughts to the imminent journey. Did I really want to know the truth? How would I be received? Was he even still alive?

What did I really know about this ghost, my father?

Nothing much, apart from what Gita told me and I knew that as she aged, many of her reminiscences sounded increasingly incredible.

Often, my recollection of events was at odds with hers. As a result, I had learned to discount some of her stories.

We could just go somewhere else. No one was expecting me to show up in Hungary. The Côte d'Azur was tempting.

Yet the yearning to reach out to this man, this stranger, was compelling. Certainly my mother painted an alluring portrait. At times, a wooden box kept on top of the wardrobe would be dusted off. With great affection, as if his very bones were entombed in the container, the lid unclasped, and the handful of grainy photos spread on the dining table.

"This is your father standing outside his factory." She sighed deeply, her finger caressed the smiling image.

"Not many people had cars, you know. He had a big, black, shiny one that went very fast. He even let me drive it on country roads when there was no traffic around. We loved going out of town for picnics." The photo showed Gita squinting into the afternoon sun, sitting on a tartan rug in a field splendid with wild flowers, her hand draped on the handle of a wicker basket. A big, black car with bulging headlamps brooded in the background.

"He was such a gentle man, educated, charming; we were so in love, treated me like a princess. I was his princess."

These glimpses were comforting to me. Was I about to shatter this image?

Too late for doubts; we were leaving in a few days.

CHAPTER 3

BUDAPEST, HUNGARY 1956

The nauseatingly sweet smell of powder rose from her cheeks. Crouched in front of me, her ruby lips formed jumbled words that hung in the air. Sloppy, brown eyes tinged with a hint of regret were wide as if she was surprised by her own utterances.

The mouth was working hard, the fingers busy adjusting the blue kerchief around my neck.

The message, delivered with earnest enthusiasm, did not distract.

My attention was focused on the portrait over her right shoulder, about halfway between the crossed Russian/Hungarian flags and the light switch.

The sepia photo of Uncle Joe, the father of our nation, looked down on me. I had never met him, but, like the dutiful, loving son that I was, I knew all about his life. As far as I was concerned he was omniscient, a towering colossus revered worldwide. His strength and wisdom comforted me in a very personal way. Not alone in this reality, I never heard the slightest dissent from people close to me or, for that matter, from anyone I came into contact with.

There was a hint of a smile on his handsome face. The jaw firm, the eyes kind, misty with compassion. He loves me and I worship him.

This man was an icon to me. I yearned for his approval.

Sometimes, when there was no one at home, I dragged my school desk into the middle of the living room, arranged a few books and loose papers on top, laid out my Russian-made fountain pen next to a carafe of water with a clean glass upturned atop, just like I had seen on the newsreels.

I imagined myself as Uncle Joe, presiding over the Party faithful, basking in adulation as I dispensed favours and granted wishes. I called this game Politburo.

What a great dictator I would have been.

A hard yank on the collar brought me back.

"Did you hear a word I've said?"

"Yes, Mama!"

"What did I just tell you?"

"Keep my mouth shut, do as I am told, follow the rules."

This seemed to be good enough summary of her lengthy tirade.

Pinned to the left breast pocket of my white cotton shirt a metal badge with a drum motif. The rest of the uniform consisted of a blue neckerchief knotted slightly higher than mid-chest, dark blue shorts in the summer, long wool trousers (also blue) when the weather got a bit nippy.

"Uncle Joe would be very proud of the way you are turned out." With a groan she straightened up, turned and checked her face in the mirror. From behind she was slim, shapely, you might say…well polished, like a cherished candlestick. All was well. We were both doing what we liked to do. She was off to Lake Balaton with her latest admirer, and I to do my patriotic duty.

This morning we were to meet outside the old church. Set in a small, leafy park, the spire still pointed heavenward but all references to the old god had been removed. The hammer and sickle had replaced the cross. No depictions of saintly activities or heavenly events were to be seen.

The new god sported a handlebar moustache and commanded the faithful. I was entirely enchanted by his message. The portraits were everywhere. I lived my life blissfully unaware of the iron fist around the throat of the nation. If you did not have a picture of Uncle Joe hanging somewhere in your home a neighbour may, on the flimsiest pretext, inform the police. A careless word could easily enmesh one in the oily gears of the state; life could turn deadly.

That was the milieu of the times.

Our day was to start by scouring the park, picking up discarded bottles, cans, assorted litter left behind by the 'night shift', a motley collection of drunks and derelicts.

Somehow, even in this socialist utopia there are those that would not play by the rules. These vagabonds contributed nothing to our cause and must be purged.

We were taught to despise them.

The words 'eliminate' and 'disappear' were thrown around. Did that mean that they should be killed? It seemed entirely reasonable to me that those that doggedly refused to be part of our struggle must be expunged from society. Harsh measures were sometimes necessary in the people's battle against infidels.

In hindsight, wholesale slaughter of nonconformists seems like a pretty harsh remedy. At the time I found myself in total accord with these notions. Our future was assured.

Bombarded by propaganda, steeped in Party rituals, reciting Party dogma, tight formation marching around the square with flags stiff in the morning breeze would easily convince any prepubescent boy. There was no doubt in my mind.

Picking up the detritus of the anti-socialists was not an activity that young boys would normally have a lot of enthusiasm for, but these were strange times.

I practically ran the two blocks to the square.

Laci was already there, a big, fat grin on his face. I yanked his earlobe by way of a greeting.

"I got mine yesterday." He pulled the folded red kerchief out of his back pocket. "I think my mother has mine, but she is keeping it from me." We had both eagerly anticipated the arrival of this symbol of our commitment to the cause; he had his, but I was still waiting.

Why had she not given it to me?

Our troop leader, a slightly older, fat boy with pus-engorged spots on his otherwise cherubic face struggled with the heavy church door, walked down the stairs, and stood in front of us.

"Get in line, stand to attention!" We lined ourselves up in neat military ranks.

For some minutes the company stood in silence waiting for 'Gomba' to emerge.

The heavy wooden church doors creaked open again and he walked down the short flight, unsteady but resplendent in his uniform. The combined weight of the metalwork on his left breast tugged at the shirt, making him look even more lopsided.

He was not a man to be trifled with.

Tall, thin and grim, he coughed heavily, producing a large globule of phlegm.

Savouring the meat of his efforts, he then expectorated the mass on the pavement. The loud splat was dutifully ignored.

Twenty-five Little Drummers stood stony-faced at attention.

We knew what was good for us. Any outward reaction would put you on your knees trimming the grass with scissors, or worse.

Inclining his mushroom-coloured face slightly he pondered momentarily on the large, wobbly, yellow-green mucus on the pavement. Seemingly satisfied, he pulled a small, red notepad from his shirt pocket, flipped it open, adjusted his glasses and started the roll-call.

Turning the pages, he stumbled through the list. When my name came up, I responded with a hearty "Present!"

Sloppily wearing what can best be described as a Communist version of a Scoutmaster's uniform, he leaned heavily on the knobbly wood walking stick on his bemedalled side.

Slightly mismatched, his shirt and trousers were shades of brown. Boots black and shiny. On his somewhat smaller than average head sat a black beret with a red star front and centre.

With effort, he stiffened his body, pulled himself to momentary attention before lapsing to regular disorder.

"Welcome, Little Drummers! Today is a glorious day." Gomba leaned forward then rocked back on his heels slightly, planting himself, spreading his skeletal legs for better balance.

"Communism is the future, YOU are the future of the Party. It is the way, as inevitable as the rising of tides, the dawn of a new day."

We had heard many of his pronouncements. The theme was routine.

Gomba paused for effect.

"We the people have the power and must have the will to determine our destinies."

The troop stood riveted in stony silence.

"Be vigilant, our enemies are everywhere!"

The process was sublime: I hung on every word.

"Now get to work!" Following a bout of mucus-laden coughing, he lit a cigarette, turned and went back inside the church.

Diligently avoiding the area which Gomba had used as a spittoon, we picked the small park clean of litter. For reasons unknown the discarded cigarette butts were separated into a small metal bucket.

The troop lined up in front of the church, waiting for dismissal.

Dripping with snot and emotion, Gomba rambled his way through the latest list of our beloved leader's accomplishments and the wonderful Communist future which awaited us. The next five-year plan should just about do it.

"Our Soviet comrades made huge sacrifices. Fought the fascists to a standstill at Moscow and Stalingrad, drove them back to Germany; we owe our freedom to the leadership of Stalin, and the glorious Red Army."

The evidence was all around and, to me at least, irrefutable.

The newsreels, reinforced by all organs of the state-controlled media, showed happy peasants reaping what they had sown. Black-faced miners hacked at coalfaces, teeth and eyes incandescent in the gloom. The flickering monochrome images of workers grinning, brimming with health, joyously sacrificing their lungs for the benefit of the people.

Glistening with the sweat of honest toil, heroically stoic foundry workers poured and pounded steel into useful shapes. A gift to the people – all to the common good.

Production quotas had been exceeded once again. Nothing could stop the rise of the workers.

The narrator was upbeat, soothing, exciting and uplifting at the same time. He stressed that young people must play an active part in the future. We were the guardians of the state, defenders of the revolution, and yes, we were eager to do our duty.

I was fully immersed; my mind was unshakeably made up, or so I thought.

Gomba again stood to full attention. Still slightly listing to port, he looked at us intensely, piercing raptor eyes searching our ranks for any sign of dissent. He saw well-indoctrinated, eager participants, standard-bearers for the cause and our people.

He finished off as always with our motto, 'Together for Each Other', adding – "Be ever vigilant, you are the future."

He lowered his voice; we strained to hear.

"Friends, neighbours and even your parents may be unwitting tools of the capitalists. Come and talk to me anytime if you see or hear anything strange."

"What does he mean strange?" I mumbled sotto voce to the kid on my right.

He shrugged and stood his ground.

Duties completed, aglow with Communist zeal, Gomba dismissed us with a final reminder.

"Be alert!" Your parents may be good people, yet, Gomba implied, 'they' may just be misguided and needed to be properly informed.

"It is up to you to give them the opportunity to be part of our worldwide movement. They will thank you, the Party will thank you, the workers of the world will thank you!"

Thus the Little Drummers were sent off to be little snitches.

We marched ourselves off to school radiant with the passion of youth.

I remember little about my early education and learned nothing that I could easily reference. The highlights of my day were the early morning Little Drummers parades reinforcing and renewing our pledges to the Party and its ideals.

And, of course, football.

When not engaged in LD activities we spent most of our time kicking a ball around the park. All that running around needed proper nourishment.

Laci picked up the ball. "Let's go back to my place, I think my mum has something tasty bubbling on the stove."

Panting, I caught my breath. "Let's go, I'm starving."

This arrangement suited me well as the food on offer at his flat was much tastier and of good variety. At home, low-grade food poisoning was an ever-present risk. Lard sandwiches even when spiced with hot paprika did not satisfy a ravenous, growing boy!

Laci's mother Mrs. Dvorak never failed to find enough food to share with her son's best mate, but I felt she harboured some disdain for Gita and, by extension, me as less than suitable companions for her precious only son. In spite of this, Laci and I were inseparable. We sat at table spooning pork and dumpling stew. In between mouthfuls we each advocated for our favourite games, he for our well-rehearsed Nazis & Partisans, and I for my new fixation Cowboys & Indians.

Some days ago, while Laci was made to stay home and do his homework, I sneaked into our corner cinema. It was a life-changing event.

On the screen, a man wearing a fringed leather jacket and trousers, pointy boots with silver tips and spurs, was singing to his horse. A white hat as big as the moon sat on his angular head.

Moments later, he put down his guitar, pulled out his pistols, and was equally at ease shooting whooping redskins. He shot most of them. The few that remained gave up and rode off. Picking up where he left off, he continued to twang and croon. The horse nodded its shaggy head in approval. I was spellbound.

"I will give you some fresh baked cherry pie if you both settle down to a game of chess." Mrs. Dvorak did her best to curb our violent tendencies but we were out of the door before she could utter. "With cream!"

The next morning I woke to a grey, rainy day. What sounded like gleeful chatter was coming from the sitting room. I tried the door. It was locked.

"Just a minute, Babili, I'm coming." Gita opened the door.

A gravelly voice over mournful music was coming from the radio.

Julius turned the receiver off.

I could tell by their demeanour that something momentous had happened.

Gita just blurted out: "Stalin is dead." I could not be sure, but I thought a shadow of a smile crossed her face.

"What are you talking about? There must be some mistake!"

Julius and Gita hung their heads.

I stormed out of the flat.

The balconies were lined with people. Some were wailing, others stoic.

I went around asking if it was true. I simply could not believe what I was hearing. Not until the black reality was officially announced on the newsreels did I start to accept this dreadful news. The whole country suffered great anguish, or at least that was what I was allowed to see. Racked by grief, a new sadness hung over my life. The sense of loss was devastating. I had lost my anchor and the only man in my life who was always there. Somehow it felt as if I had personally failed him and in some obscure way was responsible for his death. This made me ever more vigilant and fanatical in my support of the Party and all it stood for.

Eager to do my duty, for the sake of accuracy, I bought myself a small, red notebook, just like Gomba's, in which I kept a running log of activities at our flat.

I entered as much detail as I could remember. General appearance, height, weight, description of attire. A zero-to-ten loyalty coding system based on any fleeting interaction we may have had.

If strange meant a steady stream of men coming and going and a witch living in the kitchen, then indeed there were many strange goings-on in my house.

Who was this old lady and where did she come from? My mother told me she was my 'aunt', but as with many things involving Gita the precise details were kept obscure.

To this day I do not know who she was or even if she was related to us in any way.

One day she and her slinky black cat just appeared, instantly becoming a household fixture.

A small, cot-type bed was put in one corner of the kitchen under the window where she slept like a bundle of dark rags. When not cooking, cleaning or hanging laundry on a rack above the stove, her time was spent in gentle discomfort kneeling on a small rug praying, seemingly content with very little in this life, preferring to invest in the hereafter.

I cannot recall ever seeing her head exposed. For all I know she may have been bald.

The all-purpose, all-weather black headscarf tightly knotted under her chin framed the pale, deeply wrinkled face, throwing the large, hooked nose into high relief. She looked nothing like my mother; rather, as I remember her now, she was a perfect likeness for the Blind Witch.

At first I was scared to be left alone with her, thinking that I would end up treading water among the carrots and onions. I did have a good look around but did not find a pot big enough for me to sit in. With unrelenting kindness she won me over, becoming my protector and comforter; truly creative, she made fantastic excuses for my loutish behaviour, diverting my mother's rage when I knew I deserved a good thrashing.

A slap on the face was considered appropriate for relatively minor transgressions. There were many rules, most of which I could not understand and therefore certainly could not abide by.

I was told to call the old woman Neni, which simply translated means 'aunt'. She and I shared a disapproval of Gita's lifestyle for differing reasons, she on moral grounds, I selfishly just did not like to be left at home while she was out having fun running around town. I saw no reason why I should not be included.

Neni remained faithful to the old god, stubbornly refusing to embrace the shiny new reality.

Foolish woman – I thought, she was too old to understand how fortunate we were to live in a secular, Communist society. This was the future. Let her live out her days wallowing in silly notions of Heaven and Hell. I would just have to keep an eye on her.

Ever muttering unintelligibly, rolling her rheumy eyes skyward imploringly, with the patience of age she waited for the Lord to clasp her to his eternal bosom. Until that blessed day she was content to run the household while my mother gallivanted around town, Neni getting little more than room and board (such as it was), as well as having to put up with my tantrums and Gita's indiscretions.

When my mother raged at me, Neni's many-layered, long, black skirts were just the thing to hide behind, her spindly arms fending Gita off at times long enough for me to make a dash through the hall and escape out of the front door while ducking the flying footwear.

Neni did everything to protect me, but she was not above collusion, using dastardly tricks to divert me while Gita snuck out the front door on one of her dates.

"Babili, come come, sit with me in the kitchen, I will make something special for you," Neni would coo soothingly, promising to make me some 'bird milk'.

The very thought of that special treat now instantly stiffens my arteries.

Take a large mug and fill a third of it with white sugar, separate two eggs and plop the raw yokes on the sugar. Add a soupçon of milk. Beat vigorously with a fork until stiff. Eat.

I loved the stuff and her deviancy worked every time.

As far as my new pet name "Babili" was concerned, I had no idea what, why or who first started to call me that ridiculous moniker, most unsuitable for an aspiring Young Communist.

Smelling faintly of lavender water, the rosary in her blue-veined hands, she passed the well-worn beads between her knobbly fingers. Neni sat on the edge of her bed rocking back and forth slightly, making small, whimpering noises, periodically rolling her watery eyes to the ceiling.

I supposed she was praying. A habit to be deplored according to current lore.

I thought it a waste of time as, having given it a go, the results (or lack thereof) never failed to disappoint.

Certainly there were many strange goings-on in the flat but none which I could consider subversive or reactionary. These are big words but I already knew that if you were either of these things you were an enemy of the people and it was my patriotic duty to inform the authorities. That would mean a private chat with Gomba.

My mother had many admirers and there was a well-worn path to our front door, but compared to my Man of Steel these fragrant men in double-breasted suits and well-polished shoes were rusty Tin Men in need of a good squirt of WD-40!

My biological father was hardly ever mentioned around the flat, at least not in my presence. When I asked my mother about him, she just said that it was to do with the war and left it at that. It was almost as if I was Immaculately Conceived. I wondered why I did not have a 'real' father like other kids instead of a parade of 'daddies' that stuck around a while then would disappear without saying goodbye. One of the early 'daddies' was a police captain. To give me some legitimacy, she persuaded him to marry her.

Having got what she needed, Gita got rid of him within a few weeks. I never met him but he did leave me his name.

The only thing I knew to do was to throw a fit when my mother went off on one of her assignations with a potential 'Daddy'.

Gita checked herself in the mirror: she straightened the clasp holding the ruffled ostrich feather attached to her hat, set it at a jauntier angle. I still associate the smell of fresh make-up with imminent abandonment.

"You can go down to Laci's, I already talked to his mother: spend the night with them, I know you like that."

"But I want to go with you!" I wailed, pounding my puny fists on the front door in a vain attempt to stop her leaving. She just ignored my histrionics.

With one last look in the mirror, she picked up her handbag and gloves.

"I will walk down with you."

In truth, I really did like staying at Laci's flat. The amateur dramatics were just my way of getting back at her for leaving me.

After a string of spluttering failures, my mother finally managed to find a good man and was now in a committed yet scandalously modern relationship with Dr. Mihály Gyula (Julius), who visited and slept over frequently. A rich topic for the neighbourhood gossips but I saw nothing wrong with the arrangement.

At first she tried to pretend that he just stayed past my bedtime so they could have some sort of adult conversation without my childish interruptions. I suspected there was more to it.

The modest apartment was unable to conceal the realities of the affair. Comprising two small bedrooms, a good-size living room with a ceramic-tiled wood-burning stove in one corner, kitchen, bathroom and a small hallway.

Julius had a thriving practice as a dental surgeon and worked as an oral pathologist at a Budapest hospital, a man of character and substance.

He sensibly maintained a separate flat in a better part of the city large enough to contain his surgery. This arrangement suited them well, Julius being a quiet, introspective man needing a bolt-hole to get away from the pressures of family life, and Gita's frenetic lifestyle and at times entirely unrealistic demands.

I had never seen my mother so happy. He was a great prize, an extraordinary man, shortish – around 5'7" – handsome in a 1940s matinee idol way, well proportioned and manicured, spoke six languages, well travelled, played a fair alto sax, kept an overly talkative budgie in his consulting rooms, and let me play with beads of mercury on his well-polished parquet floor.

He never left the building without his homburg.

Here at last was a man I could put on the podium with my Uncle Joe. The initial resentment I felt towards Julius waned over time. His loving, respectfully gentle treatment of Gita gradually won me over. We became a family, at least for a while. I finally embraced him as my 'father' when he put me on his shoulder so that I could get a better view of the firework display over the Danube. None of the other daddies showed that kind of interest in me. I grew to love him and have nothing but fond memories of our time together. He may have been small in stature but was a giant of a man.

The then 'state-of-the-art' dental tools at his disposal would now be considered crude implements of torture – he used them on me relentlessly.

"Your teeth are as soft as butter!" He laughed as he leaned in and ground away at the caries, forever embedding the acrid, nauseating smell of smouldering dentine in my young head.

The quality of the fillings he applied were such that they will remain intact long after I am not.

Always kind to me, he did his best to rein in my uncouth, street urchin ways, setting me essays to write instead of giving me a well-deserved beating.

Gita was less tolerant of my bullshit and would not hesitate to slap or go after me with a broomstick, wooden spoon or some other handy kitchen implement.

If deemed to have been particularly delinquent I would be made to kneel in a corner of the parquet-covered living room floor on corn kernels of the type normally used to feed chickens. This inventive form of punishment left an impression on me which outlasted the indentations on my knees.

These methods of punishment were ordinary and not considered harsh by the standards of the day.

Our family situation was relatively comfortable. All my needs and some of my wants were readily met.

Until the end of the war Julius had owned a large villa on the shores of Lake Balaton. In 1945/6 the Communists took most of it and gave it to loyal Party members, surely more deserving folk, magnanimously allowing him to keep a small, self-contained section of the building which we used as a holiday home.

"Why are you getting so fat?" She slapped me hard. It seemed like a fair question, thought I, trying to erase the palm print on my face by gentle massage.

Too self-absorbed to notice the gradual changes, then all of a sudden she looked like Humpty Dumpty.

Hand on my left cheek, I waited for the pain to subside and some kind of answer from her.

"You are going to have a brother, someone to play with and very soon." She groaned, stood and cradled her belly.

This was a shock: nobody asked me if I wanted a brother. Surely I should at the very least have been consulted!

"How do you know it's a boy?" Thinking this might be a good thing, I quite liked the idea of a younger brother, a captive playmate, someone to boss around.

"Neni knows about these things, she is sure, the cross never lies."

She had used a silver chain with an ebony cross attached, dangling it over Gita's stomach area to make this prediction.

It all came down to the 'shape' of the rotation as divined by her.

These ridiculous superstitious rituals were high on the list of activities Gomba had warned us about. Surely this was strange behaviour!

To further compound her weirdness, Neni was prone to hallucinations, or as she would have it, 'visions'.

The dangly chain method was subsequently confirmed by a visitation, the Virgin Mary hovering over the gas stove in the kitchen.

"Can you keep a secret?" Neni took me into the kitchen and sat me on her bed.

"Of course!" Maybe, I thought, but if it concerned the security of the state then definitely not.

"You will have a baby brother, the Lord has spoken to me." Neni clasped her hands and looked skyward.

"He has sent His wife with a message. Look! Look over there." She was pointing to the empty space above the stove.

I stared hard, squinting, tilting my head in a variety of ways, trying hard to share her mental machinations. She became agitated with my inability to see her vision, leading me to suspect that she might not be right in the head. Perhaps she was a witch after all.

Much to my annoyance the Divine messenger never showed herself to me.

Neni continued, trying to enlist me, without success, in her kitchen miracle.

She dropped to her knees at odd times crying, "My God, My God!"

After a while, to make her feel better I said, "I do see something but it's not very clear." She readily accepted my tepid endorsement of her delusion as binding confirmation of her perception.

In due course a finely packaged baby boy came back from the hospital.

As to how he came to be in this world, some incredible stuff about storks and chimneys was as much as I could get out of either of them.

The spindly-legged bird must have found a comfortable home on our chimney as within a relatively short time my new brother Akos was joined by a baby girl soon to be named Margo.

Gita diligently breastfed both of them, even though less revealing, more convenient methods were available. Three children under the age of ten, two of whom needed constant care, did not deter her from the life of an aspiring socialite.

Neni shouldered her additional duties without complaint.

Life was unremarkable, safe and routine in spite of our somewhat unconventional lifestyle. My days revolved around school, football and marching around as a proud and dedicated member of the Little Drummers (Kis Dobos), the gateway drug to the Communist Youth League (CYL).

Laci, my best friend, was a few days younger than me, but he, too, would soon be old enough to join the CYL. He already had his red square and I was expecting mine any day.

"When will I get my red kerchief?"

"Soon, Babili, soon, maybe tomorrow."

In spite of her words she seemed annoyed at me and did not seem to share my impatience. Eager to graduate to the ranks of the CYL, Laci and I could hardly wait.

The uniform meant a lot to both of us, a significant step towards full Party membership and an outward sign of our status and dedication to the Party.

The message of unity, shared sacrifice and common purpose was irresistible.

Odd to think how important that kerchief was for me back then.

Each day I woke filled with expectation.

Within a couple of days, it was offhandedly handed to me by Julius.

I thought the manner in which he almost threw it at me strange. This on top of other signs of disdain for the Party did not go unnoticed. From behind closed doors I could faintly make out the old valve radio being tuned to foreign stations, whispered conversations taking place. Then there was the unusual number of visitors.

Surely all these activities would be of interest to Gomba.

I folded the kerchief neatly and put it away.

In essence the 'Drummers' were not much different from the Boy Scouts or the Hitler Youth, both organisations whose principal objective was to prepare boys and young men for military service, except that the LD were more honest about their aims, making no pretence about who the enemy was and what sacrifices were expected of us.

All was well and as it should be.

At the age of ten or so one could become a member of the CYL, which was the ultimate stepping stone to full Communist Party membership.

The illusion of freedom made all these steps seem voluntary, but to make a meaningful life or indeed apply to a university it was highly 'recommended'.

Secure in the Bolshevik bosom of my Uncle Joe life was well mapped and I was right on track.

"Make your canvas large and your brush broad," was the oft- repeated advice Julius had given me. I had no idea what that meant but was happy to be following the path laid down for me.

"Why don't you knock before you come in?" Julius turned to face me. "How many times do I have to tell you?" Gita gave me one of her looks.

The large dining table was strewn with 'papers'. Julius hurriedly scooped them up and tucked them in his briefcase.

This was not the first time they had acted furtively.

At times I pretended to be asleep while they held whispered conversations which I could not quite comprehend.

Then there were frequent visits from grim men in overcoats.

They shook my hand and patted me on the head before I was sent to my room.

What were they doing behind that locked door? I needed to know.

Sometimes I crept across the parqueted hall in my pyjamas to peek through the keyhole. More often than not, the key was left in the lock, blocking my view. Once, it was not.

The keyhole was of the old, pre-Yale type and afforded a good if restricted view of the room. Two overcoats, Julius and my mother, were in a heated discussion. Partially obscured by billowing cigarette smoke a small revolver lay atop a pile of papers. I shut my left eye tightly; the other bulged with curiosity. Was it possible that my 'parents' were counter-revolutionaries? This was a jaw-dropping twist to my settled life.

Pressing my ear to the door I could hear conversation but could not make any sense of the few words I could pick up on.

Did this fit Gomba's definition of 'strange'? I thought it probably did and he definitely needed to know about these meetings.

"What were you talking about in there?" I asked after the overcoats left.

I felt excluded and resentful.

"Oh, just colleagues of Julius talking 'doctor' stuff, all very boring. Now go and play." Gita flipped open her compact and checked her face. It was still all there.

Increasingly these behaviours looked 'strange' to me: the evasive answers, the furtive looks, and why would doctors need a pistol?

Torn between doing my Young Communist duty yet worried that I could get my mother and Julius in trouble, I decided to wait until the next meeting before I talked to Gomba. He would know what to do.

I went back down to the first-floor corner flat to see if my compadre Laci wanted to come out and 'play'; the partisans had wiped out the Nazis and now we would test the Cowboys and the Indians. I rang the doorbell. Mrs. Dvorak opened the door.

"Can Laci come out to play?"

"No, he has to finish his homework. Come back in an hour." I felt a twinge of pity for my mate.

This is what you get when you have two parents, two hours of homework.

The neighbours, especially Laci's parents, were always kind to me even as they gossiped and tutted about our unconventional familial situation. The frequency of gentleman callers climbing the stairs and my mother's failure to keep a tighter rein on me were a rich topic of conversation.

Being older than him by a few days made me the senior partner, yet I was a little jealous of Laci's blond, blue-eyed looks, which made him more than popular with the neighbourhood girls. Even though we went to great lengths to avoid them, they often managed to corner us: it was easier to submit briefly to their silly 'kissing games' so that we could get down to real business.

I left our building to see what mischief I could get into and headed towards the park in Republic Square. Maybe I could find a game of football.

As I walked towards the square, I ran into a small crowd gathered at a corner opposite. Crossing the street, I expected to see the man with the accordion and monkey or a troop of tumbling Gypsies. This time it was different.

This throng were not in the mood for street entertainment.

A slight, young man stood on a box wearing the ubiquitous black beret.

With the fiery eyes of the dispossessed he was haranguing the crowd. Some stuff about being crushed under the heel of the Soviets, oppression, freedom, open elections. He sounded exactly the type of subversive Gomba had warned me against. I could not believe my ears, open sedition in the streets of Budapest.

He pulled a piece of paper from his inside pocket and started to read from what appeared to be a list. Raising his voice to shrill, he began.

"We demand the immediate withdrawal of all Soviet troops! We demand…!"

Before he uttered another word two men with drawn pistols emerged from the throng.

"Go home!" one shouted, waving his sidearm as the other pointed his pistol at the speaker, grasped his right arm and they both marched him through the crowd.

"This man is a traitor, a counter-revolutionary and is under arrest. Stand aside!"

The crowd parted to make way amid grumbles and whispers of "ÁVH."

How could this be? Do these people, this rabble, not realise that we as a nation owed our freedom, indeed our very existence, to Joseph Stalin, the glorious Red Army and, by extension, the organs of the Hungarian State? How could they stand there letting this fanatic spout such nonsense making outrageous demands without shutting him up?

What is 'ÁVH'? I asked a man standing on my left. He looked over the top of my head as if I was suddenly invisible. What had I just witnessed? Forget football; I headed back home to get some answers.

"Mama, where are you?" Then I heard her cough in the sitting room.

She was arranging the flowers in the pitcher which also doubled as a vase, fussing with the placement on the lace doily.

"I have just seen some strange things on the street that maybe you can explain to me." I told her what I had just witnessed, ending with, "What is ÁVH?"

There was a discernible shift in her demeanour; her eyes darted left and right. The power of the Party was strong within me. To my enjoyment she squirmed in her chair then stood and paced the room.

All those hours at the cinema had not been wasted.

"Stop! Sit down!"

Shifting to my role as interrogator I held my gaze steady and watched her flounder. She knew something that she was not letting on about. It was my duty to find out what she was hiding.

Swallowing heavily she said, "I don't know. Probably some Party organisation or something." Her voice trailed away; she looked ashen. The fact that she was upset emboldened me.

"Don't lie to me! You must know, ask Julius or one of your other 'friends' in overcoats." I had never seen that look before, unbridled fear.

There were a few days before the next meeting of the Little Drummers. Gomba will be pleased; I would show my loyalty to the workers and the Party. Gita needed to be properly informed. There was something not right about her attitude; she gave every appearance of not being fully committed to our glorious struggle. I would do my duty. Gomba would be able to make her see the error of her ways!

I almost felt sorry for her.

Seemingly overnight the streets became less pedestrian and more hostile.

Groups gathered into crowds that a couple of men with handguns could no longer contain. I decided to follow Gita's warnings and kept my mouth shut, not even telling Laci about the revolver.

The nature of the ÁVH was finally revealed to me (in hushed tones) by Laci's father.

"They guard the security of the nation and deserve our help. We should be grateful to them for their dedication and diligence in rooting out the enemies of the people."

Inadvertently he had just condemned Gita, Julius and Neni. Even her cat Lucy might be part of this subversive cabal.

I would do my bit.

I was within hours of taking my notes to Gomba, then this.

Stevan and his wife lived in the corner flat just a few doors down from my place.

They were a childless couple living what seemed to be a 'normal' life, kept pretty much to themselves. I had very little to do with them, just the odd few words when I ran into them in the stairwell, polite greetings from afar.

Stevan going off to work early. His wife took on sewing jobs to literally make ends meet.

Sometime during the night there was a kerfuffle on the balcony outside, shouts, shrieks, the screech of boots on tiled floors. Lights came on all over the building.

Doors opened, people came out to see what all the fuss was about.

I made it out of our front door just in time to see Stevan's wife lose her grip on her struggling husband.

He put up a pretty good fight.

It took four men in large, black boots to subdue him while others kept the neighbours at bay with sub-machine guns. The shackles snapped shut on his wrists.

"Leave him alone. Why are you taking him!?" shouted a neighbour from across the yard, more people emerged; emboldened by numbers, a small crowd formed as the ÁVH dragged him down the stairs and into the courtyard. By now the whole building was awake.

One of the abductors fired a short burst in the air. It was enough to scare most people back into their flats. Gita was not so easily intimidated. At that moment she shook off any pretence, making no attempt to hide her loathing for the powers that recently she had made such a show of admiring. Driven by sheer hatred of the regime, she vented her fury without regard to consequences.

I knew how to swear and thought I had a pretty good lexicon but what was coming out of her mouth was a revelation. Julius tried to drag her back in, pleading for her to shut up.

"Fuck your prostitute mother!" she screamed at the ÁVH, throwing in other helpful suggestions like a "may a carthorse's dick stretch your arseholes!"

Not sure who was more shocked; the neighbours, ÁVH or me.

Like I said, she could never be accused of nonchalance.

That was the day the veneer cracked on my rosy portrait of Uncle Joe. Confused and conflicted, perhaps I should wait a few days before talking to Gomba.

Yes, on reflection…I thought it would be a good idea.

CHAPTER 4

THE BEGINNING

The brutal arrest of Stevan was symptomatic of what was going on in the streets. More openly defiant crowds roamed the streets. The spontaneous student protests were soon joined by workers as they marched on the Parliament building in Pest.

From my perspective the upheaval was a welcome change. The city became exciting. Rowdy, banner-waving mobs filled the streets. The gaping hole left by the hacked-out Communist 'coat of arms' in the Hungarian flag added a fresh anxiety.

This new symbol of defiance was suddenly hanging from windowsills and balconies all over the city. Confusion and chaos arrived seemingly from nowhere.

I blamed Western agitators.

Laci and I waited as usual outside the church for one of our scheduled LD meetings. Some other kids showed up but we soon realised that we were waiting in vain.

There was no sign of Gomba.

To cool the Blaupunkt Gita had placed a fan on the sideboard, the reciprocating control in neutral, speed at maximum. The potential generated by the friction on the streets seemed to be wired directly into the well-twiddled radio. As a testament to good German design and construction, both fan and radio stood up well to round-the-clock operations. Gita and Julius scoffed at the proclamations of the government stations, preferring to surf the long waves to find foreign transmitters.

Even as we slept fitfully, the hushed Art Deco-style radio continued to broadcast the undulating voice of Radio Free Europe. What was going on? Out of habit I still made notes in my little red book. Gomba, when he returned, would be very interested to hear about these antisocial activities.

The neighbourhood gossip mill was abuzz with rumours, reports of violent clashes with police, the ÁVH ramping up their activities, raiding offices, snatching people from their beds.

As the street violence intensified, increasingly strident reports on the government-controlled airwaves broadcast warnings of dire consequences if the streets were not cleared and order not immediately restored.

Martial law and a curfew were imposed then immediately rescinded to allow people to get out to try to find food. In the days that followed many contradictory announcements were made, what was forbidden one day was compulsory the next. Where nothing is true, everything is possible.

The world had gone mad.

I badly wanted to be involved in the street activities but Gita kept the front door locked; the key on a cord around her neck made it almost impossible for me to get to it.

Almost... She had just taken a bath and carelessly left the key momentarily unattached.

This was all I needed. I was out of the door to join the action.

The swirling mob carried me around the city. Trying to understand what was unfolding before my eyes, I asked many people many questions but the answers, if I got a response at all, were evasive. In these turbulent times who could be trusted?

When a student delegation entered the 'radio building' wanting to air their grievances, they were detained by the ÁVH.

The crowd chanting outside the building were fired upon, resulting in the death of one student. I watched as the body was wrapped in a defaced Hungarian flag and paraded through the streets.

The revolution had its first martyr.

As the news spread the pent-up anger of the people was unleashed. Disorder turned to insurrection as some units of the Hungarian Army sided with the rebels, opening up their armouries. Eager hands reached for power.

So it began.

I instinctively knew something momentous was happening but hunger drove me home.

As I neared my building the crackle of automatic fire from the direction of Republic Square drew me. Curiosity smothered hunger. Recklessness overcame fear. I just wanted to be part of it. My mother and rumbling stomach would just have to wait.

The Square was less than half a mile from our flat and was a favourite hangout for kids from the neighbourhood. There was a playground with swings, slides, roundabout, sandpit and an open, grassy area which bore the scars of numerous feet hacking at a football.

That day, I was drawn not by the prospect of fun and games but by the impulsive inquisitiveness of youth. The boom of tank guns and the chatter of automatic weapons grew louder as I walked towards the Square.

Many happy hours were spent playing in the shadow of the imposing, Soviet-style building (now at the centre of the action), totally unaware that it was the headquarters of the Hungarian Workers' Party. The two top floors were occupied by a contingent of the ÁVH.

The building took up most of one side of the square and was topped by a large, red star over a bronze relief of triumphant workers, their uplifted faces set in grim determination, marching in lock step towards a Communist utopia.

This symbol of everything I held dear silhouetted against a clear blue sky made an excellent target for the machine guns of the WWII-era T-34s of the Hungarian Army.

Large chunks of the metalwork were chewed away, riddled with holes but still standing. Secure in ignorance and assured of invulnerability, my immature, feeble, yet highly permeable brain surveyed the tableau as I strolled around the square.

Fully detached from the awful reality of the death and mayhem that surrounded me, I imagined myself to be the central character of any number of the many 'war' films that I had consumed. Somehow, the scene was like an old movie to me.

The three rebadged tanks lined up directly in front of the building, firing their main guns at close range. Small arms fire pecked away at the masonry.

Huddling behind the armour were a motley collection of 'freedom fighters' firing a variety of weapons at the upper windows, pock-marked walls framing the glassless openings.

Deployed alongside modern, Soviet-made weapons liberated from Hungarian arsenals cached World War II-era small arms, German Mausers and MP 40s were given a second innings against the Russians and their lackeys.

Preserved in oily rags, these well-engineered weapons needed nothing more than a quick clean and fresh ammo to become lethal in the hands of desperate men.

Under the smouldering hulk of a burnt-out APC lay three charred corpses, their arms angled grotesquely, as if in prayer. The relatively thin armour of the APCs lacked the power to stop the larger-calibre munitions; perhaps they died by gunfire, the bodies then burnt in the ensuing inferno. I hoped that they were dead before flames engulfed them; the thought that they were roasted alive was an inconceivable horror even for me, though I considered myself battle-hardened by all the war movies I had seen.

In a mild, self-induced trance I continued to patrol the area, stopping periodically to watch the drama unfold. The trapped and outnumbered ÁVH returned fire from the upper floors; they must have known that they were fighting for their lives. Barring some intervention, they were doomed. The firing became sporadic, as if the trigger fingers needed respite, stopping completely in the late afternoon when for reasons unknown (lack of ammunition maybe) the occupants began to surrender, some donning regular police uniforms in a vain attempt at disguise. They were the lucky ones; the fighters, in no mood to take prisoners, shot them as they approached, hands high in the air clutching white rags. The man at the front of the terrified group waving what looked like a white bedsheet on a pole was the first to fall in a spray of bullets; the rules of 'civilised' warfare were, as is often the case, ignored in the adrenalin-fuelled killing frenzy and heat of the moment.

Watching from the upper windows, those that did not surrender, seeing their comrades massacred below, knowing that nothing could save them, fought to the last round.

Abruptly, firing stopped from the building, the crowd below swirled, buzzing like angry hornets.

Then a voice from the crowd: "The bastards are leaving through the 'tunnel'!"

I had not seen him before; he must have just arrived. Gathering a small group of fighters around him, he told them that there was a secret escape tunnel leading from the building to one of the houses nearby. He claimed to have been involved in its construction and knew roughly where it ran. The possibility that some high-ranking ÁVH officers might just slip away was a fresh boost to the fighters exhausted by combat. Pickaxes and shovels arrived in a lorry.

People streamed into the square and at the direction of the 'new arrival' a dozen men rolled up their sleeves and set about the hard ground. The grassy area which had been our football 'pitch' became a large hole in the ground. We all had to make sacrifices.

The dig was slow; many stood around offering unwanted advice. Arguments were breaking out as to where exactly their efforts should be concentrated.

Then the unmistakable sound of a heavy tracked vehicle squeaking and clattering on cobblestones from around the corner sent the mob running and the fighters to their weapons. The Hungarian Army T-34s swivelled their turrets in the direction of the approaching menace and waited. The metal monster rumbled, squeaking on the cobblestones, grinding its way towards the square.

From my hiding place in the sandpit the first glimpse I got of this behemoth was a large, metal 'bucket' of the type used for excavation. There soon followed an articulated arm attached to a giant, tracked vehicle driven by a worker. Trigger fingers relaxed, a cautious cheer rippled through the square. The machine had been liberated from a nearby building site and would be put to work.

Under the direction of the informant the dragline bucket was positioned precisely where indicated. The hole became larger with each scoop. The diggers, admiring the marvels of modern mechanical excavation, stopped work to lean on their shovels. Onlookers stood around in clusters.

Several hours and large holes later, when our football pitch looked like a Godzilla-sized, star-nosed mole had been on a feeding frenzy, the excavators gave up; the men searching nearby buildings for the exit end of the tunnel found nothing.

In frustration, the fighters turned their attention back to the building and the one-sided skirmish continued from where it had left off. There was no incoming fire from the windows or indeed any sign of life.

We later heard that there never was a secret tunnel, and to enrage the mob further the man who started the whole pointless exercise was nowhere to be seen. Was he sent in to obfuscate?

When nothing is true, anything is possible.

In the late afternoon the few remaining ÁVH men, in a desperate effort to escape, made a dash from the HQ building.

They did not get far, run to ground by the mob and beaten with savage fury; pleading for their lives, screams and protestations only served to enrage the rabble whose frenzied attack continued long after the bodies lay lifeless.

They died on the hard ground where just 24 hours ago a well-used, less than spherical leather football had been the focus of my attention.

Using electrical wires, the bodies were stripped to the waist and strung up by their feet. The image of lamp-posts festooned with dead bodies still haunts me.

New arrivals to the Square, denied the opportunity to vent their collective anger on the living, kicked the hanging bodies and spat on the battered corpses.

"What are you doing here?" I recognised him from my building.

He was smashing his fist into the bloodied face of a swinging corpse. Paused for a moment. Grinning manically he lashed out at the body once more, then without looking at me melted into the crowd. Was he appalled by his actions?

Mob mentality took hold of what had been, just a few hours ago, ordinary law-abiding workers, students and housewives. I recognised some of them as neighbours, their faces distorted by rage, the bile of hatred oozing through their pores.

Not immune to the contagion, I, too, spat on a mutilated corpse. I immediately felt ashamed, looked around to see if anyone I knew had seen me. Such confusion: the upheavals in the streets had shattered my happy, carefree life.

Blind hate exhausted, the mood changed suddenly as the mob sobered to the thought that the body rotating gently in the late afternoon breeze was somebody's father, son, brother, a casualty of war and a victim of circumstance.

It later came to light that many of the victims of the street justice meted out by the mob were either young (and perhaps innocent) rank and file ÁVH conscripts or just regular Army officers in the wrong place at the wrong time. Such is the fog of war and a graphic example of the mentality that sadly these days we have become accustomed to.

When I returned to the flat I expected to be punished but Gita was preoccupied with shuttering the windows using hefty planks of wood she had acquired from somewhere (she was an accomplished scrounger). To barricade the front door, sturdier pieces of furniture were piled against the opening. This did not facilitate easy access but was deemed necessary as a neighbour had been wounded by a stray round coming through a door.

Sensible precautions had to be taken.

I said nothing about the day to my mother, not wanting her to worry unduly. She just looked at me blankly and went about her task. Having wriggled through the barricade, which also blocked access to the coat hooks, I threw my jacket on the floor and went into the sitting room.

The outline of the space from where the portrait of Stalin used to look down on us was now occupied by a smaller frame. The Man of Steel was gone. Instead Charlie Chaplin the vaudeville clown grinned coyly from the space recently occupied by my hero.

I looked at Charlie then at Gita. She smiled and went to the kitchen to see why Margo was wailing.

Akos tottered into the room. We both stood looking up at Charlie. I slipped his little hand into mine and gave him what I hoped was a reassuring squeeze.

My core beliefs were laid to waste on that day.

The creeping shadow of doubt was made substance. I had been lied to and deceived by the people I trusted. Sense of betrayal turned to anger.

Angry at the Party and its lies.

Angry at my mother for allowing me to wallow in my delusion.

Angry at myself for being so gullible.

From that day on Stalin became the object of my hatred.

In the space of a few short hours I had become a turncoat.

Where could I go? Who could I trust? Could I even trust my mother? I had to get some help from somewhere. I decided my best bet was to thrash this out with Gita. In the light of recent events a cosy chat with Gomba might turn into a disaster for my family. I was fully aware of the peril we were all in. Indoctrinate for Stalin no more.

"So, Mama… I need the truth from you!" I was overstepping the mark but the feeling that something momentous was about to happen emboldened me.

She looked defeated. I was unused to seeing her out of control.

Shakily she said, "Please trust me… all will be well and

I shall explain everything very soon. I love you. Do not tell anyone anything." She kissed me on the forehead, stood up, shuddered slightly, regained her composure and left the room.

Feeling helpless and dejected I sat in my room wondering what else was around the corner.

Unexpectedly, the streets became silent.

In contrast, the noise level in our flat grew. Julius and Gita danced in the sitting room; throwing caution to the wind they twirled and chanted like children. I became sombre, serious, thoughtful. The adults became children. The child came of age.

Overnight my carefree life had ended.

"They're leaving, the red bastards are leaving!" They danced around the flat. I was sick of hearing it!

The meetings with men in overcoats were becoming longer and noisier, too. I was still excluded but now had a better understanding as to what was going on. It was just as well that I dithered about talking to Gomba: the little red book was full of what I considered to be strange goings-on. My indolence surely saved Gita and Julius from being dragged off like our neighbour Stevan. He never did return. I once glimpsed his wife, head lowered, hurrying towards the staircase. She wore a black band on her left arm.

The Russians had, as if by magic, disappeared overnight and the demands of the revolutionaries were being taken under consideration by the now teetering government.

It was too late for concessions.

The people, for once, had the upper hand. The old guard were rapidly ousted, and the new government began to implement the reforms demanded by the leaders of the revolution.

Citizens emerged from their basements and hiding places to a bright new day full of promise. Free from Russian domination?

Blinking in the sunlight, wiping grime-encrusted faces, many wept openly, struggling to grasp the new reality.

A new smell in the air, that of freedom, gusted through the city.

The streets were crowded with people overjoyed and stunned in equal measure. Could it be true? Had we really sent the Russkies packing?

On the 30th of October 1956 Russian forces withdrew from Hungary. Was this a fiendish trick? A dastardly ploy to wrong-foot the rebels? As we know, the celebrations were premature. In less than a week the Soviets would return, a few little stings not enough to drive the bear from the honey.

"Can Laci come out?"

Mrs. Dvorak, as I had expected, replied with a firm "No!"

Standing outside my building I watched a steady stream of people heading north towards the park.

Two men pushed a wooden handcart loaded with metal cylinders down the cobbled street.

I ran after them. "Can I help push with you?" I wanted to be involved somehow.

"Does your mother know where you are?"

"What are these tubes for?"

They both laughed.

"We are going to cut him down to size."

"Who?"

"Stalin!" They both spat on the cobbles.

Saying nothing, I backed off but continued to follow the cart. If only I was a bit older; just a few months would have put me in the fight instead of merely a witness. I so badly wanted to swagger around with a gun, stick grenades poking out of my belt.

Városliget (City Park) was just a couple of kilometres up the road and was the site of a giant statue of Comrade Stalin standing 8 metres tall atop an even taller stone plinth.

As the park came into view I could see clusters of men hard at work; there was feverish activity around the statue.

Workers on ladders were fastening steel cables around the neck of my soon-to-be fallen ex-hero while the men with the cutting torch went to work. More and more people arrived. Even as the torches were doing their work angry men were straining at the cables.

The massed power of the heaving proletariat finally toppled the colossus, pulling it crashing to the ground. Swept up in the moment, I cheered as the crowd rushed forward to vent their rage on the fallen effigy.

Using hammers and crowbars, the angry, the joyous and yes, the newly empowered set about the statue.

The dictator was dismembered and broken into souvenir-size pieces.

The dishevelled crowd celebrated, linking arms, singing, faces bright with hope. Some danced on his belly while a large man wielding a sledgehammer smashed off his nose.

I picked up a fragment, slipped it into my pocket and headed back home. Stopping momentarily, I sat on a bench to collect my thoughts. What did all this mean? How would this change my life? Just a few days ago the world was right by me and my role in it was settled. That was gone. Everything was different now.

What happens next? Where would we go from here? The felling and dismemberment of the Stalin statue had left me empty and afraid. How could I have been so stupid? How could I have been so blind to not see and more importantly feel what must have been simmering just below the surface pretty much all my life?

He had been my father, personal hero, someone I could rely on and trust, the 'man of steel' in a gleaming white uniform, godlike.

I had been taught that he was a military genius, directing the destruction of Hitler's armies at Stalingrad, driving the Nazis out of Russia. The glorious Red Army under his brilliant generalship had, at great cost in lives and treasure, liberated the whole of Eastern Europe, making the world safe for Communism.

As I sat rerunning the newsreels in my head, coming to grips with the new reality, I remembered how I had often seen him as kindly, smiling, pipe-puffing Uncle Joe visiting the halcyon fields of Georgia, fondling ears of corn and bouncing young girls on his knee (or was it the other way around?) before, that is, these things were frowned upon. His open-top car had been filled with a cascade of flowers carefully lobbed by joyful peasant workers.

That was what I knew.

This is what I learned later: the overly zealous or wilfully reckless pitcher might have to develop a liking for gulag soup.

Uncle Joe, smiling, waving in the manner of malignant dictators everywhere, was, under the façade (as we all now know), a shrewd manipulator and mass murderer.

His Cabinet lived in fear. Life in the inner circle hung by a thread: the towering tyrant cast a long, dark shadow.

Stalin encouraged his cronies to drink to excess while he abstained, watching for signs of dissent ' – in vino veritas – ' ever-vigilant in his paranoia, needing little excuse to ship one of his ministers off to Siberia when caught in a rare good mood or to the Hotel Lubyanka, conveniently within screaming distance of the Kremlin, for a slow session of nail-pulling before the inevitable bullet to the back of the head.

While he ruthlessly crushed his own people he was well loved, and seemingly all goodness flowed from the man.

He famously said, "One death is a tragedy, a million deaths a statistic."

Propaganda is a seductive mistress: ask the other Joe, Herr Goebbels.

I had loved this man deeply enough to die for him.

Now he lay shattered on the ground and I had a piece of his nose.

All that remained of the giant bronze of Joseph Stalin were his empty boots.

"Where have you been?" asked Gita angrily. Under normal circumstances I would be in the corner kneeling on chicken corn by now.

"Nowhere much, just looking out of the window at number 18," I lied (the home of a friend overlooking the street). She was too distracted by events; the window barricade complete, she got busy rattling the old Singer again. Why was she so focused on these damn coats? I did not dare ask so I grabbed a quick snack, thickly sliced fresh brown bread liberally smeared with lard. A generous sprinkle of paprika to make it less anaemic. The lard-covered slice, when viewed at certain angles in poor light, was a winter scene from the Eastern Front, at least in my imagination. Fantasies of war, heroic battles, triumph in the face of overwhelming odds were never far from my mind.

I took a large bite. Headed back to the streets.

A sense of 'normality' had returned and the clean-up began.

Groups of insurgents, some with weapons, others armed with nothing except their simmering rage, united by their desire to be rid of the Russians, stood around uncertainly on street corners, smoking, talking and waiting. Waiting for what? Leadership? Direction?

Some looked hopefully skyward. Were they expecting paratroops or divine intervention?

If so, neither was forthcoming, no break in the storm clouds, no host of angels riding heavenly chariots, no sword of just retribution raised high to smite the evil oppressors, and of course no paratroops.

It was all so bewildering. How could we know our enemy, which Army units were on 'our' side, and which were still under the command of Soviet sympathisers?

Danger lurked everywhere.

I latched onto an older man (perhaps around 50) wearing the ubiquitous black beret adorned with a variety of metal badges. He reeked of strong liquor and had, in my imagination, the hollow-eyed look of a killer. Cradled in his arms, 'Stalin's guitar', as the standard-issue Russian sub-machine gun was known to the Magyars.

I wanted it badly. Not enough to want him dead, just enough to see him taken off on a stretcher.

In my imagination he would be shot in the shoulder, sag to the ground, left hand covering the wound, fresh blood seeping through his coat and oozing through his fingers.

As he lay gasping, imploring eyes fixed on mine, he would raise his good arm to pass the weapon, Olympic torch-style, to my eagerly outstretched hands, instantly promoting me from observer to combatant.

This scenario was entirely real to me.

Swaying gently, he nipped at a bottle, hugged the weapon to his chest, the leather strap secure around his neck; I would have to wait to prise the weapon from his cold, hard grip.

"Hey, boy, fuck off, stop following me around!"

I retreated a few steps but kept him in sight, dogging him at a respectable distance. He moved down the block, periodically ducking into doorways, glancing nervously up and down the street.

In time other fighters joined him and they formed a 'street squad' of around 20 armed civilians. There were many rumours swirling around the city: Western (American) intervention by land and air was imminent, a popular theme.

The prospect of nuclear Armageddon and news of a Soviet army massing on the border were much more probable scenarios but were taken less seriously. There was no one in charge and they had no orders; to bolster morale and to keep focused many of the insurgents, joined by unarmed citizens, prepared defensive positions, thinking it impossible that the Russians would not return.

I closed the distance and was again at his elbow eyeing the sub-machine gun and weighing my chances of getting my thin, young finger around the trigger.

"I will not tell you again, boy, go home, your mother..." It ended right there.

There was a strange yet somehow not unfamiliar sound like that of a cabbage being cleaved in half. Jellylike pieces of brain splatted on the side of the yellowing stucco wall. Stalin's guitar clattered on the pavement as he sagged to the ground.

The game had turned deadly. Did I cause this man's death? Did my stupidity and selfishness cost him his life? I convinced myself that the horror I had seen play out right in front of me was somehow my fault. I stared at the body transfixed for some time, then spun on my heels and ran as fast as my legs could carry me in the direction of home. This was not how it happened in the movies.

Obviously I was not ready for combat.

Back to the relative safety of my building, I climbed the stairs to the third floor.

I knocked on my friend Zollie's door. No answer. The door was slightly ajar, it pushed open easily.

"Zollie, are you there, anybody home?" Nothing.

Crunching over glass and rubble I made my way to a street-facing window.

Peeking over the sill I watched defences being readied for the expected return of the Red Army. A small lorry towing a large- calibre anti-tank gun was unhitched and manoeuvred into a prepared position behind the sandbags; cobblestones were also piled up to form fire bases. Abandoned vehicles and tramcars were manhandled into position as makeshift barricades. Jars and bottles collected and lined up to be filled with a mixture of petrol and motor oil, a paraffin-soaked rag stuffed into the bottle top to make a fuse, the classic Molotov cocktail.

There seemed to be no co-ordination or communication between the various militias; confusion reigned and fear stalked the streets. The drunk fighter lay where he fell, his head, what was left of it, still partially covered by his beret. What had I done? From the window I watched as an older boy picked up the weapon and was now bent over taking his belt, extra magazines and grenades.

He laid out the colour-coded grenades neatly on the stacked paving stones. Like lethal lollipops the red one could have been strawberry, the yellow a tangy lemon; they all had a lethal purpose, some anti-personnel, fragmentation, others magnetic anti-tank, phosphorus or thermite.

I knew about these things as it was part of our training. Little Drummers were well-versed in military matters.

I put two fingers in my mouth and whistled. He looked up at the window, saw me and turned away.

I felt somehow that he owed me at least a nod, a wave even, as he now had the gun that rightfully, I felt, should have been mine. I ran down the stairs, then casually, to show how brave I was, sauntered slowly out of the building to the barricade.

I avoided looking at the drunk fighter's lifeless body.

As I approached he met my gaze and our eyes locked. We may have played football, even on the same side, but I could not be sure. He could not have been more than a couple of years older than me, but already had the look of a seasoned fighter.

"Can you tell me what is going on?"

"I don't know… but for sure the Russians are coming back." His grimy face inches from mine, breath garlicky. "You!" He tapped my chest hard with his index finger. "Go home, NOW!" Another hard tap for punctuation. "You can do nothing but die here. If you stay here you will never see tomorrow."

The last statement, delivered flatly without a shred of emotion and coming from this boy, was enough to frighten me into leaving the scene.

A fresh rumour that a Soviet armoured column was heading for the city swept through the barricade builders, adding urgency to the preparations.

Up to this point I had ignored being told to 'go home' by many people.

Yet as I walked towards my building past groups of fighters working in grim silence, making use of whatever was at hand to reinforce their positions, I felt like I not only may have caused the death of the drunk fighter, but was now also a deserter.

Torn between being a hero, standing and dying with my new comrades as I had been programmed to do, or going home, the choice was not as obvious as it now seems.

That boy may have saved my life.

I would be home in relative safety in plenty of time to enjoy a fried fish dinner while he crouched behind a pile of sandbags with 'my' sub-machine gun. What must have been going through his head, on maximum alert, scanning the top of the street looking for signs, a wisp of black smoke, a plume of dust, ears straining for the distant rumble of the awesome might of the Red Army bearing down on their position?

He would not have to wait for long.

At 3 am on the 4th of November, a day before my 10th birthday, a Soviet Army of around 32,000 combat troops and 1,200+ tanks were sent back over the Hungarian border. By first light they were on the outskirts of Pest and by the time I got out of bed the sounds of war were close enough for me to hear the distant rumble of big guns.

I just had to see what was going on. Everyone was asleep except for Neni, kneeling at her shrine in the corner of the kitchen. She was so intent on the dismal image of the Blue Virgin that she did not see me leave. I walked back along the balcony to number 18: the door was still open

The tenants may have been taking shelter in the cellar or had left town until things quietened down.

Heading for the window, I crunched through their best china. A glass-fronted cabinet, which had housed a collection of ceramic dogs, had fallen and spilled its contents. Undamaged among shattered poodles and headless basset hounds, a fist sized English bulldog peered dolefully at me.

It went in my pocket as a spoil of war.

Curiosity overcoming fear, I crawled to the window, peering over the sill to see what was going on in the street below, fully aware that I could easily be taken for a combatant and shot at.

Ironically you were more likely to be a target skulking behind walls than out in the open.

The lead tanks of the Russian column were rumbling steadily towards my building and into the sights of the anti-tank gun emplacement almost directly below my hiding place.

The four-man crew worked the load-and-fire sequence like professionals; they must have been deserters from the Army, way too slick for amateurs. The lead tanks were quickly disabled, crew scrambling out of the turret hatch through the billowing black smoke immediately cut down by withering small arms fire.

I could just see the top of his head behind the cobblestones. The 'boy soldier' was emptying the 71-round drum magazine in long bursts.

When he changed mags he looked up and saw me at the window. Incredibly he smiled and waved. I waved back.

Some distance down the street a steady stream of firebombs rained down on the halted tanks. Molotov would have been proud; the surprisingly effective cocktails smashed on the armour plate, spreading liquid fire, setting a number of Russian tanks ablaze.

Several tanks elevated their guns, targeting the top floors of the building.

Mostly I kept my head down but from time to time I managed to overcome my fear to take a quick peek over the windowsill.

Intense tank fire had collapsed the whole front of the building down the road. I don't know if any of the cocktail makers managed to escape.

In the street below a seemingly endless column of Soviet T-54 tanks were stopped in the middle of the street, the disabled lead tanks halting the column momentarily.

The anti-tank gun crew got off another couple of rounds before being overwhelmed by concentrated machine-gun fire. Many were killed; those that could still walk melted away, leaving the severely wounded to a fate unknown.

Eyes wide, trembling with fear, I still managed to poke my head over the sill from time to time. At the top of the road, what were unmistakably Red Army shock troops advanced on both sides of the street.

An explosion below drew my eyes back to the silent A/T gun. The shattered boy soldier's body lay some feet behind a pile of cobblestones. His left arm and most of his shoulder were gone. This boy gave up his life for reasons beyond my understanding; the child-sized fingers of his right hand still held a firm grip on 'my' gun.

The knocked-out tanks were bulldozed aside and the awesome parade rumbled on, turrets rotating robotically, searching for targets, firing at anything that moved. There was a lot of ordnance flying around, the skirmishes fierce, tracers ricocheting off armour in a spectacular display of fireworks.

Nothing could stop the relentless march of the monster machines.

What chance did a ragtag, uncoordinated insurgency have against the might of the Red Army?

Resistance collapsed after a brief, bloody fight, which left the neighbourhood littered with the detritus of war, spent munitions, abandoned defensive positions and mangled bodies.

The reinvading Soviet juggernaut continued to grind forward, unstoppable, scattering the resistance as it crawled relentlessly down the street.

Hastily erected street barricades served only to annoy the Russian tank crews; cars and trams, like the abandoned toys of a petulant child, were crushed under their tracks.

Fear parched my throat. I crawled through the smoke and dust back to the landing and then a quick dash along the balcony to my front door.

Neni let me in. It was sheer luck that my mother was at a neighbour's a couple of doors down and would probably not know that I had been out of the flat.

"Please don't tell her." Neni just looked at me with great sadness as she stood aside to let me in.

I locked the door of my room and climbed into bed.

Before my head touched the pillow, she banged on my door.

"Bring all your bedding and pillows to the bathroom right now!"

She must have learned something, probably just another rumour, but she came back highly agitated, shouting and banging around the flat for all of us to gather in the bathroom. Dragging our bundles, we crammed ourselves into the tight space. From the street, the sounds of war grew ever louder. My mother held Margo to her breast, rocking back and forth gently. Whimpering noises came from the bundled-up baby. Gita tried to hide the fear in her eyes by soothing us with a lullaby.

Periodically she would reach out and touch my brother and me in an effort to stop us from shaking. Neni wept; a cascade of tears rolled down her craggy cheeks, the beads slipped through her fingers at a greater than customary speed.

"Hush! Don't make a sound." Gita's nipple finally managed to silence Margo.

We cowered in our padded cell, silent in the dark.

Russian shouts and scuttling boots on the tiled landing seemed to be just on the other side of the bathroom door.

How could I have been so blind? More to the point, how could it be that I was so engulfed by the party system that the whole insurgency, the rising anger of the people, the seething discontent that must have been just below the surface had been so well concealed from me? Many must have harboured utter hatred of the Soviets, their dogma ridiculed behind closed doors. What about the men in suits? The revolver? The furtive meetings? Whispered conversations? What did all this mean?

We sat mostly in silence for ages. When the gunfire subsided, seeming to move away from our building, Gita eased the furniture aside and took a look outside. I followed her to the landing. The roof above the flat opposite where I had skulked and watched the street fighting was smoking heavily, then an orange flame leapt through the shingles.

Before long the roof was properly ablaze.

Priding herself on being a 'woman of action' and inclined to be bossy by nature, she took immediate charge, descending into the bowels of the cellar to find recruits for her bucket brigade but only managed to get a few reluctant volunteers. She told those that chose to remain in the 'safety' of the cellar that they would all be asphyxiated or be cooked crackling crisp if we did not put the fire out. A few more were bullied into joining our little brigade. "You will all choke down here, we need you, come and help us!"

"Look at this boy!" She pointed at me. "He will fight this fire. Why won't you?"

What is the definition of a volunteer? Someone who did not understand the question!

I had no choice but to puff out my chest and follow her lead.

Collecting all the buckets, larger saucepans and working hoses we could find, the reluctant troop led by Gita set about the blaze. My job was to keep filling the empty buckets as they came back through the window.

Gita, sweating profusely and covered in grime, would periodically return to the basement to try to recruit extra hands. The speculation was that the Reds were using 'phosphor bombs' and it would be impossible to put the fire out. Confusion fuelled by rumours were rife.

"You stupid bastards, you sit here while your house burns down around your ears. If we do not put the fire out you will all be cooked like slices of pumpkin! There is no help from the outside: we either put this fire out or the whole building will burn to the ground."

She could not get any more help. Returning to the bucket line, Gita and Julius exchanged a brief glance; something, some understanding on a level beyond my comprehension, passed between them.

Eventually, after hours of back-breaking work, we managed to extinguish the flames and proudly declared ourselves heroes. Physically exhausted, Gita and Julius fell into bed and were asleep in seconds.

I had other concerns.

Now that the fire was out and those that had chosen to hide in the cellar felt safe enough to go back to their homes, I went down to the basement to check on my booty.

A cinema, a haberdashery, pharmacy and a toyshop made up the street-side frontage of my building. All heavily damaged and wide open; much too tempting a target for the young looter.

The previous day I had waited for the cover of darkness to start my criminal activities. In a couple of highly productive hours I had systematically cleaned out all the cash drawers of the shops that fronted my building. These retail outlets were state-owned and therefore legitimate targets for the criminally inclined aspiring revolutionary, especially those too young to bear arms. Happily, I fit into both categories, needing little justification to embark on nefarious activities. The newly pilfered plastic wallet bulged comfortably against my right buttock.

Our storage space was soon stacked floor to ceiling with sacks full of toys and around a dozen or so bicycles.

I had no use for the pharmaceuticals but did liberate several cartons of perfume and cologne, making my mother an unwitting accomplice by gifting her a couple of bottles of rare '4711' Eau de Cologne, which I found hidden in a back room cupboard at the pharmacy.

She was delighted but knew me well enough to be a tad suspicious.

"Where did you get these from?"

"I found them in the rubble outside." That seemed to satisfy her, no further questions.

The rest I sold very cheaply door-to-door: the neighbours smelled better as the plastic wallet became fatter.

Julius asked to see me in the sitting room.

I knew this meant trouble but wasn't sure which of my activities had come to his attention. Did he know about my forays into the cornucopia and the loot in the cellar?

"What is all that stuff in the cellar and where did it come from?" he asked, answering my unspoken question.

At some point earlier he had stumbled on my treasure trove of looted goodies. Why he went down to the cellar was unclear. All I knew was that I was busted.

He was not angry, just deeply disappointed that I would do such a thing, not to mention the possibility of dire consequences for the family if the state/police got involved.

My main concern was the safeguarding of my newly acquired riches; avoiding punishment was a distant secondary issue.

"You must return everything to where it came from – the cellar must be empty by tomorrow morning." To my relief there was no talk of punishment.

"Yes, Papa." I left shamed but determined to make the best use of my time. The last time he chastised me was for spitting at another kid in the stairwell. He gave me five hundred lines, something like "Spitting is antisocial, unhygienic and may spread diseases".

He was a doctor, after all.

The shooting was almost over. What resistance remained had moved south away from my part of the city towards the Danube and Buda.

A few curious folks were starting to emerge from their hiding places.

One by one I wheeled the bicycles into the street, scrawled a price on a piece of cardboard, threaded the cardboard through the spokes and stood in the street right in front of my building. The prices were such that I sold out in minutes.

Who would not be tempted by a Steyr 10 speed with drop handlebars for the equivalent of a tenner?

Selling stuff that one did not pay for was much more to my liking than the prospect of 'real' work. Did this make me a capitalist/profiteer or just a thief?

No time to ponder these things, I was too busy counting the cash!

Smaller toys I gave away by the armful to the neighbourhood kids and my posse of mates.

The job was done, the basement was cleared. I headed back upstairs.

The next morning I was able to tell Julius that the cellar was empty. He laid a hand on my shoulder, nodded gently, opened his mouth as if to speak. A shadow passed over his face, he turned and walked away. What did he decide not to tell me? Why was everybody being so evasive?

I consoled myself with the thought that stuffed with cash the plastic wallet was fat and safe under my fat and safe pillow.

By now it was obvious, even to the most optimistic, that in spite of desperate appeals to the 'West', no American paratroops would be falling from the skies. Patton would not come roaring through the streets of Budapest; his chrome-plated six-shooters would remain holstered.

There would not be any help from outside.

The few remaining city blocks held by the rebels were squeezed ever tighter by the serpentine coils of the Red Army; it was just a matter of time.

Their choices were bleak: stand, fight and die, surrender to face an uncertain future; or the preferred option of many: pretend you had nothing to do with any of it, abandon or hide your weapon, go home, pin the red star back on your lapel and go back to the streets throatily cheering your second liberation from the reactionary agents of the despised capitalists.

Back to the status quo: point the finger at your neighbour before he could raise an arm and point at you.

For those that may have exposed themselves by getting actively involved, few options remained. Rough justice in the form of the heavy fist of the state would come down hard on those merely suspected of some anti-socialist behaviour.

Drawn by unidentified impulses, I set out in the direction of Elisabeth Bridge, trusting that my boyish charm and naive innocence would protect me.

Sporadic gunfire could still be heard as I walked towards the Danube. Destroyed and abandoned tanks and APCs both Russian and Hungarian sat smouldering at major intersections, evidence of the many fierce engagements.

Flies were already exploring the bodies which lay grotesquely angled in death.

Turning a corner, a Russian tank opened up in my direction from about 1000 yards.

Were they really shooting at me or were they aiming at another target somewhere behind me?

I had become numb to cruelty, carnage and death. Somehow I was able to insulate myself from the awful things that I had seen. Maybe because of, or in spite of this, I felt untouchable. Nothing could happen to me. I continued to saunter down the street, the red kerchief around my neck.

The sounds of bullets whizzing past me had a cinematic quality. It was exactly as depicted in the movies. Did they not see I was wearing the red YC neckerchief? If the bullets bouncing off the kerbstone at my feet was any indication, then the answer must be no.

Coming to my senses, I took cover in a doorway. Not so much scared, more puzzled: were they really trying to kill me? Why? What had I done? Did I somehow deserve death?

Waiting for the tank to trundle on, I continued towards the bridge, walking slowly in plain sight. Why would I be a target? I was just a child strolling through a battlefield!

A Russian heavy machine gun (DShK) mounted on a tripod squatted menacingly at the Pest end of Margaret Bridge. The sinister-looking weapon poked its voracious muzzle over the plump sandbags. Fresh-faced Russian 'boys' manned the position. Like a troop of meerkats they eyed me with curiosity – I continued walking steadily towards them not knowing what else to do; turning and running could be seen as a hostile act, an open invitation to the trigger-happy. Grinning insanely, too stupid to recognise the peril I was putting myself in, I walked up to and straight past them as they enjoyed a private joke at my expense but made no attempt to stop me. There was no 'destination', just a feeling that I should head for the wooded hills of Buda.

On the other side of the bridge I kept walking until the city gave way to country, the terrain steeper, the vegetation denser.

The wooded hills drew me on. Driven by some inner disturbance I kept walking.

The mid-afternoon sun barely managed to poke through the canopy; fading day giving way to dusk, it became noticeably cooler. Unfettered by rational thought I had left home in a shirt, light jacket, tracksuit bottoms, plimsolls with long knee socks. Not even enough sense to pack a lard sandwich. Hunger pangs rumbled in my stomach as I walked deeper into the woods. The thought of my cosy bed with newspaper-wrapped warm bricks by my feet was becoming more appealing by the minute.

Then I stumbled into the man with a gun.

CHAPTER 5

BUDA 1956

He blended into the forest so well that I almost bumped into him. Mud-splattered, encrusted with leaves, small branches and twigs sprouting from the top of his head, the man with a gun stood blocking my path.

The camouflage and his general state of disrepair made it hard to guess his age, maybe around 30. His feet entirely hidden by the greatcoat hanging on him like a shroud gave the impression that his torso was rooted to the forest floor.

Thin to the point of emaciation, his gaunt face was topped by the ubiquitous black beret, the twiggy head foliage held in place by an unravelled, repurposed length of gold braid.

It would have been terrifying if it was not so fantastic. The arms dangled limply at his side, right hand gripping a large, black Colt .45.

For what seemed like minutes we just stood there.

"What is that around your neck?" My hand instinctively went for the knot.

Before I could come up with a good answer he said, "Did the Russians send you?"

Tucking the gun into the military-style leather belt which held the coat tight around his frame, from his left pocket he pulled a spare magazine, from the right a handful of bullets. We stood inches apart as he fed the shells into the mag, his wild eyes sizing me up.

What did he see? A skinny kid dressed like he was on his way to the playground.

For the first time I faced the possibility that my short life, with so much undone and the cash in my stash unspent, could, with a gentle squeeze of the trigger, end right here.

Paralysed, barely able to process what was happening, I opened my mouth but nothing came out. Coughing dramatically to buy time, I loosened the noose to free up the vocal cords.

"No!" The word choked in my dry throat, the red kerchief around my neck seemed tighter somehow. "I live on the other side of that big hill. My dog chased a rabbit into the woods. I ran after it and got lost." The lies tasted good in my mouth, more palatable than the truth. "If you could please point me in the direction of the main road I think I can find my way home from there."

He grunted, shoved the spare mag back in his pocket.

Suddenly he lashed out and grabbed me by the lapels. Pulled me close so that our noses were almost touching.

"Are you stupid? Do you have any idea what is going on?" I looked at him stupidly so as not to disappoint. "What is a snotty-nosed little kid doing wandering around alone? Does your mother know where you are? Go home and hide behind her skirt." Or words to that effect.

How could he know that I would hide behind Neni's skirts from my mother!

"Get rid of that rag around your neck," he spat. "There are partisans in these woods, go home before you get shot." He released his grip. I stepped back.

The next thing I knew I was on the ground choking on dirt and seeing stars.

Then a gravelly voice from behind.

"What have we got here, a little Russian spy?" As I staggered to my feet, I was cuffed again, on the other ear this time, hard enough to knock me back to the ground.

This time, I stayed down and thought about making a dash for the woods while the two men argued about what to do next. Skinny tried to defend me. "He's just a kid lost in the woods."

The older man swore. "Why is the little shit wearing that red kerchief, eh-eh? Get up! Start walking."

Not daring to look up I rose and brushed off my knees.

By way of encouragement he prodded me in the back with the muzzle of his gun. It was looking decidedly sketchy for me at this point. I had no idea what to do so just meekly trudged along.

The skinny, young man was upfront leading, me in the middle, the older guy close on my heels, the MP 40 dangling from his right shoulder. For about an hour we wound our way through the forest in silence, the older man wheezing as we scaled a steep bank.

Deeper into the hills we climbed. I weighed up my chances of making a run for it again but decided it was not a viable option given the prospect of a bullet in the back, as well as the fact that I had no idea where we were.

At the crest we stopped to rest. Sitting in silence they both lit cigarettes, sucking heartily; nothing like a fag to revive flagging lungs.

Sitting on a fallen tree I asked, "What is your name?" The thin, young man did not hesitate. "Akos."

"That is my brother's name," I replied, glad to find some common ground, get him on my side perhaps.

The older man was having none of it. Glaring at me, "Shut up, you little shit, no more silly chit-chat."

I used the cigarette break to take a better look at the nameless one.

Between 50 and 60 years old, over six feet tall, slightly stooped, with two large and very bushy black caterpillars marching across his brow, below which a curly mess of greying hair formed a full beard.

Small, dark eyes buried in deep hollows, nose large and crooked, grey clumps sprouting from his nostrils and ears, face set in a habitual scowl.

Curly head of greying, wiry hair, headband Che Guevara-style.

The jumble of military outerwear was topped by a Sam Browne on which leather-trimmed canvas pouches housed the spare magazines for the MP 40.

No hat.

In silence they sucked deeply on their cigarettes, inhaling the unfiltered smoke as if it were the very essence of life.

"Let's move!" Pinching the minuscule fag remains and pocketing them, the old man stood, looked at his compass and led off. We followed, Akos now bringing up the rear.

The terrain levelled out but dense vegetation slowed progress to a snail's pace. We pushed through a final thicket onto a trail which eventually led us to a clearing.

There were around twenty armed men sprawled around a smouldering campfire. My arrival did not cause much reaction. The men seemed listless, resigned, almost like the crap had been knocked out of them and they just wanted to go home. Some were freshly bandaged, others nursed deeper scars not readily seen.

The pall of defeat covered the encampment.

Given the circumstances I thought it odd that the partisans did not seem unduly bothered by my presence.

I, on the other hand, was terrified of being at the mercy of a ragtag group of heavily armed, desperate men.

They sat me down with my back against a tree and told me not to move. A visibly twitchy young man holding up an enamel mug offered me a drink.

The water loosened my fear-parched tongue.

"I just want to go home, I am not a spy, nobody sent me, I just got lost in the woods," I pleaded.

"Shut up, boy! Tomorrow we shall see if you are telling the truth." Unibrow threw a greatcoat at my feet. "In the meantime this will keep you warm."

The fire was rekindled and when it got going wedges of pumpkin on sticks were toasted for the evening meal. The young fighter who had given me water earlier brought over a steaming slice and sat next to me.

"My name is Adam." I told him mine and we sat, blowing on the steaming pumpkin wedges. Hunger overcame prudence. We burnt our lips nibbling at the soft, orange pulp, even devouring the rubbery skin. Hunger will rapidly turn picky eaters into ravenous savages.

My mind turned to Soviet documentaries about the siege of Stalingrad.

I had no experience of real hunger but well knew that the denizens of that besieged city had endured a hunger so acute that it drove them to eat just about anything. The family pet, being readily available, was often the first to go. Farm animals, goats and horses were high on the menu. Rat stew could be tasty spiced with hot paprika. Even leather boots could, in extremis, be turned into something to chew on.

"Adam, what will happen to me?"

"If you told the truth we will let you go, if not then…" His voice trailed away. Tying a rope around my leg he attached the other end to his.

"Now go to sleep, we shall see what tomorrow brings."

I shut my eyes but my mind was vividly awake. Almost everything I had told them was a lie. How could they find otherwise?

I thought about escape again but there was always at least one man on guard. Whether poking at the fire, nipping on a bottle, or roaming around the camp smoking with the gusto commonly seen at the wrong end of a firing squad, a bleary eye was always kept on me.

I tried to stay awake, worried that something dreadful could happen at any moment, but my lids grew heavy and eventually, enfolded by the smelly greatcoat, I fell into a deep sleep.

The next morning a sharp yank on the rope woke me up. "

Get up, boy, we have to move right now."

Just then two men walked into the camp. One was limping, the other bandaged around his wrist.

Unibrow joined them and they walked out of sight. Returning a few minutes later they would not meet my gaze.

I was yanked up by the arms, and a blindfold was roughly tied around my head.

This was not looking good. It was quite possible that my life was about to end so why hold back? Gulping air, from somewhere deep inside I let go of what we were later to learn was a 'primal scream', thrashing and kicking until hands gripped my legs and someone stuffed a handful of leaves in my mouth.

"Keep quiet or I will give you something to cry about!"

By way of punctuation, Unibrow cuffed me to the ground again. Dragged back to my feet, what felt like a rope was tied around my neck. Was I to be hanged? I sometimes wondered why those standing on a scaffold with nooses around their necks or on the edge of a pit with cocked pistols at the back of their heads did not try to make some effort to save themselves. The answer is that one cannot comprehend what is taking place, the brain shuts down, the arms and legs will not respond: effectively one goes into shock.

A tug on the rope and I was led away like a small, scared dog.

Were they really going to just kill me?

I simply could not grasp what was going on. This could not be happening to me. Behind the blindfold images of my short life looped through my brain, my mother and Neni wailing over my limp body. Laci would have no one to play chess with. Who would spend the cash secreted under the stairs? What if my body was never found? Just another tick in the 'disappeared' column.

Terror, the fear of death, must somehow change the electro/chemical soup, revving up the synapses. Of course I knew nothing about human biology as I stumbled along in shocked silence, tripping and falling at times. All I knew was that I did not want to die.

Ages seemed to pass then he spoke.

"Don't worry, I will not harm you." It was Akos. "Just keep walking, you will be OK."

My life was to be spared? Or was he just saying that to keep me walking?

The skinny young man led me through the forest for what seemed like ages.

We stopped. He took off my blindfold.

"You don't know how lucky you are." He pulled the kerchief from his pocket and unexpectedly handed it back to me.

"Why are you giving it back?" I asked.

"It nearly got you killed, now it may help save your life."

Blinking, rubbing my eyes, trying to focus, I stuffed it in my pocket.

Using the big black weapon as a pointer, he said, "Just keep going down that trail, follow the stream downhill: that will get you back to the road. Go home! It is not safe to be out here." He looked scared and angry. For a moment I wanted to fall at his feet to thank him for sparing my life, but instead felt vaguely sorry that I had to leave him out there, knowing that he was fighting for a lost cause.

Casually, he released the safety, raised the .45 and fired into the air. The sharp crack reverberated through the hills.

Our eyes melded for a second. Turning, he started to climb back up the embankment.

I set off in the direction indicated and did not look back.

When I felt he was out of sight, I sagged to the ground trembling, sobbing out of sheer relief. I was still alive.

Finding the way out of the woods was harder than expected. I soon got lost again, winding trails ending in thickly tangled bushes or opening up into clearings offering a choice of directions. As the temperature dropped the prospect of getting back to Pest and home faded with the light.

The thought of spending another night in the forest was much more frightening than the Red Army tanks.

I had to find shelter as it was getting really cold and darker by the minute.

Finding a warm gingerbread house, even if inhabited by a snaggle-toothed crone with a black pointy hat, would be a happy thing.

As night fell I chanced on a woodsman's hut in a small clearing; the door was secured with a bit of string.

The musty, old hessian sacks lying neatly folded in a corner would make a crude mattress; the thin, scrappy blanket hanging on the door would have to do as a cover.

I rearranged some of the logs to make a platform bed and used the larger pieces piled against the door to make a barricade in case the partisans found out that Akos had not shot me and were out there looking to kill me. Shivering I lay on the log pile in the dark, afraid of everything. The cloak of invisibility loses its magic when you can't see your hand in front of your face. The logs did nothing to keep out the terrifying night sounds of the forest.

The lumpy bed pressed on my puny frame: the bones yearned for oblivion.

It was a bitterly cold night and as tired as I was I could not sleep until light started to seep through the cracks, the events of the last few hours swirling in my head. Did I let myself down by crying and pleading pitifully? Or given the circumstances was I a brave little comrade? Could I still call myself that?

The morning chorus punctuated by the crowing of a rooster finally opened my crusty eyes. Having removed all evidence of occupation, I set off down the narrow path knowing that where there were cocks there would be people. The smell of woodsmoke grew stronger as I followed the trail, shivering, teeth chattering.

In a few hundred yards I came upon a large clearing in which sat the woodsman's cottage, smoke rising from the chimney, offering the prospect of warmth and nourishment I so needed.

If only I had had the courage and energy to walk a little further instead of sleeping in the woodshed I may have had the possibility of a warm and cosy bed in a pleasant peasant cottage.

Hesitantly, I knocked on the door. After a pause a metallic bolt slid back, the door opened.

A waft of warm air gently touched my frozen face.

Stooping slightly a tall man looked down at me. There was a mellow kindness in his brown eyes. I felt an immediate rapport with this woody giant. He wore a weathered fur hat in the style of the Russian military, the earflaps tied over the top of his head. The star outline still clearly visible on the front, a reliable indicator of its provenance.

Dressed for work in heavy boots, wrapped in woolly layers, scarf and overcoat in hand he was ready to leave the cosy warmth of the cottage and start his day.

Shivering, through chattering teeth, in my friendliest voice I said, "Good morning. I wish you a good day." Smiling pitifully, I waited.

He looked me up and down, taking in my general state of disorder. I peered past him to the glow of the open fire, catching a whiff of the food still warm on the stove.

He took pity on me.

"Come in, my boy." He stepped aside to let me pass. "What are you doing here? What happened to you? How did you get here?"

I told him about my meanderings, the hard night in his woodshed, my fear of maternal retribution when I got home.

Prudently, I thought, omitting details like the Soviet troops on the bridge and the encounter with the partisans in the forest.

"My name is Zoltan, what's yours?" He enfolded my soft, outstretched hand in his heavily calloused paw.

He introduced me to his wife Anna and daughter Sylvia. They went to the kitchen while he and I sat chatting at the roughly hewn table drinking hot, weak coffee.

Keen to know what was going on in the city, he had many questions to which (if I had any answers at all) I only gave him a sketchy, neutral outline of recent events, unsure of where his sympathies lay. Gita had repeatedly drummed into my head, "Trust no one, keep your mouth shut, you know nothing!"

Anna produced a hearty breakfast of scrambled eggs with spicy hot kolbász (sausage), fresh baked bread, cheese, ham and home-made apricot jam. It was the best breakfast ever, made even better by the attentions of Sylvia, who, I guessed, must have been a couple of years older than me. She and I took sideways peeks at each other when her parents were diverted.

Very awkward around girls of any age, I fell in love immediately but could not look at her directly. I knew that if I sat next to her and our bodies inadvertently touched I would be reduced to a quivering idiot. The blush on my cheeks could be blamed on the proximity of the stove and the coffee. The babbling could not.

These outward manifestations of hormonal upheavals were something new to me, as only days ago I thought girls were too silly to bother with, to be avoided at all costs.

What a lovely family, kind, gentle, simple. Vaguely I wished my family were more like them, uncomplicated, open-hearted and joyful.

Replenished, warmed by the fire and Sylvia's lopsided smile, they sent me on my way with directions and an old overcoat to keep the morning chill at bay.

A crisp, sunny morning and a full belly did nothing to allay my fear. Not of the bullets, Russians or sinister swivel-eyed men in the woods; the fear that gripped me was anticipating my mother's wrath and the beating I was expecting when I got home.

Looking down from the top of the hill I could clearly see the city below. Taking the kerchief out of my pocket, I tied it loosely around my neck and followed a downward track, hoping that it would take me back to the main road. Trudging on through the thinning vegetation I could now make out the river and one end of the bridge.

The Soviet Army emplacements now on both ends of the bridge had been improved and reinforced, taking on a hint of permanence.

Comfortable in victory, the young conscripts manning the machine guns stood around casually, smoking and chatting. They paid me no heed as I crossed the bridge walking towards Rákóczi út. and home.

The grim reality of the crushing defeat the rebels had suffered was evidenced by the devastation: familiar buildings scarred by bullets, some crumbled; gaping holes in the façades; burnt- out trams and cars; destroyed armour. The aftermath of street fighting was everywhere.

Bodies lay unattended; the acrid smell of burning rubber mingled with diesel permeated the air. A few stunned and bewildered citizens could be seen wandering through the rubble-strewn streets.

I entered the dark portal of Rákóczi út. #82, leaving my footprints in the light grey dust. With a bit of luck she would not be home.

Fearfully, I knocked on the door. "Who is it?"

I was in for it. Damn! Was hoping I could sneak back in without repercussions.

"It's me!" Grunting and scraping noises came from behind the door.

The barricade shifted and the door opened.

Like a trapdoor spider on a cricket she leapt, enfolding my thin frame, literally squeezing the breath out of me, pressing salami-scented kisses on my head and cheeks.

Suddenly remembering her ordeal of the past 24 hours she came to her senses: smile turned to scowl and she pushed me away roughly, making a dash for the kitchen.

I ran in the opposite direction, taking up a defensive posture on the leeward side of the dining table.

There were muttered curses, a clatter of household objects. She swept into the living room preceded by the business end of the broomstick. When roused, as she was right now, one would be forgiven for thinking that that was her normal mode of transport.

This routine was, well, routine. The chase began.

My mother loved me dearly but if I crossed some ill-defined line she would lay into me relentlessly. My babushka-like protector Neni would try to intercede on my behalf and at times would take on the role of a referee standing between us, taking a few random blows as I dodged around the furniture.

Gita was fast but I was faster and more agile. After a few cartoonish minutes I was laughing hysterically, enjoying the dance secure in the knowledge that as long as I kept the table between me and Gita, the broomstick could not touch me.

Perspiring, flushed with anger and the chase, slowly, slowly my contagious laughter eventually got to her and she started to chortle through gritted teeth, cussing me out colourfully. I knew then it was over. We fell into each other's arms and the laughter turned to tears. Sobbing, she said, "How could you put me through such worry?"

I promised never to do it again – again.

I spent the rest of the day scheming: there must be a way to take advantage of the chaos in the streets.

The more you have, the more you want! Rich beyond my wildest dreams and still I wanted more. How can a spoilt, greedy, selfish little runt add to his hoard?

In the space of a few days I had rejected Stalin and become a bourgeois capitalist pig, oppressor, profiteer, looter, thief.

Under the old regime I would have had to denounce myself and be sent off to a 'Young Communist' re-education facility.

But not today: I was flush with the prospect of spending the contents of the plastic wallet.

In common with many of her peers, Gita had no real 'work' skills but she could sew. In those days it was all about finding a good man, preferably one that had a bit of status, a steady job, or at least some prospect of gainful employment. Drunken rages and domestic violence were only exceeded by chess and stamp collecting as popular pastimes for the Hungarian male. There was no guarantee that even careful vetting would expose those that were inclined to beat their women senseless in an alcohol-fuelled rage.

Pálinka and cheap red wine turns gentle men into raging bulls.

In a jiffy she could stitch up a nice summer frock or a fairly passable shirt for me on her well-oiled Singer. From some unknown source she got hold of several yards of thick, brown, plastic-coated material. As soon as the street protests started she had set about making us all overcoats. Work now resumed on the coats with a sense of urgency, and the old machine was getting a good workout. Three identical coats of differing sizes were in production, one for her, one for me and one for my little brother Akos. Margo was only about 16 months old and had no use for such a bespoke luxury item.

The plastic resisted mightily but was cruelly manipulated, literally bent to her will and eventually reformed into collars, buttonholes, pockets (with flaps) engirdled by an unyieldingly stiff belt. A large Bakelite buckle was used for fastening.

Possessed by the sewing demon she worked with the urgency of an editor on a deadline. Not until her fingers bled did she take a break to apply a home-made bandage made from a strip of old bedsheet.

"I could nip down to the pharmacy for some bandages."

"Ha, you are not leaving my sight!"

"What about dinner? I'm starving!"

"Go talk to Neni. I have to finish these coats." A nasty fishy smell crept under the kitchen door, the hiss of the frier punctuated by the clatter of saucepan lids.

What was it with these damn coats? She had done nothing but sew for the last few days!

Julius sat in his leather armchair occasionally peering over the top of the paper, staying aloof from our little squabbles.

Neni staggered in with a large tray loaded with steaming platters, plates and cutlery. Muttering, she placed the tray on the table.

"Hard to find anything decent to cook in these godless times." Her mumblings followed her back into the kitchen.

Battered fish deep-fried in lard, one of our regular favourites, parsley potatoes, boiled carrots and red cabbage.

In all the excitement of the past hours food had been all but forgotten. I fell upon the oozing mess like a ravenous hyena on a fresh wildebeest carcass even while the rest of the family were lining up at the bathroom sink to wash their hands (with soap) – a ritual Julius insisted upon but I largely ignored.

The reaction was swift. I had barely taken the third bite of fish when a peppery burning sensation in my mouth and throat stopped the fourth forkful from reaching the bottomless pit. My face flushed, and tiny beads of sweat moistened my brow.

The fish was off: my greed had saved the rest of the family from what for me at least turned out to be a life-altering event.

From that day on I had to cross the road to avoid displays of wet fish. Even now I cannot tolerate any kind of seafood. I know that I have missed out on a vast range of culinary delights. My life is poorer for that. Would it be possible to survive on coconuts on a desert island? Let's hope I never have to find out.

With all that I had seen and learned in the preceding few days it was easy for me to blame the Russians for everything wrong in my life and the world in general, so it was not a great stretch of the imagination to blame them for the bad fish.

Dr. Mihály's professional care and convulsive vomiting soon had me feeling better and I was packed off to bed with a large glass of water.

"Goodnight, Mama." Her back arched, bearing down on the sewing machine with elbows splayed; breathing hard, she barely looked up. I went to my room and locked the door.

The plastic wallet was so well stuffed that it exceeded the design specifications of the manufacturers.

I was unable to fold it.

It lay dormant between the pillow and case, not the most original of hiding places but it was still there, so good enough.

With trembling hands, eyes wide with greed, I spread the contents on the bedspread. The pastoral scene depicting shepherds in tall black hats leaning on knobbly sticks was partially covered by the spoils of my opening gambit into the world of capital.

Full of promised value I start to arrange the notes into neat piles. Before I could finish, a voice: "Go to sleep now, we have a busy day tomorrow." She tried the locked door.

"OK, Mama, I am going to sleep. Goodnight!"

There was more cash than I had ever seen in private hands. I would have to find a better hiding place. Stuffing the notes back into the wallet, it fattened up like a tick on a Labrador.

This was how rich people must feel: now that I had it how could I protect it and stop others from taking it from me?

A curse, yes... that's it, I would include the Gypsy curse Neni had taught me. She was an endless source of what may be described as folklore. Home-made infusions, incantations and herbal remedies for whatever ailed you; she always had a potion simmering on the stove. Not so many years ago practising this ancient lore would have had her corn-encrusted feet warming on a bonfire!

Tearing a page out of an old exercise book, I scribbled the following:

"Be warned o seeker of secrets,

Disturb this spirit at your peril

The hand that touches this (insert appropriate item)

Shall turn dry and die

The arm will shrink, the brain rattle in the skull, teeth will rot, lips wither" etc. Slipped it in with the banknotes. That should do it.

The flat was quiet except for an odd gurgling noise from the kitchen. Hard to tell if it was Neni or the plumbing. Either way this was a perfect time of night to sneak down to the communal basement. Getting dressed in silence, I crept out to the kitchen. I would need a few things.

Neni was lying on her back; the knotted headscarf prevented her mouth from opening sufficiently for natural slack-jawed sleep. As a result, unearthly noises breezed through the graveyard of her teeth. I eased past her to the pantry, took a box of matches, a stump of a candle, serving spoon, ate the remaining crumbs in the biscuit tin and tucked it under my shirt. Perfect. I tiptoed past Neni and out of the kitchen.

The steps to the cellar were dark and the lights, as expected, did not work. My intention was to 'go deep' but a shiver of fear ran up my spine and I dared go no further than the steps. This would have to do.

In the flickering candlelight I started to dig a hole in the soft dirt under the stairs. Periodically stopping to listen, all was still; some muffled noise from the distance, a barking dog somewhere upstairs. I was alone, unobserved.

In fear of what may be lurking in the dark behind me, using the spoon I dug a pretty good-size hole in less time than it took me to scribble the curse, then put both wallet and note in the tin box, placed it in the hole and covered it with dirt, spreading the top layer around to obliterate the evidence.

Safe from vermin and robbers, the notes buried in the dirt behind the wooden stairs held my dreams.

I could hardly wait to dig it up. When things returned to normal the cash and I would be ready.

I didn't know exactly how much I had but surely I had enough to buy anything.

A horse, an aeroplane, a suit of armour...

I saw no signs of life on my climb back up to the third floor, crept into the flat, slipped into my fluffy bed, and fell into a satisfied slumber.

The clatter of the Singer woke me up. She looked like she had been at it for a while. Facing the large window with her back to me, Gita was bent over the machine, making best use of the early morning light.

Neni came in with some tea on a tray. I watched my mother kneading the hard plastic, cursing gently. I sipped my lemon tea wondering what the devil had gotten into her.

"Can I try mine on?"

"Give me a bit more time...nearly ready."

Neni brought me a plate of bread and butter generously smeared with home-made plum jam.

After I munched my way through breakfast Gita let out a triumphant hoot, straightened her back, and turned.

"They are finished!" I think I was more relieved than her as the constant whirr of the machine was getting on my nerves. To say nothing of parental neglect.

I was rather looking forward to trying on the new coat, fancying myself as a pint-sized KGB officer.

In later years I wondered why the well-cut, smartly tailored leather overcoat was preferred by the merchants of terror. The Gestapo, petty criminals, nightclub bouncers and rank and file Mafiosi also favoured the garb.

Perhaps they were a tad more intimidating than regular old wool or serge.

Or could there be more sinister practical considerations, the slick surface making the removal of bodily fluids easier?

No need to bother the dry-cleaners after a gory session in the dungeon, just wipe with a clean, soapy sponge. This is all just speculation on my part. They probably all (even the Gestapo) went to the same Jewish tailor. Who knows?

Our brown plastic coats were formidable. She helped me put it on. Shoulders sagged, knees buckled under the weight.

Mumbling distractedly, she struggled to force the carved-horn buttons through the holes.

I stood in front of the full-length mirror in the hall and admired her work.

Although I could not fully lower my arms or bend my elbows more than a few degrees, it looked great and would have intimidated a despot.

The coat's double-breasted frontal armour consisted of large, round buttons, triple-stitched collar with lapels the size of a baby elephant's ears. The Bakelite buckle attached to the thick, wide belt completed the picture.

The fact that I was barely able to move, jerkily at best, and looked like a robot going on an intergalactic holiday, weighed lightly on Gita. In spite of his protests Akos was also encapsulated in his coat, the belt adjusted to maximum efficiency. Finally, she put hers on and we three stood in a line like Gestapo babushka dolls waiting for a bus.

In spite of the diversions I sensed a change on the wind. The hogo of anxiety hanging in the air even as the adults around me made a fine show of normality. There were anxious glances between Gita and Julius that I was not expected to detect.

"Can I go and play at Laci's?"

"Only if you promise to stay there."

Making the right noises, I dashed out of the door and ran down to the corner flat on the first floor.

"He is doing his homework." Mrs. Dvorak told me to come back later.

Why do they have him working so much? What a waste of valuable play time.

I headed back to the streets.

In that sweet spot of life where mostly I was ignored, too young to be a threat, old enough that I could roam freely without being challenged.

There were uniforms everywhere, Russian mostly. Some units of the Hungarian Army were scattered around to lend some semblance of credibility to the invaders.

Heavily patrolled by Soviet troops, the streets seemed to be calm and somewhat normal, armoured vehicles stood at intersections, a grisly reminder of the heavy hand that crushed the revolt.

The ÁVH were back in business with renewed vigour. If they didn't like the cut of your jib they would 'invite' you into one of their mobile interrogation units. Not much more than a blue box on wheels in which sat an ÁVH officer accompanied by a guard. This is where preliminary investigations were made. If you carried any kind of a wound or your answers did not satisfy the interrogator, you would be arrested, shackled and loaded into another vehicle. When the van was full it was driven off to someplace where more intensive inquiries could take place. I hung around, coming and going so as not to attract attention, and had plenty of time to observe the process. I got a fleeting glimpse of the officer inside the box. He looked grim, all business. After a while he noticed me hanging around and had one of his stooges shoo me off. The events of the last few days had shattered my world. Nothing made sense anymore. The smile had been wiped off my face.

I thought a lot about what I had seen today and in the days leading up to the Russians rolling back into Budapest. Foolish child, all this must have been happening around me and I was unaware or chose to ignore anything that did not fit in with my indoctrinations.

This was the end of innocence.

The streets were busy with clean-up crews shovelling, sweeping the rubble and broken glass into piles, waiting for lorries to transport the detritus of war to destinations unknown. Hands deep in pockets, trudging back towards my building, I spotted Laci's father, Bruno.

Bent over, focused on the job, he did not see me until I tapped him on the shoulder. Great clouds of dust rose from the ground.

Laci's father looked at me blankly. "I cannot talk to you, Ati, please keep moving." Looking around nervously, he turned his back on me, white knuckles gripping the broom handle.

I stood there for a moment blinking in the dust and walked away.

This man was a fixture in my life. He and his wife took me in like a second son. Unlike all the other 'daddies' he was always there, kind, considerate and wise, someone I could count on when things got too weird upstairs. Now he would or could not speak to me! What had happened to change what I always considered to be an unbreakable bond between us? Strange times.

Sad and confused, I climbed the stairs to the third floor.

My mother was generally relentlessly cheerful. That being said, she had turned it up a notch, demonstrating alarming symptoms of a full-blown certifiable maniac.

"Sit sit sit… eat!"

"Are you trying to kill me again?" She did not see the joke. " Clean your plate and get ready for bed."

"It's only 7 o'clock! I'm not tired."

"Just do as I say, I have no time for your games!"

Locking my door I consoled myself with thoughts of the stash safely buried in a shallow grave and occupied myself with fantasies of frenzied consumerism, my head spinning with images of all the things that I would be able to spend my money on.

Being woken (even gently) at anytime will always be an intrusion into my dreamworld, especially at 4 am.

"Whaaaat? What time is it? It's still dark outside…Why are you waking me up?"

"Get up, get dressed, we are going on a trip to the country." Gita had laid out the clothes I was to wear.

"Where are we going?" She ignored my whining question and went about rousing the rest of the family.

Rolling sluggishly out of bed, I headed for the bathroom.

Gita had prepared everything: spare clothing, toiletries and a few treasured possessions were stuffed into small knapsacks; the plastic coats on stout, wooden hangers hung stiffly in the hallway. They looked intimidating even before we climbed into them.

Margo started to wail for no apparent reason.

I wondered if it was because she didn't have a plastic coat. Just a baby, how could she know that she was lucky not to have to bear this newly imposed burden cruelly thrust upon her older siblings? Akos and I were at times used as fashion accessories. In spite of spirited resistance culminating in screaming hissy fits, we were made to bear the indignity of wearing the 'sailors' outfit inexplicably popular those days with parents bent on humiliating their children in front of their mates!

Gita silenced Margo by putting a teat in her mouth.

It did not seem to matter how often she drained those fleshy orbs, somehow by some mysterious means they were replenished. Female physiology held many secrets and I wondered how the milk got in there in the first place. When she drank a glass of milk did that simply refill the tank or was there some other arrangement with the milkman that I was unaware of?

Those magnificent breasts used to be mine, then my brother suckled happily for a span, now my sister was the current (and final) leaseholder.

While my mother fussed around us and made sure we had as much as we could reasonably carry, Neni prepared breakfast. If the amount and variety of the food on our plates were any indication, we were in for a long day. "Eat everything on your plate, I don't know when we shall be able to eat again." Following her own advice, Gita wiped her plate clean with a piece of fresh, crusty bread; I did the same, wondering why we had to stuff ourselves.

Julius was nowhere to be seen. I assumed he must have stayed at his flat on Tégla utca. No matter, he would no doubt join us shortly.

At first light three plastic coats plus Margo and our meagre bundles trundled to the railway station.

"What if the trains are not running?"

She turned to me. "The stationmaster told me yesterday that all was back to normal. I know his wife, he would not lie to me."

If Gita's intention was for us to blend in with the general population she would have had more success if we had been wearing high-visibility vests. Perhaps they were admiring glances – but no, I did see two ladies exchanging glances and giggling at us.

Gita, oblivious to ridicule, focused on her task, purchased tickets and we boarded a train. There was still no sign of Julius.

"When is Julius coming? Where are we going?"

"Stop with the questions, I will tell you later!" Why was she so angry?

Surprisingly the carriages were not very crowded; Gita had expected a lot of people would be heading to the countryside for a 'holiday' away from the turmoil in Budapest.

In those days train interiors were much more luxuriously constructed: hardwoods, wrought-iron brass fittings and well-upholstered seats. The windows could be lowered into the door recess by sturdy leather straps so that the overly inquisitive could lean out and get a boulder-sized lump of soot in their eye. The corridors ran the length of the carriage with compartments to one side with seating for around eight people.

She found an empty compartment.

I had the good sense to stay silent, having experience of likely repercussions when Gita was in such a high state of agitation.

After an hour of tense waiting the train pulled out of the station. Now that we were actually moving, I settled into the journey. A few days at the lake would be a welcome change from the mayhem in Budapest.

Jolted out of my musings by the compartment door sliding open, we were joined (much to Gita's annoyance) by a young man and a girl who could have been his sister.

They looked to be in their early twenties, well dressed, polite, asking my mother's permission to join us, then lapsing into an uneasy silence.

Shortly thereafter a slightly built, distinguished-looking gentleman entered our compartment. I noticed that his hands seemed large in proportion to his build. He took the window seat opposite Gita, tipped his hat, ignored us children.

I looked him over, mid- to late-thirties, clean-shaven with nicotine-stained fingers.

He wore a good-quality grey suit, starched white shirt with shiny metal cufflinks, plain red silk tie and polished russet brogues.

On the small, brown leather suitcase which he now used as a makeshift lap table he neatly arranged two pipes; one straight stemmed, the other curved. The curved one suited his mood, and he fondled it in a sensuous way. From his jacket pocket he produced a leather pouch, a tool for poking/tamping the tobacco, and a box of matches.

These items were arranged neatly on the valise. Ceremoniously he filled the bowl, tamping with his thumb and leaving the tool unused. With well-practised ease and anticipatory delight he struck a match, waited for the phosphor flare to subside, and applied the flame to the bowl.

Puffing loudly, enveloped in a cloud of blue-grey smoke, he sat back with a smug, pensive look on his face. The smoke curled around his head. Suddenly he looked vaguely familiar but I could not place him.

Gita glared at him and opened the carriage window, letting in a chill blast.

We all complained. Prolonged, noisy negotiations between my mother and Mr. Pipe ensued. The window was to be left open a couple of inches.

Compromise reached, harmony restored.

Unlike Gita, I quite liked the smell of his burning shag, bearing in mind that in those days I enjoyed the smell of petroleum and would deliberately inhale great lungfuls of the noxious stuff. It's a wonder I have any brain cells left.

The collar of the coat had started to decapitate me, the rough plastic sawing at the back of my neck, and I started to complain.

"Shut up! Here, put this around your neck and sit still!" She handed me the square of red cotton. Recognising it immediately as my Young Pioneer neckwear, I folded it corner to corner as I had been taught and tied it around my neck, wondering why she should have had it in her pocket. I thought about what the skinny partisan back in the wooded hills of Buda had said before he melted back into the forest.

"Pin this on your shirt." She handed me my Little Drummers badge.

"Where are we going? Can I take this coat off?"

"I told you! To the countryside, and yes, you may take it off."

"But WHERE in the country?" I whined. "Are we going to Lake Balaton?"

The carriage door slid open.

A large, round man, the conductor, hesitated at the threshold then, turning sideways, sucked in his stomach with a grunt and launched himself into our compartment.

In his wake two young Magyar soldiers, one with a slung rifle, the other a junior officer with a sidearm. Suddenly the space was oppressively crowded.

This was not normal – these were not normal times.

"Tickets and papers please," said the conductor politely.

Gita had ours at the ready and handed them over with a big smile.

"What is the purpose of your trip?" asked the officer. The red kerchief around my neck and the 'Little Drummers' badge on my chest did not go unnoticed.

"As you must know, the city is not a good place for children right now so I am taking them away to visit relatives." Gita smiled seductively.

The smile and explanation proved to be sufficient. The trio turned their collective gaze on the pipe smoker. The young couple were becoming agitated, making a brave show of searching their bags and pockets for non-existent papers. It was increasingly plain that they did not have travel permits.

Mr. Pipe handed over his ticket, tucked in the pages of a passport-type document, hard cover embossed with what appeared to be the emblem of the Communist Party.

All three stiffened slightly, the soldiers saluting, showing him a certain deference after examining his papers. No questions asked.

Why? Who was he? I was wary and suspicious.

The young couple without the right papers were arrested, handcuffed and, despite their protestations, bundled out of the compartment.

We were now alone with Mr. Pipe, the heavy silence broken by a voice from behind the smoke.

Looking at me, "That was very clever of your mother, the badge and all!" For the first time I studied this slight, well- turned-out man and his leather valise and noticed that, even though I could not put my finger on it, there was something not quite right about him.

"Szombathely is a beautiful city, but why go there now? I will tell you," continued Mr. Pipe. "It is because it is close to the Austrian border." He grinned broadly, showing tobacco-stained teeth. There was something strange about his top lip. Was it a trick of the light? It seemed to be a shade lighter than the rest of his face.

"If you have the right papers and a convincing story nothing is impossible," he added, grinning.

I turned to Gita. "What is this man talking about, Mama?" I was pretty sure the lakeside villa was nowhere near the border.

Gita shot Mr. Pipe a fierce look. With a loud click he clamped his yellowing teeth on the droopy stem, retreating behind the smokescreen.

None of these events made any sense to me. The further we travelled away from home, the more uneasy I became. What was all this 'Austria' talk anyway? I just wanted to go home. Failing that, some idea as to where we were heading could have eased my mind. The prospect of a few idyllic days on the shores of Lake Balaton would have suited me perfectly.

Gita was in no mood for my questions.

"We are just going on a short break in the country, get away from it all for a while."

Her demeanour suggested that any further enquiries were pointless.

Still, I thought, even if we were not going to the lake, a few days in the country would do us all good after the bedlam of Budapest.

Every turn of the wheel took me further from home and the cash buried under the stairs. I was deeply troubled by recent events; something was not right. A sense of foreboding roiled my brain. I wish I had been able to nip down to the cellar and dig up the booty before we left for the station – alas, too late now.

I hoped the Gypsy curse worked and it was all still there when we got back.

What could be keeping Julius back in the city? I so wanted his calm, measured words to soothe me.

The rest of the journey was spent in uneasy slumber. Even Margo slept like a little angel. Mr. Pipe smoked steadily, dozing between refills.

The metallic clickety-clack of steel wheels on shiny rail were now spaced further apart. The train was slowing; we were approaching the terminus and our destination.

I was anticipating a country holiday, looking forward to exploring the grounds, poking around bothering the beasties that surely lurked in the bushes, a bit of swimming in the lake, maybe some kayaking.

I had plans to initiate my brother, expanding his horizons and doubling the membership of the Explorers Club. There were adventures to be had, mysteries to be solved.

The feeling that this Balaton holiday would be like no other I put down to the general upheaval, the discombobulation of the times.

Climbing back into our plastic coats and gathering our meagre possessions, we prepared to alight.

Mr. Pipe had no luggage apart from the small suitcase he had used as a table – come to think of it, the case never left his grasp. Strangely he seemed somewhat attached to us also, almost as if we had the same destination.

We left the carriage and headed for the exit. He and Gita exchanged quiet words which I could not make out but there was a noticeable shift in the relationship, a secret shared; the intimacy of fellow-travellers? We stood outside the railway station and waited.

"Where are we? What are we waiting for?" This plainly was not the station for Lake Balaton.

Gita took my hand, asking Mr. Pipe to watch A&M, and led me back into the now deserted station. She squatted to level our heads, placed her hands on my shoulders and with the searching intensity only a mother is capable of looked me in the eye.

"You are now the man of the family and have solemn and serious responsibilities – are you up to the task?" Although you could not tell under the inflexible coat my chest swelled with pride. I listened with rapt attention, becoming increasingly deflated as she explained what was about to happen.

"Son, I know that all this must be very strange to you, but please trust me. Austria is the safest place to be right now. Besides, you love to ski and the slopes are just about perfect right now. Julius has booked us a lovely little cabin at a resort just a few kilometres over the border where we will wait for him to join us. I know that I have not been completely truthful with you, but the less you know, the less you can tell!"

"Why does this have to be such a big secret? Why do we have to go there? What's wrong with spending some time at the villa?"

Ignoring my questions, she stood, turned and walked towards the street to rejoin the others.

I ran after her. None of this was making any sense. "Why Austria? Why now? How long will we be there? When is Julius coming?"

"Just trust me, all will be well. Tomorrow I will answer all your questions."

How could I trust her after all the lies and deceit? The prospect of rampant consumerism was, for the sake of a stupid holiday, slipping from my capitalist clutches.

A tall man wearing a Cossack-style fur hat and heavily soiled work clothes approached our group. Smiling, he greeted us warmly, as one would visiting relatives. He hugged each one of us in turn.

The piggy smell reminded me of a time when Gita went away for a few days with one of her admirers, leaving me with some country relatives on their farm.

One morning I was woken by dreadful squealing noises. Looking out the upstairs window into the courtyard below just in time to see the knife open the pig's throat did nothing to endear these peasant relatives to me. The spurting blood was collected in a white enamel bowl as the poor pig continued to struggle before going limp.

Not a sight a city boy was used to.

A few days later I tucked into the best sausages I had ever tasted.

Years later, I made the connection.

This smelly man, this bumpkin, was here to help us... apparently. I just wanted to go home. The last time we went skiing the hardest thing we had to deal with was crabbing up the slopes. Now we needed the services of a 'guide' to show us where the snow is? The word 'coyote' had not yet been applied to people smugglers.

I yearned for my bed, my room, my old building and especially my friend Laci. Every step took me further away from the comforts of home. Whatever Gita had in mind was disconnected from my reality.

It was just as well that at this stage I did not really understand what was going on or I may have been inclined to sell out my family in the naive expectation of forcing us to return to our normal lives.

With urgent hand movements, Mr. Hat indicated for us to follow him around the corner.

A horse and cart stood waiting, steam rising from the body of the huge, brown beast, its head deep in a feedbag, grinding the contents contentedly.

The open cart was fitted with leaf spring-mounted wooden benches. We clambered up. Mr. Pipe sat upfront with the driver, Mr. Hat.

The whip cracked above the wide chestnut buttocks. The horse, taking up the slack, straining at the harness, lumbered down the dirt road without interrupting his lunch.

A long, bumpy ride later we arrived outside a large farmhouse flanked by an assortment of outbuildings. A horrific piggy squealing resounded in the courtyard. Mr. Hat's pork-fed wife opened the front door, smiling coyly, and waved us in.

Gita asked me to wait with her outside. Mr. Hat took the others into the house, shutting the door behind them.

She took a deep breath. "The time is right, I will tell you everything."

As I had suspected, things were not as they seemed.

She made it sound as if this was a good thing for me.

"Julius and I have decided to give you the gift of life. I do not expect you to fully understand this now but you and your siblings will live in freedom. We are going to America and will never return to Budapest."

Even though I knew this convoluted trip was not going to be a regular holiday, this was still a stunning revelation. How could I stop this madness? This was a bad dream and I wanted no part of it.

She took my hand. Angry and confused, I snatched it back. In silence we walked through the doorway to the start of a new life. There were around 15 adults in the crowded room. Idle chit- chat and nervous laughter filled the air. There were no children apart from us and no introductions were made. Mr. Hat showed Gita into an adjoining room. As he turned to shut the door I caught his eye and he winked at me.

I later found out that she had paid him with two diamond rings and a multi-string antique pearl necklace which had been an heirloom and had adorned the necklines of generations of female relatives. Such was the price of freedom.

"Mama, I have to tell you something." Maybe this would somehow change her mind. She waited while I collected my thoughts.

I went on to tell her about my looting spree and the treasure buried under the stairs.

"Darling boy, my liver, my heart, the money has no value. I am so sorry, even if we went back for it you could not buy a Turks slipper or even a pretzel with it anymore."

Could it be true that money had suddenly become valueless? How was this possible? Was she just telling me this to make me feel better, or was this just another ruse to shut me up? Many things had changed, unprecedented events, mysterious and strange happenings, but money was, at least in my experience, never without value.

A few coins would buy an ice cream or a loaf of bread. These were absolute tenets of daily life.

This whole escapade was incredible. I simply could not accept that my hard-looted cash was worthless!

Mr. Pipe followed Mr. Hat into the room to make his arrangements.

When both emerged Pipe was looking glum. Mr. Hat, hard on his heels, was grinning widely.

It was plain to see that whatever went down in the back room was to Mr. Hat's advantage, as one could almost see him mentally rubbing his palms together.

I turned to Mr. Pipe. "Excuse me, sir, I was always taught to be polite even to people I did not like. May I ask you a question?"

"Certainly, my boy, fire away." Until now he had virtually ignored me. Now he was all chummy and smiling. What a prick, thought I. Anyway...

"Is it true that money no longer has any value?"

"Who told you that?"

"My mother."

He rubbed his chin in the manner of thoughtful people.

"Well, how can I put this? That is not 100% accurate, as of this moment, right now with so much uncertainty it is hard to spend the forint. Of course you are too young but right after the war we had the pengő as our national currency. It devalued so fast that you needed a wheelbarrow full to buy a box of matches. It is not like that now but there is a lot of fear so…" Gita entered earshot so Pipe stopped talking but he had told me enough.

Even though this new information made me feel less distraught about the buried wallet, I was still annoyed that I had not had a chance to disinter it before leaving town.

I did not like what was going on. I did not like Pipe, I did not want to be here in a room full of strangers but I was hungry (as always) and whatever Mrs. Hat was cooking smelled delicious. Putting aside my feelings for the moment, anticipating a good bowl of grub, I edged towards Mrs. Hat and the food.

She used both hands on the ladle to stir a large cauldron of steaming goulash sitting on the black-iron range. The delicious smell of loaves baking in the oven permeated the house.

I was right there first in line, roughly fired earthenware bowl at the ready, spoon in hand Oliver Twist-like. She ladled the stew into my outstretched bowl, a dollop of sour cream on top, big chunk of brown bread on the side; the noisy room gradually turned from chatter to clatter.

I greedily attacked my bowl, already eyeing the pot for seconds.

In silence, Mr. Pipe sat on the floor with us, his bowl on top of his suitcase. Pursing his lips, he blew on the first spoonful. I imagined he was taken by the group to be 'the man of the family – ' the role so recently bestowed and accepted (albeit reluctantly) by me. My mother had warmed to him and might even have batted her eyelashes a little.

The oversized hand lingered a little too long on her elbow. She sat a little closer than even the crowded conditions demanded. The eyes locked a nanosecond longer than normal.

I had seen and now recognised what was going on. They were flirting.

This bizarre journey and Pipe's involvement pissed me off. Why did he keep hanging around? His creepy presence was an unwelcome intrusion into our little family unit.

"When is Julius arriving?" Gita gave me one of her looks. "He will meet us later," is all she had to say.

As evening fell the children were put to bed on cots in a small room. This included me, even though I was now the nominal head of the family.

"Get a big sleep, we have a busy day tomorrow." Gita shut the door on us.

CHAPTER 6

THE BORDER

These surprise awakenings were starting to hack me off. I would never get used to being woken (however gently) from a dream where I had some control over what went on – always managing to wake up before I hit the canyon floor.

In a trench waiting for the onslaught, the barrel of my gun became a garden hose, a recurring theme, just as the tip of the enemy's bayonet touched my chest I could push the abort button and rouse myself.

Unfortunately 'reality' is not so easily managed.

It was still dark outside A light rain beat gently on the window panes. The gaggle were abuzz. Dressed and ready to go, belongings gathered, we stood around nervously.

"Where are we going with all these people?" Petulance personified, that's me.

"Just a short walk, darling, there is a firework display and we need to get there early so that we get good seats."

That seemed reasonable to me, I loved a good display. What kid doesn't?

Two-legged on a three-legged stool Mr. Hat stood, bumping his hat on the ceiling light, sending the single unshaded bulb swinging. It was a comic moment, light relief if you like; as the giggles faded he regained his composure, lowered his voice to a conspiratory whisper.

"As we walk, spread out, do not bunch up. I will stop from time to time to let stragglers catch up. When a flare goes up stop immediately, lie down and do not move until I make this sign." He removed his hat and circled it above his head.

"It is very important that we maintain silence. The baby," he pointed to Margo, "must be kept quiet. Our lives will depend on stealth and luck."

This must be the mother of all firework displays, stealth, luck, our lives! Again I got the feeling that Gita was not giving me the full picture.

She assured him and the others that 'the baby' had been given a mild sedative and should be no problem. Margo would sleep through the whole ordeal.

I opened my mouth to protest but one look from Gita shut me up.

At this point it finally dawned on me what that little chat Gita had with me back at the station was all about. The life- altering significance of those words, about taking responsibility, stepping up, being a man etc. None of which I was ready for and certainly did not want.

It meant: Leaving that crone Neni behind, I had grown to love her.

It meant: Never again seeing my friends. I did not even say goodbye to Laci. Whatever must he think of me just disappearing suddenly? The thought of leaving him behind was acutely painful.

My neighbourhood, my building, my flat, my room, my possessions and my fat wallet. In short, a life abandoned. For what? Some stupid adventure dreamt up by Gita and Julius. What were they running away from? And what were they running to? Why did I have to go? I liked my life just the way it was.

The group was subdivided into units and under the cover of darkness slipped out the back of the house to a copse about 150 metres away where we regrouped. The rain stopped and under our impermeable plastic coats we were still dry.

I fumed silently. The others just stood around. What thoughts troubled them were theirs alone; I had my own concerns.

When Mr. Hat deemed it safe he set off, leading. We were to follow in single file, like rats following the piper.

The woods provided good cover and the going was easy. Mr. Hat stopped just inside the forested area and waited for everyone to catch up. Gita with Margo, head lolling, swaddled on her back, me dragging my stoic brother Akos, already struggling to walk weighed down by his slick plastic coat, bringing up the rear.

"That was the easy part. The rest is open country and the ground will be muddy and uneven. When you see a flare go up (that had to be the fireworks she was alluding to) you go down, and stay down until it dies." Mr. Hat looked grimly serious. The flight of refugees looked agitated, fearful.

Why was this happening to us? What was so wrong with life that made Julius and Gita decide to go on this reckless escapade? Where was Julius anyway?

I had become a victim of circumstance, a pawn in a game for which the rule book had not yet been written.

The reluctant refugee took his first faltering steps.

The plastic coat was gnawing at my neck again but under the circumstances I thought it best to just suffer in silence. Nothing but open fields from here as predicted, rutted and heavy with sticky clay, criss-crossed by deep ditches and water-filled gullies. We trudged for what seemed like hours, Gita with the drugged baby girl on her back, me holding my brother's hand, making slow, plodding progress towards an unknown future.

Periodically from somewhere in the distance a white parachute flare would shoot up into the night, illuminating the ground below as it slowly descended. The changing angle of the light source cast eerie shadows on the rain-soaked ground.

As instructed, we immediately dropped and lay flat until the flare reached the ground and was snuffed. Each dive into the slush added another layer of the sticky stuff.

Feet clumped with mud balls, we dragged ourselves along, stopping periodically to scrape. It was slow going, each step harder than the last until finally Akos got stuck and could not lift his feet. I tried cajoling him. "Come on, little brother, we are nearly there. I think there is some ice cream and some proper fireworks just over the next hill. Can you smell the candy-floss?" I took a deep breath. "Can you smell it?" He was not convinced by my clownish attempt at humour and looked at me blankly.

Exhausted, every few yards we had to stop and scrape, rest for a few seconds then plod on. Within a few steps the lumpy clay built up around our boots again. Back to Frankenstein feet.

Stopping frequently, we continued to fall further behind.

Ahead, Gita sat on the soggy ground, breathing hard, clouds of steam rising from her head. She was at the end of her tether and asked me if I would carry Margo for a while. "Where is your new friend, Mr. Pipe? Why is he not helping us?" Gita, legs splayed, sat in the mud; head downcast, she pointed ahead. "I think he is upfront helping Mr. Hat." Already she was making excuses for him.

Akos, wide-eyed, stood rooted to the spot like a plastic-covered tree stump; somehow he sensed that this was a time to be brave and made no complaint.

As the 'man of the family' I was determined to shoulder the responsibility I did not want but could not refuse. Stepping out of the mud-caked plastic coat I used the opportunity to abandon it; the refugee shed his first layer. My whole body felt light; relieved of their burden the stick-like legs found new bounce. That is until Gita strapped Margo's inert body on my back papoose-style, scraped the mud off my boots before uprooting Akos.

Swivelling to the left, I looked over my shoulder at the discarded coat standing, so stiffened by the layers of caked mud that it just stood erect, a resentful sentinel in the gloom eyeing me accusingly. I felt a twinge of guilt. After all her work, how could I leave it behind so callously? Too exhausted to argue, Gita looked at me, then at the coat in which she had invested such time, effort and love. Her hand reached out to touch it, but before the fingers made contact, with a splat it collapsed into a puddle.

The abrasion on my neck, combined with the weight of Margo on my back and the balls of mud on my boots, soon dispelled momentary remorse. I clenched my jaw and plodded on.

Gita took Akos's hand, dragging him along, trying to keep in visual contact with the other stragglers in our group.

Mr. Hat led the group like a foraging column of army ants, halting at a tangle of rusty barbed wire to allow us to catch up. He placed his index finger on his lips then pointed to crudely stamped metal signs attached to the wire at intervals graphically depicting what would happen if you stepped on a mine. What about the border guards? They were known to be more fanatical than the regular Hungarian Army troops. Would they just shoot us on the spot? If not, would we be separated? The children sent to re-education camps and Gita to a smelly, damp cell? Still no sign of Mr. Pipe. Had he gone ahead alone? If so why?

Near-total exhaustion, Mr. Hat allowed us a few minutes to rest, scrape boots, then he led off through a gap in the wire. As instructed we kept at 5m intervals, making sure that we followed in his footsteps which, by the time we got there, were well marked by the 20 or so pairs of feet that went before us. We were at the back of the flight, carefully avoiding untested ground. Striding ahead, Mr. Hat seemed unconcerned; obviously he knew the lie of the land well.

Another flare went up and again we threw ourselves into the mud. No thought to the bone-shattering devices which surely lay somewhere below the gooey ground.

Clearly illuminated now, in the distance was a narrow canal with two soldiers on the opposite bank.

It looked like our adventure was coming to a bad end.

I was ready for anything, ready to be shot, run through, beaten with rifle butts, clubbed unconscious, anything short of death really. I wanted this nightmare to end. Maybe, hopefully, they wouldn't let us in and we could pretend this whole thing never happened, all go back home and wind the clock back to 'normal'.

My stash, even if severely devalued, must still be worth a fair whack. I would have happily given it all away to be snuggling under my duvet, head resting comfortably on plump, fluffy pillows.

Alert, peering intensely in our direction, the soldiers unslung their rifles and unexpectedly laid them against a tree.

As the flare sputtered out they waved at us, frantically indicating that we should hurry. The exhausted, mud-caked group raised themselves as one and made an adrenalin-fuelled dash for the canal.

"Run! Freedom is just across the water!" Gita heaved her steaming body up and a last-ditch effort was made to cross the last ditch. I found all this incredible and felt that I already had all the 'freedom' I could handle. Why could we not just take the train to this resort like normal people?

Mr. Hat vanished into the night.

Running over the uneven ground shook Margo awake and she started to cry.

Following the rest of our wretched band, we plunged into the waist-deep, icy water. The soldiers reached their rifles down the bank. One at a time we grabbed the barrels and they helped us clamber up the slippery slope. An invisible border had been crossed.

One life ended, another began. I felt sure she was the main driving force behind this escapade and that Julius, like me, would have been happy to stay home. Did she fully realise what she had done?

"Willkommen in Österreich!" The soldiers greeted us with beaming smiles, arms hustling us to join the rest of our shivering group.

Up to this juncture I was still hopeful that some event, some intervention, would cancel this whole insane adventure; we would go home, all would be well and forgiven, our lives would resume; I could go to the park with Laci, put the ball on the spot and kick off a new game.

It was not to be.

We were now officially refugees, a word I would learn to despise.

The border guards handed our group over to a 'reception committee – ' seemed as if they had done this before and it was all executed with Teutonic efficiency.

Our shattered, stunned group huddled for safety.

The Hungarian interpreter reassured us that we were indeed safe.

"You are now on Austrian soil." She smiled welcomingly. "Be patient, we are waiting for transportation."

There was a collective release of tension – laughter, hugs and kisses all round.

The events of the last several hours were fleshed out with personal detail and thoughts as a Niagara of pent-up emotion spewed forth in a torrent of babble. Many, including Gita, could hardly believe how well it all went considering the potential for disaster.

As the sky lightened Margo started to reassert herself and demanded to be fed.

My mother's inexhaustible nipple quieted her just as a rickety, old Army truck loomed out of the mist. Stopping directly in front of us, a grinning Mr. Pipe helped us into the back of the lorry.

Where had he been and why was he already here?

The truck soon filled with animated refugees; excited chatter, names and contact details of likely destinations were exchanged. Promises to keep in touch made knowing that the chances of meeting again in this big old world were slim at best. "When do the fireworks begin?" I knew we had already seen the fireworks but wanted to needle her a bit.

"I'm sorry I had to lie to you, but we are going to where the cowboys live: you know you love cowboys!"

That at least was true. My grief at having to leave the buried treasure under the cellar stairs was tempered by the prospect of life as a cowboy. Perhaps it would all turn out well after all. I could definitely see myself roaming the range, shooting tomahawk-wielding savages, bringing justice to evildoers.

I would have to learn to play the guitar and to sing, at least well enough to entertain a horse. Should be easy, I had ten fingers and there were only six strings.

After a long, tiring day of derring-do, I could see myself poking at a campfire, watching the sputtering wood launch its sparks into the star-spangled sky. Picking up the guitar, I would serenade my trusty steed into righteous slumber.

The truck lurched down the bumpy dirt road until intersected by a two-lane paved highway.

To my dismay and continued irritation Gita and Mr. Pipe had become somewhat closer, sharing intimate moments, sly touches; this did not make me happy and as the head of the family I looked for some means to break the growing attachment.

"Julius will not be pleased to hear about your 'friendship' with this man Pipe! I want to go home! What about poor Neni, what will happen to her? Why can't we go home? These people don't speak my language, I have to go back to school, I miss my friend Laci!" I mined this vein until I ran into bedrock.

"Shut up!" Gita hissed through gritted teeth. "Be grateful you are free!"

I did not like this so-called 'freedom' but did feel anger towards her. As for Mr. Pipe, I feared and hated him in equal measure.

Approaching an open barrier manned by more soldiers, the truck entered a fenced compound, turning towards what appeared to be rows of wooden huts lining both sides of the narrow street. Stopping in front of a larger building, we were ordered to line up for 'processing'. High expectations were brutally shattered. This was the new reality. Why should we be treated like the heroes we felt ourselves to be?

This was Auschwitz light.

A Jewish couple in our group were visibly shaken and the woman started to sob inconsolably, perhaps recalling recent history.

Someone somewhere said, "When you walk the crooked mile, watch where you tread, look ahead from time to time so that you know where you went, when dead."

We went through the 'welcome' process and were each given a package containing a towel, soap, toothbrush and paste. Gita answered the 'interrogators' to their satisfaction and we were shown our quarters.

Essentially it was a wooden barrack room with around twenty beds lining the walls on each side and a communal area in the centre in which stood a squat, black-iron pot-bellied stove, the only source of heat for the hut. Highly effective within a radius of around 3 feet, there was no Goldilocks zone; standing with your back to the stove, the thermal radiation was capable of inflicting first-degree burns on exposed areas of skin while the tip of the nose was in danger of frostbite.

The accommodations were good enough for the Austrian Army but not good enough for Gita – her sense of entitlement could not be contained and she harangued the 'staff' until they put the four of us in a small, private hut, even though the 'protection' of a man, namely Mr. Pipe, was lost to her.

I was happy with the outcome.

We set about making ourselves at home, stowing our possessions in wooden lockers. Within days the new regime became routine.

Meals were taken in the mess hall; it was good, solid grub and plenty of it. There were no surprises; Austrian and Hungarian cuisines were much of a muchness, at least until the wily Austrians rolled out their secret weapon: tropical fruit.

This is where I met my first banana.

Eastern Blockers (as we were to be named) had no experience of such exotica and knew only locally grown fruit: apples, pears, plums, apricots etc.

The belated celebration of my 10th birthday and first encounter with strange fruit did not go well.

My mother had nothing to give, no money to buy anything, let alone indulgences like cakes or cookies; there were no presents and little fuss. The lovely ladies in charge of the mess hall kitchen baked a small cake, stuck a single candle in the top and gave me an unripe banana.

Craving sugar, I greedily ate the whole cake (reasoning that there was not enough to go round), slipped the banana into my pocket for later. When alone back in our hut I pulled it out and instinctively used it as a gun, shooting up the room while posing in front of the cracked mirror, the mottled silvering aptly reflecting my new life.

With the banana tucked into my waistband I practised the quick-draw technique. Even with many hours of rigorous observation and practice I could never match the lightning speed of the gunslingers I had seen at the movies.

Ignorant of cinematic techniques, editing being one of them, I was easily convinced that what was depicted on the screen was unquestionably true.

Repeatedly being used as a six-shooter was starting to affect the structural integrity of the banana so I decided it was time to eat it.

Not used to dealing with fruit that had to be peeled, I bit into the curvy, yellow product of the tropics and was shocked that people actually enjoyed these things.

Fit only for monkeys, I thought, and threw it away!

Clearly, the brain damage I had inflicted on myself sniffing petrol had taken its toll as I repeated the scenario with an orange.

Newfound playmates would disappear to be replaced by fresh faces on a steady basis. Most of the adults we arrived with had left. Even Mr. Pipe stopped showing up: it gave me a large shot of glee not to have him lurking around. There was something sinister about this smooth-talking, dapper little man.

Hopefully he was gone for good, out of our lives. Gita would just have to do without him.

At first there were lots of kids in the camp and we soon got organised.

Early on there were enough of us to make up small teams but as time passed there were only three of us left: one named Barnabas, thick glasses, two left feet, and Daniel, a Jewish boy who was forbidden by his parents to participate in sporting activities. We harangued this gentle boy into being our goalie.

"All you have to do is stand there and guard the goal so technically you are not 'playing'." Impossible to know whether the ball was made of pigskin or aardvark hide. Either way, he was doomed. Then even he vanished.

But why were we still here? Would there be any white horses or shiny six-shooters left by the time we got to America?

Some weeks went by and we were still in our little hut, settled into a routine like the inmates we were.

Unbeknown to me, Gita had refused offers of resettlement in Germany, France and Denmark and was holding out for a flight that would take us to the land of the singing cowboys.

That enchanted land where milk and honey flowed in the streets, where men lived in freedom and harmony, where everybody lived in a big house attended by grateful, polite, black servants.

While gentle hands rocked the cradle of their future masters, bejewelled lace-clad ladies fluttered fans and sipped mint juleps. The gentlemen, overdressed for sultry southern climes, smoked cigars and drank bourbon from heavy bottomed lead crystal glasses.

The beautiful antebellum mansion sat on a hill surrounded by a well-tended formal garden. A small fleet of cars parked in the curved driveway awaited their pleasure.

This was the image and was exactly what Gita was expecting.

I had rather more modest expectations. My America was where the cowboys roamed, lived in log houses, ate biscuits, polished their pistols and passed the gravy. At least this is the impression I had from the few American movies that made it to my local cinema.

Convinced that huge Russian armies were poised to invade and overrun the whole of Western Europe, so any continental settlement would only postpone the inevitable, Gita stubbornly held out for America.

Turning down many offers of resettlement even as far away as Australia, of which we knew virtually nothing but heard from trusted sources that it was a vast desert full of snakes, spiders and crocodiles, the whole continent governed by professional criminals in boldly striped suits.

Not much has changed. The suits are now pinstriped, well tailored and worn with ties. Why would anyone want to live there?

None had the appeal of the USA, that fabulous land where surely the King of America would reward handsomely anyone brave enough to rise up against the Communist menace. Perhaps a modest estate and a couple of Cadillacs to get around in would be a good start.

At quiet times I still missed my old life. Laci, the other kids, the streets, the cosy, comfortable little flat in Pest; it was already fading but I still clung to it, vaguely hoping something would happen or that Gita would have a change of heart and we would just go home.

The mythical land of Merka was calling! My mother remained steadfast.

By week ten her patience was wearing thin. The next flight was going to England and we would be on it. She studied the map and deemed the channel separating the UK from the continent sufficiently wide to keep the Soviets at bay. It worked against the might of the German armies so why not the Reds?

There would be no ranch, fancy cars or the cowboy life I had set my heart on. This human drama would not have a Hollywood ending.

"There are no more flights going to America. You will have to make up your mind or you will just have to stay here." The man in charge of these things twirled the biro between his fingers, looking at Gita with an expression that, to me at least, made it look like this was his final offer. He was more than ready to get rid of us, especially her, always bitching about something.

CHAPTER 7

ENGLAND 1957

As the runway rose out of the mist, the refugees let go a mighty cheer. Clapping and foot stomping drowned out the squeal of tyres.

Unwarranted applause is a habit to be deplored.

The Britannia turboprop landed heavily at Gatwick. I know this because it was and still is the only airport in Sussex able to accommodate large aircraft. Relieved to be back on terra firma, the passengers, in spite of being told to remain seated, could not contain their excitement. Some danced in the aisles, others stood and sang the old national anthem, as the pilot reined in the shiny beast, stopping with a wobble on the wet tarmac, the refugees suddenly silent.

Outside it was grey and dark; a well-settled band of rain irrigated this green and pleasant land.

'Welcome to England' read a makeshift sign over the terminal in which sat a row of bureaucrats ready to process our planeload. This was when I spotted Mr. Pipe. My heart sank. If he was on our plane why had he not shown himself? Waving, he headed in our direction. They were both smiling. I was not.

"Is Julius here?" I already knew the answer to this question. She looked away, unable to face her duplicity.

"Get back in the queue please," a polite Englishman said to Mr. Pipe. He returned to the back of the line. The young official with reddish hair and freckles, wearing what was later to become known as John Lennon glasses, asked Gita a series of questions. Fuming over Mr. Pipe, I paid little attention to the many questions coming from the young man but do recall that through an interpreter he asked her the fateful question.

"What is your religion?"

"Roman Catholic!" she said with conviction.

Standing off to one side, my ears pricked up. This was news to me – she turned her head away from the desk and winked slyly at me. I went along with this seemingly innocent deception.

This small lie would have huge implications for our future.

Back in the Old Country we never attended church. Out of curiosity I did look around a couple in our neighbourhood. In true RC style they were fiendishly garish, demonically ornate, almost as if they were designed to impress and oppress. I will admit that there was something beguiling about the smell of the incense. The candles casting flickery shadows could spark the imagination. Essentially, I was unconvinced. Gomba and the Party, at least in this regard, had done an exemplary job.

'Young Communists' were taught to despise religion. Our leaders and educators poured scorn on the priesthood. Parasites and relics of the Dark Ages had no place in a secular Communist society.

The official with the Lennon glasses stamped our papers and we were told to join a group sitting by a window overlooking the runway.

My recollection is a little hazy, but certainly we got shunted to one side, inadvertently joining the ranks of the faithful. This is how we became accidental Catholics and thence we were, if not in God's, at least in the hands of the Church.

Further down the hall, to my delight Mr. Pipe was receiving special attention and was taken away for reasons unknown.

The twenty or so 'Catholics' were loaded on a bus and driven to a large country house in Sussex (I think it was Gerston Manor in Storrington but I cannot be certain).

Now this was more like it! We were given a large room with fine period furniture.

Oil paintings of expressionless worthies stared down on us. There were full suits of armour standing at decent intervals down the corridors; tapestries depicting heroic deeds and notable events decorated the walls.

There was a large room set aside for communal use. The inglenook fireplace framed by rough stone slabs was big enough for me to stand in comfortably. Even piled high with blazing logs it struggled to keep the room moderately heated.

My eyes, drawn by movement, fell upon a small cinema screen in one corner of the room upon which a masked cowboy on a white horse accompanied by an Indian on a slightly smaller grey and white steed were at full gallop in pursuit of a gang of banditos.

I had not noticed it before as the magic machine was hidden behind a sliding wooden door effectively obscuring its function, which indeed was the purpose; 'the box' (as it would be known) was considered vulgar by most of those that could afford to buy one.

What magic was this? How could there be a small cinema screen in a house? How did it work? Where was the projector? Alone in the room, using a butter knife to loosen the screws, I prised open the back cover. A warm updraft brought a distinctive ozone tinged smell, like the aroma which lingers when the instructions of the 'Toxico Chemistry Set' (much loved by boys of my age) were ignored.

Close examination of the alien landscape inside gave no clue as to where the participants engaged in the action on the screen kept their horses or indeed where they would go for lunch. This, for now at least, would remain an enigma.

The interior of the 'box' was dimly lit by bulbs neatly arranged in rows, clusters of unidentifiable cylindrical shapes and components colourfully painted with dots or stripes connected by neat bundles of multi-coloured wires. The overall effect reminded me of the science fiction classic *Metropolis* by Fritz Lang, which I had seen several times back in my very local cinema in Pest. It had left a lasting impression.

The dystopian nightmare as depicted on the cinema screen was the future of capitalism, this straight from Gomba's mouth therefore immutable.

That day I instantly became a huge fan of the Lone Ranger.

Curiously he was never alone unless one considered Tonto to be a non-person who just tagged along to hold the reins and do the cooking.

As gullible as I was, I still wondered how he kept his outfit clean and pressed, and his pistols polished, what with all the ranging about in clouds of dust and sleeping on canyon floors. Not to mention the inconvenience of taking a piss in what (in black and white at least) appeared to be a 'onesie' with a gun belt.

Later in life I was shocked to learn what 'Tonto' meant in Spanish.

On the screen the exchange of gunfire between the goodies and baddies would put a helicopter gunship to shame, yet miraculously there were few injuries, maybe a grazed knee or a nick on the forehead.

Most of the action took place in the saloon which, it seemed, was diligently avoided by the less than competent Sheriff. The inept lawman spent most of his time in his office, feet up, lolling around in his chair.

An ever-changing cast of characters appeared at the office (which seemed to serve less as the seat of law and order than as a social club for the townspeople) with a variety of complaints and lists of grievances. Life had been all very black and white for me and I was bothered by the lackadaisical approach to the enforcement of laws, contrasting deeply with the well-regulated society I had so recently been forced to abandon. Yet, I could feel my attitude shifting, slowly, gradually; my rigidly Communist world view was eroding.

When the dust settled, at worst the baddies would clutch at light shoulder wounds easy enough for the town doctor, in between swigs from a half-empty bottle of whisky, to patch up well enough for the sullen and remorseful to do the 'perp. walk' to the town jail, conveniently located at the back of the Sheriff's office.

The bungling lawman was routinely upstaged by the Lone Ranger. The townspeople turned out in droves to cheer their masked hero as he rode out of town.

"Kemosabe, did you pick up the rice and beans like you promised?"

"Sorry, Tonto, I forgot. You will just have to go in the morning. Now what's for dinner?"

"It's gonna be just tortillas again, I am so sick of tortillas!" Tonto sighed, turning to camera, a pained grimace on his bronze, chiselled visage.

Promptly the next morning, blind yet well balanced Lady Justice meted out retribution in commensurate doses as the town returned to humdrum with nothing but the thunderous farting of horses and the occasional dust devil to disturb the peace. I was mesmerised.

The Lone Ranger was a perfect substitute for my fallen hero, Joseph Stalin, a timely arrival in the life of a boy. I sat in front of the TV as much as they would let me. The magic box was my teacher.

Queen's English ("Good evening, here is the news read by Richard Baker") and cowboy lingo ("Aw shucks…I guess so!") jostled for space in my head.

I was soaking it up.

LR episodes in particular were a quick learn, easy to follow with linear storylines.

"Drop the gun!" The baddie complies. "Put your hands up!" The baddie complies. Good visual aids to learning.

Bang in the middle of an LR episode an adult walked in and switched channels. I threw a mighty fit, driving him out of the room and switched back to the Masked Man.

That was how it went.

Just as I got into the habit of a regular ride with the Ranger we were told that we were to be relocated a few miles up the road. By now, I was so used to being shunted around that without protest we packed up ready to board a bus the next morning.

"If they have TV at the new place will the Lone Ranger be on it?"

"I don't know, darling, ask the bus driver."

I climbed the steps to do as Gita suggested but before I could open my mouth I spotted Mr. Pipe about halfway down the coach.

My heart sank. The bus driver looked at me helpfully but I just got back off and hissed at my mother, "Mister Pipe, your 'friend', is on the bus."

Where he had been and why he continued to haunt us were a deep mystery.

Akos and I sat in the seat behind him, Gita taking the seat next to him with Margo clamped onto her left nipple.

It seemed Mr. Pipe had been expecting us. Before the doors closed two men boarded the bus.

"Mr. Victor Grandpierre, if you are aboard please show yourself."

Mr. Pipe stood up, looking a little shaky, and went forward. A few words were exchanged and to my delight Mr. Pipe, or should I say Victor, was escorted off the bus.

Back in Hungary I would have pegged them for plain-clothes police but here in this country where they drove on the wrong side of the road, drank milky tea from dainty cups, and inexplicably the police wore funny hats and were unarmed save a short stick hidden in their trousers, it was impossible to be sure of anything.

Packed with refugees and their belongings, the bus pulled away bound, surely, for someplace better than the draughty heap we had just vacated, with a private kitchen, separate bedrooms and our own TV without the news but with extra LR episodes.

This man, Victor, why did my mother never utter his name? She must have known it, just called him 'darling', fairly innocuous you would say but every time she used that endearment it was a poke in the eye to me, my siblings and above all, I felt, Julius.

Surely he must be on his way by now.

Her dalliance with him was another persistent betrayal; she lied about the 'holiday', the firework display, the instant devaluation of the currency and probably many other things.

Her increasingly cosy situation with Victor was even harder to accept.

Not to mention my role as a junior patriarch steadily undermined by this man who stubbornly turned up just as I thought we were rid of him.

Perhaps he was some kind of a criminal or even better a Red spy sent to establish a sleeper cell; with a bit of luck he was sitting in a prison somewhere.

Then like a bolt it struck me, Mr. Pipe aka Victor aka Captain Victor Grandpierre was the ÁVH officer from the interview booth back in Pest. Of course, back then he sported a fine handlebar moustache, but though now clean-shaven it was unmistakably him.

Surely he was busted and would get a taste of his own medicine from these men; they looked like cops so they must be cops. No other conclusion was possible.

History lessons had taught me that the English were particularly innovative when it came to torture; I knew all about the rack, the iron maiden, being hanged, drawn and quartered and any number of pain-inflicting devices finely calibrated to cause the maximum amount of discomfort. The red-hot poker up the arse would be just about right for the Captain, I thought.

I was convinced we would never be troubled by him again.

Our short stay at 'Camelot' in leafy Sussex was over and again we were shunted off to ramshackle accommodations. There was no privacy, no TV; therefore, crucially, no Lone Ranger.

The new digs were very similar to the Austrian Army barracks. Rows of closely packed wooden huts surrounded by a barbed-wire perimeter fence designed to keep people out rather than in. The same basic accommodations, tissue-thin blankets upon hard mattresses, brick-sized bars of soap infused with some sort of abrasive material explicitly formulated to last all eternity. Translucently threadbare towels the size of pocket handkerchiefs.

In spite of these minor hardships we were made to feel welcome and were grateful for all that we were given.

The signs were in English which did not inform us any better than those in German, as none of us spoke anything other than Hungarian.

To say that the food was less than enticing would be an understatement.

Although I could not claim that my palate was anywhere near refined, it had been somewhat awakened by the generosity of our neighbours back in Budapest. My mother had little interest in domestic routines, preferring to entertain herself in more mysterious ways. Thus Neni was saddled with providing nourishment for the family. Her offerings were nutritionally adequate but uniformly bland so I tried to make a point of being elsewhere around mealtimes in the expectation of being asked to stay for a meal.

English food found me totally unprepared.

Everything available at that time, bearing in mind that rationing had ended less than 18 months previously, was slowly, with unintentional malice, boiled to death. Meat products encased in gelatine oozed from cans. Puddings were made of rice, all very curious.

"I wonder when Victor will come back. Why did they take him away? This country is no better than the one we ran away from," Gita rambled more to herself than to me. I stayed silent.

To borrow a phrase from Vonnegut: "So it goes"…

Gita continued to complain. I was sensing that she was having doubts about the whole escapade; it was not working out as expected. No word was coming from behind the Curtain; I kept pushing her for news but there was nothing from Julius or anyone.

"He will be here soon, has some things to do before he can leave." In spite of the optimistic statements her voice was tremulous and there was fear in her eyes.

Victor was gone. She was segregated, friendless and very much alone.

I knew when to stop; turning, I headed out of the door. There was football to be played.

Back home she was used to the attention of many admirers but had found it hard to make friends with other women. I think she saw them all as potential rivals so when Marta, newly arrived with the last batch of refugees, tried to befriend her, she was suspicious.

Life had taught her to be wary.

However, these were strange times. Gita needed a friend, an adult she could actually talk to, a companion, some support.

When my mother found out that Marta had lived a few blocks south on our street back in Budapest and was a 'cosmetician', she slowly opened up to the possibility of a new friendship.

I was unsure what a cosmetician actually did, but knew for a fact that it involved a lot of cream slathered on the face. I had seen Gita do this at home. What a waste of time sitting around for hours with white goo on your face, I thought.

As far as I was concerned there was no discernible difference between 'before' and 'after'.

Gita, however, firmly believed that Nivea cream was endowed with mystical properties packed with rejuvenating enzymes working hard to obliterate the ravages of time.

Who was I to argue?

Marta was allowed into our lives and they became fast friends.

There was another much more compelling reason for their friendship. She was also waiting for her husband. Many late-night discussions about how and when their menfolk would arrive. They were both convinced their fortunes would immediately improve, the ladies would take their rightful place in society, and joy would blanket this new land.

Gita and Marta were, in many ways, products of their time, shared prejudices poured into short, round moulds. Gita took up smoking to further seal their friendship; eventually hacking her way to full blown nicotine addiction. Even the hairstyles started to coincide.

As much as they were a couple of bookends they differed in one key aspect. Marta was a hustler in her own right, whereas Gita needed the support of a man.

Continuing to be a thorn, I asked, "I have not seen Marta around for some days, is she OK?"

"Her husband arrived and they left. I think they moved to London." Her face belied the offhand attitude. I could feel her pain, sorrow tinged with longing for the arrival of her man. She was alone again.

Except for Victor.

Much to my dismay and Gita's apparent delight he just showed up as if nothing had happened. Where he went or what he did was never discussed, but he always had something nice for Gita and small toys and sweets for the kids. As far as I knew he never stayed over, bunking down at the other end of the compound with all the other single men.

Then he would disappear again for a few days without explanation, only to resurface just as I started to think he was gone for good.

Steadily, with unrelenting purpose he became a fixture in our lives and I must allow that he was persistently, annoyingly charming and made a great effort to win us (the children) over, paying particular attention to me, buying stuff, pressing coins into my grubby little hands. Aware that he was manipulating me I played his game, convinced that as soon as Julius showed up he would be gone. Akos in particular was asking for his dad.

"He will come any day now. Here!" Gita pulled a chocolate biscuit out of the packet and twirled it between her fingers... Easily diverted, my little brother, with a few words and a digestive.

I also loved the plain chocolate discs but was less easily sidetracked.

She took a second bite, looked blankly at the wall. "He will be here any day now." She had lied about many things. Was this just another lie?

I think she truly believed he would arrive anytime soon, take charge of the situation, send Victor packing and all would be well.

In the meantime Gita was walking a fine line fending Victor off while just flirty enough to keep him interested. He hung around tenaciously, talked the talk and came across like a decent bloke.

As time went by, I resented his presence less, chipping away at my hostility with flattering attention, trinkets and small cash bribes. More importantly, he made my mother laugh, something that I had not seen for a long time.

Slowly, almost imperceptibly, relentlessly and with great perseverance he infiltrated our little family. He had grandiose plans, each more fantastic than the last, the least of which was to open a Hungarian restaurant along the lines of the Gay Hussar in Soho, London. It must have been quite the place for it to be known by the likes of Victor. He told Gita that he had heard that it was popular with certain classes and doing good business.

Apparently, goulash and schnitzels were to the taste of London's more intrepid citizens.

Gita found all this talk convincing. I did not.

In spite of his 'charm offensive' he would, for me at least, never replace Julius. I had many reservations about this slight man with the large hands.

Should I tell her about 'Captain' Grandpierre? A couple of times when I was angry at her for something I almost blurted it out. Not sure how long I could keep my little secret from her or even if she would care. Victor, on the other hand, well, it never hurt to have some dirt on your adversary. Gomba had taught me well.

Of course he could just deny it and it would be my word against his.

For now... I decided to hold my tongue.

Needing the support and protection only a 'man' could provide and the fact that he spoke a little English went a long way with her.

As we languished in this gulag the RCC (Roman Catholic Church) were hard at work behind the scenes looking for somewhere to put us.

As an interim measure and to give my mother a break, arrangements were made to send me off to a good Catholic family in the country. My protestations, as anticipated, brushed aside. I did not want to go; the thought of leaving the family, especially with Victor making himself comfortable, feet well under the table, was not a happy one. I had no say in the matter.

The Church sent a 'minder' to deliver me to Chelmsford. Malcolm shook my hand a little too warmly and patted my head.

On the train we sat opposite each other by the window. In silence, he lovingly ran his fingers over the black leather-bound Bible on his lap. The train pulled out of the station. Malcolm made a half-hearted effort to engage me, but I was suspicious and resentful, mostly ignoring his efforts to be sociable and answered him in monosyllables or just sat in silence.

Finally he gave up on me. Opening the Bible, he ran his sinuous fingers along the page. Mouth moving slightly as he read the script. His cherubic face settled to a beatific smile as the train picked up speed.

He did look a bit like Victor. There was the small head, bad teeth, big hands.

Put me in mind of a previous train journey and first encounter with Mr. Pipe.

Why did we have to become refugees? I hated that word. Was there some point in the future when the word no longer applied? I did not want to be a curiosity in somebody else's circus. I just wanted to live a normal life.

The train pulled into Chelmsford station.

Waiting on the platform, Mr. and Mrs. Farley greeted me warmly, seemed genuinely pleased to meet me. We got off to a good start. I resolved to be on my best behaviour.

The bus dropped us off near their house; a short walk around the corner put us in front of a large, semi-detached mock-Tudor house. Mr. Farley opened the door and held it for his wife and me.

Pretending to be a Catholic and sitting through a mass once a week seemed like a small price to pay for this unexpected adventure. Not to mention that they also had three beautiful, lively daughters aged 12, 13 and 14, as one would expect from good Catholics. I think they really wanted a boy and that may have been the reason I was there. The girls also seemed rather pleased to have me in the house.

Anyway, there I was, school was out and I was enjoying my role as the 'proxy son', getting more parenting than I had ever been accustomed to. This was also my first encounter with real English home cooking.

Welsh Rabbit, Shepherd's Pie, Toad in the Hole, Pigs in a Blanket sounded more farmhouse than town house. These uniformly bland offerings did nothing to excite my palate. The 'pudding' that went along with the Sunday Roast was equally disappointing.

Real puddings, at least in my limited knowledge of these things, usually involved sweet concoctions, cakes, chocolate sauces, cream and custard. I already had a mouthful of mercury-laden fillings as a tribute to the sugar god.

I longed for a slow-cooked Paprika Chicken.

Painfully shy, blushing like a baboon's arse at the slightest hint of anything to do with the nether regions, did not mesh well with the stirrings of puberty.

One sunny afternoon we played hide-and-seek while the parents were busy digging up weeds in the long, narrow back garden. 'Somehow' the two older girls and I ended up in the cupboard under the stairs where the laundry bags were kept, the three of us lying on the soft bags, me in the middle, our bodies touching; it was pitch black with the door closed so my flushed cheeks and boyish erection went unnoticed.

The youngest sister, the 'seeker', did not find us at all (perhaps called away by the parents). We lay silently, our bodies pressed close in the dark; my hands, as if out of control, crept onto their thighs, squeezing gently and inching higher until I could feel the heat radiating from that dark, damp, forbidden place. Neither made any attempt to stop me. Even as a 'mature' 11-year-old I had no idea what I was supposed to do with one, let alone two!

This was scary; what primitive hormonal impulses were driving me to that mysterious kernel which was to me, at that particular moment at least, more stimulating than a trip to the beach and a ride on a donkey!

Not knowing how to proceed I kissed them clumsily on the cheeks and escaped through the trapezoid door.

Hiding the puny yet insistent bulge in my pants, like a fleeing felon I ran to my room and beat the nascent member into submission.

Guilt and shame immediately wrapped me in its sticky, cloying embrace. Not only had I failed as a 'man' but worse still, I had spilled my seed into a Kleenex. The spurt of pleasure was immediately followed by deep remorse. Certainly, I thought, such an opportunity would never again present itself. I felt my disappointment (if not guilt) was shared by the girls.

Regretfully I do not remember any of their first names but the lady of the house (I shall call her Janet) in a futile effort to divert my growing fixation with the eldest daughter decided I had to get out and socialise.

A visit to the local youth club was arranged.

She gave me some money and walked me to a bus stop, instructing the conductor of the 27 bus to let me off at the club. She had also written a note, pinned inside my coat which I could not read but was instructed to show to an adult if I got lost.

Please help me, I am a Hungarian refugee and do not speak English.

I am lost and cannot find my way home.

My address is:

My phone no. is:

Thank you Kindly

So off I went to be a socialist, an activity, I thought, I was well practised in. The conductor dumped me at the stop and pointed to the club entrance a few yards away. Getting off the bus I paced up and down outside the entrance trying to pluck up the courage to go in. What was this place and why was I here? Would they see me as just another kid with ill-fitting clothes or one of those damn refugees?

It started to drizzle.

"Well, you coming in or what?"

Adopting what I imagined would pass for the demeanour of a 'bad' guy off 'the Lone Ranger', I drawled, "Guess so." The kid laughed, went inside. Not a good start.

This club for youths had to be an RCC-run centre; surely they would not leave me with a roomful of infidels! The sound of kids at play inside only made me feel even more like a friendless stranger.

I took a deep breath and walked through the bendy rubber door.

Having faced and overcome my greatest fear, the rest should have been easy.

There were 20–25 kids of various ages supervised by an adult wearing a charcoal grey suit; around his neck, his badge of office, the dog collar. Surely no harm could touch me here.

Indeed it was an entirely unexpected event that was to leave a painful memory.

I strolled around casually then stopped to watch the to and fro of the ping-pong ball, trying very hard to look as if I belonged. I had no idea how to get in the game or to register my interest in playing so just stood around waiting and watching.

The skinny kid decided he had had enough, carelessly threw his bat on the table and went over to see what was happening at the snooker table.

I jumped in to take his place. On the other side of the net, a fat kid, somewhat older and taller than me, was wearing an orange and black horizontally striped sweater which made him look like a bumblebee with a paddle. Pointing at him with raised eyebrows, a silent question on my lips, I made the universal sign for drinking, the raised hand, thumb inclined towards the mouth.

I bought two Cokes while he held my place at the table and gave him one; he took it, raised the bottle, drank and burped without a word.

I did the same.

This was how communications were established. We started 'knocking up', no words were necessary.

I had him at a disadvantage as ping-pong was way up there with chess and mathematics on the list of stuff that Hungarians were traditionally good at. I had been a junior league player in the Young Drummers and had beaten some visiting Chinese kid who was supposed to be hot shit back in his village. So, the bar was pretty low but nevertheless...

Warming into it, I let him win the opening games knowing I could beat him easily. Gradually I ratcheted up my game, letting him win a few points to keep him at the table.

The Coke did its unintended best to erode the enamel on our teeth, while the relentless diuretic effect steadily distended my bladder. Suddenly I needed to pee.

We continued to bat back and forth until my need became urgent.

I spoke to Bumble Boy for the first time.

"Gentlemen?" The 'G' pronounced as in GILL, the respiratory organ of a fish or a measure of liqueur. He shrugged and served.

I tried several slightly different pronunciations – he just did not understand me!

Getting desperate, my bladder distended beyond capacity I needed to find a 'Gentlemen' very, very soon. Quitting the game I tried the priest, perhaps he would be divinely inspired to discern my need and point me in the direction of a WC.

Pining with unrequited love, head tilted slightly to the left, he listened to my incoherent plea for help. In spite of his intimate connection with the Almighty he, too, was unable to understand what the fuck I was on about!

Distracted by a minor dispute back at the ping-pong table between Skinny Kid and Bumble Boy, he flounced over to take charge of the situation.

I stood exposed, a wet patch in the crotch area of my trousers crept steadily down my left leg. The warm liquid flowed freely, soaking my socks, pooling in my shoe.

Immediate relief was followed by profound shame and disgust. The reaction in the hall was as expected. I would have hooted and jeered, too, if I had been on the other side of the equation.

Grabbing my coat, I headed for the door. Laughter followed me to the street and I still had to get home on a bus.

The coat covered most of it; the wet trouser leg could be taken for spilled lemonade or some such thing. No one would notice. But I knew and was ashamed.

Waiting in the shelter, it started to drizzle, then came down hard.

I stood on the edge of the pavement and let the rain wash away my humiliation.

The bus arrived. I showed the note to the conductor, he nodded and told me to sit.

"Don't worry, laddie, I'll tell you when to get off."

I never set foot in a youth club again until disqualified by age. In my thirties I felt the need to lay that ghost to rest and helped out as a volunteer at various facilities for unruly kids. To this day the words 'youth club' immediately trigger that memory.

Even though, by now, I was thoroughly soaked the thought of knocking on the front door and one of the girls answering was more ignominy than I could bear. In the event Janet let me in.

I ran upstairs to my room to wash and change, burying the urine-soaked clothes in one of the laundry bags under the stairs.

Janet's efforts to divert my obsession with her eldest daughter by sending me on another visit to the YC was met with stubborn resistance. I simply refused to go. I could not explain why.

I pulled every trick out of my shallow bag to get her daughter back under the stairs. We flirted constantly; sometimes she let me hold her hand and occasionally kissed me chastely on the cheek, but the 'below stairs' opportunity never again presented itself.

My behaviour did not go unnoticed by Janet and the middle sister, who increasingly turned on me. I was too stupid to realise she was jealous.

Suddenly, Janet and her husband decided that perhaps a pubescent foreign boy in the house full of girls was not such a good idea. My stay in Chelmsford was over. I was delivered back to the camp to rejoin the family.

Maybe the visit was some kind of evaluation; if so, then I must surely have failed on pronunciation, violation of Catholic morals and bladder control.

I had learned my lesson and can now pronounce Gentlemen and Toilet perfectly.

CHAPTER 8

BAD NEWS

"There is a letter for you at the office." The message was delivered to our hut by Linda, one of the office ladies.

She looked at Gita blankly. I noticed the change from her usual chirpy self but did not make the connection.

We followed Linda back to the office in silence.

Edged in black, the unopened envelope was on top of the pile in the in tray.

The blood drained out of Gita's face. She swayed a little, looked at me blankly, shakily reached for the letter.

Tearing open the envelope, she scanned the letter rapidly before breaking into sobs followed by uncontrollable wailing. She started tearing at her hair, collapsed, thrashing on the floor.

I prised the letter from my mother's fingers and read the short note.

Paraphrasing: we regret to inform you that Dr. Mihály Gyula's (Julius) body was found hanging from a tree in the vicinity of Lake Balaton. Verdict: Suicide.

It was a short, formal note from some Hungarian government department.

My first thought was, how did they know where we were?

I had to read the letter twice to make sure I understood it properly. I could not believe what I had just read, this was not possible. For the past months we had all lived fully expecting him to show up at any time. The family had been counting on his arrival to take charge of our lives once again. Get us out of this camp, back to some semblance of a 'normal' life. I also knew that when he arrived Victor would rapidly be shown the door.

My mother was on the floor convulsing. I tried to pick her up and comfort her, but she was inconsolable and pushed me away.

She sobbed, gulping huge lungfuls of air as she thrashed on the hard linoleum floor.

Kind hands helped her to her feet, stroking with soothing words, until she was able to just sit in a heap whimpering quietly. I embraced her and joined her in tears.

I was totally unprepared to deal with this latest twist in our turmoil-filled lives. The imminent arrival of Julius made the chaos, the dislocations, the strange language and bad food bearable. Repeatedly Gita had told me that when he arrived all our problems would disappear. In spite of my protestations I was sternly told to go back to our hut and not to say a word to A&M.

There was no one there. Filled with foreboding, I lay down on my bed and stared at the ceiling.

Hope turned to anger; this was all my mother's fault. She had taken the family from what was a good, comfortable life to this strange land where we had to live in a wooden hut surrounded by barbed wire. Did Mr. Pipe have anything to do with this? I needed someone to blame and he was an obvious target.

All the pent-up resentment over the previous weeks now poured out of me. I hated her for what she had done to our lives and saw nothing but bad food and misery ahead. Wallowing in despair, I refused to eat or get out of bed.

After a couple of days of threats and cajoling they gave up and sent for 'The Exorcist'.

The young priest came and sat on the side of my bed.

"I hear you are good at football." He offered me a chocolate biscuit. Without hesitation, I reached for it. Several visits and packets of biscuits later he finally banished the demon possessing my body. Slowly I returned to the world, coming to terms with the new reality.

This was my life now, there was no going back. All of our hopes had been pinned on Julius; the letter changed everything.

Not immune to the scourge of estate planning, he had delayed his escape attempt in a largely futile effort to liquidate his assets but left it too late. By the time he was ready the Austro-Hungarian border was as tight as a drum. The official verdict was suicide, took his own life while mentally disturbed. That at least was the implication as outlined in the letter but Gita knew that this was a lie, had to be some kind of a cover-up; she was convinced that he was murdered by the regime for his activism. With hindsight I am inclined to agree. Why would a doctor go out in the woods, put a rope around his neck, opting for a possibly slow, agonising death when he had a medicine chest full of lethal toxins right there at his surgery? He was a thoughtful, methodical man, not the type to risk slow strangulation over an expeditious dose of poison.

Incredibly, within a few weeks Gita's smile was back and her boundless optimism returned. Her actions belied the depth of her despair; when she thought we were all asleep she sobbed into her pillow.

Life was not going according to plan, the man she loved was dead; alone, stricken with grief, burdened by three children in a strange land, unable to communicate, her prospects severely limited by a lack of marketable skills.

What would become of us now?

After an indecent interval of mourning Gita sought solace in Victor's arms.

Somehow he had wangled his way into a job as a waiter at a fancy restaurant, namely Cunningham's in Curzon Street, Mayfair, and found accommodations in a less than genteel area of West London. Gita eventually talked the powers that be into releasing us and we all moved into the 'flat' in Shepherd's Bush.

Indeed it was flat, that at least was an accurate description, without features, bland, devoid of convenience.

The habitable area was crammed with random sleeping arrangements, lumpy mattresses patterned by mysterious brown stains on the floor for the children, a convertible sofa doubling as a bed for Gita and her lover. The metered gas stove on the landing just outside the door was shared with another family upstairs. This arrangement did nothing to promote neighbourly bonhomie as incredibly 'them upstairs' were inclined to eat their meals at times dictated by convention. The revolving door to the shared bathroom and toilet up the first flight of stairs was lubricated by the excreted misery of the residents. With great foresight my mother had bought a pretty Victorian chamber pot from a Portobello Road market stall. It stood in a corner covered by a plank of wood piled high with stuffed animals.

Again, I had been somewhat misled. The medium-sized room that Victor, abetted by Gita, had parlayed into a 'flat' was nothing more than a miserable rathole.

She went to work for a small West End workroom as a seamstress.

Though more than adept on the old Singer, the 'rag trade' demanded a whole new set of skills. Seamstresses were expected to do piecework; deadlines and quotas had to be met.

What passed for high fashion at the better department stores took many hours of hard labour to produce. Even by the standards of the day, she was very poorly paid. It had to be done, there was no alternative; if it meant working late into the night to meet her quota she downed a couple of shots of espresso and got on with it.

While they were both at work I was left in charge of A&M.

This must be the 'responsibility' she had asked me to shoulder back at the station in Szombathely. I did not want it then and certainly did not like or want it now.

Victor's work kept him out late. He often returned after midnight so I mainly saw him in the mornings, when he was sober. We never knew when Gita would get home but there was always plenty of yellow cake and instant coffee in the cupboard. We pretty much lived on the stuff.

We were to be taken into 'care' and shipped off to the country.

I explained the gist of the letter when she came home. "They are coming for us on Wednesday, that is four days from now, what are you going to do?"

She looked at me dolefully, her big, brown eyes underscored by dark circles. There was no fight left in her. Not fully able to hide her relief, she took a breath, sighing deeply.

"I think that might be the best thing for you. You have to go to school, get to sleep in nice, clean beds in a warm house; you will be together, at least."

This was devastating news for all three of us. No matter how dire the situation she always gave me the impression that, if not in total control, she at least had a light finger on the rudder. Now it seemed life had manoeuvred her into a corner and she was helpless.

The 'Flat in The Bush' was far from ideal but there was a slummy charm about the room, a place of safety where we could cling to each other and pretend that the world cared about us.

A refuge for refugees where, buoyed by the relentless optimism of our mother, we felt safe.

"You will all be fine. They will have nice clothes and lots of good food, probably a garden to play in with other children. It will be just for a short while."

Being away from her for the first time in our lives was hard for any of us to contemplate. I think harder for me as the mere mention of the word 'orphanage' conjured up images of diabolical cruelty and depravation.

I kept my fears private and with profound sadness prepared for our impending departure. On top of all this I would have to leave behind that battered, rusty, powder blue bicycle. Even though it had been the cheapest on offer, Gita still haggled ferociously.

"I don't want that one, it's a ladies' bike!"

She ignored me and paid the man. "This one has good saddle, you will not get sore bum."

Even though it was a made to be ridden in skirts, I loved tooling around the streets in pursuit of my fantasies. The only thing that I could put down in the plus column was that Victor would be out of my life.

CHAPTER 9

THE ORPHANAGE

A long train journey and series of buses took us to our new home. Our escort swung open the large, wooden gate, telling me to go ring the bell, turned and left.

I was angry, confused, afraid. Akos and Margo were sobbing quietly, repeatedly asking for Gita. Dumped like empty milk bottles on a suburban doorstep, we stood at the threshold.

What was a home without her? We lived in disarray: our crammed hovel may have been an amusement park for mice, but at least we had each other.

I was emotionally spent, wrung out and had nothing left.

The front door opened. Sister Conchita greeted us warmly and led us into another dimension.

It was a large Edwardian house on a corner lot with rambling gardens front and back, snuggly situated in the quiet seaside town of Bexhill-on-Sea in East Sussex.

The next few days were tough on A&M. I tried to be brave; the stony-faced expression I hid behind could well be seen as just another surly, resentful kid in need of a good dose of Jesus. No shortage of surly kids here in Osmunda, the name on the gate hanging on a rusty chain. We stood huddled, waiting in the hallway. The sisters, appearing as if on cue, greeted us in turn. Those that did not speak laid their hands on our heads in some kind of benediction. All went well until they tried to split us up. The mask of stoicism slipped off my face.

I only knew three English curse words, bloody, bugger and damn. In a short burst, I per mutated them without visible effect on the sisters. Falling back on my native tongue, I spewed a torrent of Hungarian invectives that would have curled the toes of Satan himself. We clung to each other but were dragged apart and in turn made to take baths, the first of many indignities.

Over time, A&M settled in. For me it was a little harder but in short order life had taught me to be adaptable, flexible, compliant.

Chameleon-like I blended into my surroundings.

There were around 18 kids living at the house, various ages, mostly boys; the few girls in residence were segregated as far from the boys as was physically possible. Margo, now two years old, slept in a cot in the 'big' girls' room.

The boys had bunk beds in the other two bedrooms.

The whole enterprise was a tight ship run by Spanish nuns dressed in civvies, their habits only worn on high holidays, thereby indistinguishable from the general populace of this moribund seaside town.

In spite of open-armed and mostly compassionate treatment by the sisters we all missed our mother very much, especially Akos. Margo was fussed over and seemed quite content. With all the relocations in the last few months we had learned to take each new adventure in our stride.

I was given a new set of used clothes which fit fairly well but would have appalled a fashionista. Everything was freshly laundered, third or fourth hand, either too big or fitted so snugly that my recently dropped testicles were having second thoughts. The only new item was the school blazer, just oversize enough to attract derision (room to grow, she said). The school emblem was slightly crookedly sewn onto the breast pocket by Sister Anna Maria.

Before I was to start school there was time to explore my surroundings. It was easy to wander around town on the way back from mass without having to account for time. If they quizzed me, my ready answer was that I stayed behind to pray. But it never came up. Bexhill, a typical, compact sleepy town a few miles west of Hastings, offered little excitement for an energetic boy. No pier, amusement arcade or indeed much to divert a scallywag city dweller.

The hiatus was over; the next day they packed me off to St Richard's to be tortured.

The school was almost next door to the church, also called St Richard's, where I would spend hours on my knees waiting in vain.

Thanks to the BBC and the Lone Ranger my English had much improved. I could now string a sentence together and my accent was disappearing rapidly. Just as well.

My first day at St Richard's was a test.

Not only did I have to suffer the treatment meted out to a new boy joining mid-term, but also endure the taunts and mimicry of the other boys due to my less than perfect English.

In the classroom the well-meaning teacher, ignorant of playground politics, had me stand and introduce myself, telling the pupils to 'be nice' to me as I was a Hungarian refugee.

This was a very bad idea. Well intentioned? Possibly, but had the opposite effect.

I had a fight in the first break. The boy was roughly my size, with dark hair and complexion, his most prominent feature a nose that would not look out of place on a Roman senator.

Not sure what started the ruckus but we ended up on the hard asphalt, thrashing.

"Git him, Manny, he needs a good kicking!" Obviously I was the enemy and needed to be reminded of my newcomer status.

"Will you give it up!" Manny gurgled.

My nose was bleeding but I now had a choke hold on his neck.

"You give in…give in!" Squeezed with all my might.

We lay on the ground entwined in a bloody stalemate.

He tapped my leg, I eased my failing grip and let go.

As is often the case, my adversary Manny Cohen became my best friend. "Can you play football?" asked Manny. I simply said, "Yes."

The 1950s were the high water mark for Hungarian football. The national team was ranked number one in the world and had a run of 24 unbeaten international games, including the trouncing of the complacent English side 6–3 in 1953 where they were shown to be technically and tactically inferior to the Magyars.

As good as I was at ping-pong, football was really my first love. I had played street games almost every day since I could swing my stick-like legs, all those hours kicking balls of various sizes and degrees of inflation stood me well in playground games. Very quickly I became the number one pick when it came to team selection, not only for my novelty factor, but also for my dribbling skills and ability to dance the ball up and down the playground.

"Dixie or whatever your name is, boy!"

One of the masters shouted in my general direction, a raised arthritic finger beckoning. "The headmaster wants to see you!" The delivery more suited to a parade ground than a playground.

Although caught in mid-dribble I moved smartly towards the headmaster's office; dawdling could be seen as insubordination.

By way of an introduction and 'Catholic' welcome the headmaster told me in no uncertain terms that I had a duty to God and right after school I was to present myself at the church. The RCC was an institution that not only traded in souls and absolution, but also demanded a return on their investment.

The parish priest, Father O'Reilly, met me at the church door with a smile, a handshake and a friendly tweak of a cheek.

"Come inside, my lad, we can start your instruction right away."

He gave me a lengthy sermon echoing the 'duty to God' bit, went on about the Church of Rome, the Pope, confession, absolution and many of the more obscure edicts of the RCC before handing over to Brother Luke, who was to instruct me in catechism, teaching me parrot-fashion the responses to the Latin mass, how to swing the thurible and when to ring the altar bell at mass and benediction.

I became an instant believer; the Church, like a giant anaconda, was swallowing me head first. The need to belong and the insidious nature of the indoctrination turned me into a pious little shit and for the first time a proper Catholic.

The Spanish sisters were delighted and did everything in their power to encourage me in my delusion. It seemed to them that I had the 'calling' and they groomed me accordingly.

I served at morning mass before school and benediction after, hardly off my knees long enough to confess to the pixilated figure behind the screen that I had stolen stuff, namely a pair of shiny metal cufflinks from Woolworths, even though I did not own a shirt that they could be used on, told some lies and had a couple of wanks.

Never admit to more than two.

Was it my imagination or was that a groan from behind the screen?

It seemed so easy – go away, mumble a few Our Fathers and Hail Marys, pass the beads through the fingers, head bowed in pious supplication, start the week with a clean slate.

I sang in the choir, polished the candlesticks, sampled the altar wine, determined to serve God in expectation of spiritual guidance unto rapture.

Succour came in the form of silver. Most times, after mass, the Father would slip me some coinage.

For reasons that at the time made no sense he would insist on putting the money deep in my front trouser pocket, for safety – "So that you don't lose it on yer way home," in what I later learned was a heavily musical Cork accent. Did this constitute abuse?

Perhaps, but at the time the cash was a welcome addition to the pocket money I had been squirrelling away for the 'Lone Ranger' gun belt and matching pair of six-shooters that I so wanted.

Some days on the way home I would take a slight detour past the toyshop, stopping to admire the pistols in the window, counting the days and the pennies until they would be mine. A few more masses and I shall be the masked man!

Although deeply torn between the priesthood and the life of a cowboy, this minor fork in life's road I justified as convergent. A mere detour. I could see myself as a 'priest- at-large', dispensing absolution and rough justice, a kind of frocked warrior sustained by the gratitude of town dwellers while I went about the Lord's work.

It would be necessary to find and enlist to my cause a faithful "Tonto"-type character. In keeping with Masked Man tradition I felt that somehow my sidekick should have a name ending in 'O'. Shouldn't be difficult to find a Mexican with a suitable name.

Naturally, he would have to have frontier skills that would complement my needs. Cooking, cleaning and laundry came immediately to mind but I was certain there were many other unsavoury chores that he would happily undertake.

The outfit was almost complete; all I needed was a mask and a hat. I traded a wind-up toy car with one of the kids for a hat that had a passing resemblance to the one worn by my hero. I made the mask out of a moth-eaten black blazer, carefully trimming out the eyeholes by folding the fabric in half and cutting semicircles. The two long bits at the sides would be used to tie it at the back of my head.

In the meantime, I was diligently praying that Father O'Reilly would continue to thrust coinage deep in my pockets until the day, allotted by the Lord, when I could confidently walk into the toyshop and buy the guns, holsters and several rolls of caps.

The big day finally arrived.

I was back in the vestry after mass.

"Look what I have for ye today." Father O'Reilly fished two large silver coins out of the collection plate and held them up, twirling one in each hand.

It looked like two half-crowns, a whole five shillings. That would put the fund into surplus, even a bit left over for sweets!

"Turn round so that I can make sure you don't lose them." I did as I was told.

He stood behind me, reaching around to thrust the coins deep in my front pockets, a coin in each, accompanied by a certain amount of fumbling.

I thought I could feel a finger prodding me from behind but his hands deep in my pockets would scupper that notion.

This ritual of his struck me as odd and I could not understand why he seemed to get so much pleasure out of what to me seemed like money for nothing.

Annoyingly, I had to wait until Monday to buy the guns. Pockets heavy with assorted change, I told Manny that I had to go to confession and veered off towards the church; he continued homeward. When he was out of sight I turned towards the toyshop in the high street. Another lie; I would just tack the extra to my 'bundle'.

No point in confusing the good priest with a confession about confessing, was there?

The man behind the counter seemed to be expecting me. "I have another set of pistols and holsters in black, same in every other way, except for the colour," he said, smiling.

I had a dilemma... did good guys wear black? The priests and nuns certainly did and they were about as close to perfection and to God as is possible in this earthly realm. I went for the black matching set complete with realistic-looking, silvery metal bullets arrayed in leather hoops around the gun belt.

Barely able to contain my excitement, I practically sprinted back to the orphanage. Rushing through the door I ran into a barrier in the awesome form of Sister Anna Maria.

"NO run in de 'ouse! 'Ow many time I tell?" She glared at me. Frozen with fear, stock-still at the foot of the stairs, I waited for divinely mandated retribution which would never arrive.

This withered crone was in the wrong business if indeed she was fully aware as to which order she had prostrated herself or why she had sacrificed her secular life at the altar of Jesus. Never to this day have I had the misfortune to be in the clutches of a more miserable, mean and intolerant human being than this particular 'Sister'. At least not until Brother Francis wielded absolute power over me as my form master and dormitory supervisor at Mayfield.

Both seemed to delight in the power (derived from God) that they had over the children in their 'care', strong advocates of corporal punishment, earnestly and vigorously applied in spite of the covert disapproval of many of their Brothers and Sisters.

"Go to room! Wait!" Luckily that was exactly where I wanted to be. Obediently I waited for what seemed like ages, then, the sound of a bell. Strange, I thought; normally a gong would be struck summoning us to meals.

The ambulance took Sister Anna Maria to hospital. There was power in prayer after all; she never returned, shipped back to Spain to meditate on the imminent meeting with her vengeful, jealous god.

Good riddance! I had other concerns.

Opening the locker I took out my regalia, laid it out on the bed. White felt cowboy hat, shirt with metal pop studs, white jeans, black rubber boots (wellies), red bandana, mask and guns: I dressed and admired myself in the full-length mirror. I had become not just any cowboy but a pretty good likeness of the Lone Ranger. Joining the ranks of the ordained should be relatively easy compared to the hours I spent on bony knees, the weight of unalloyed guilt pressing on my skinny body as I prayed for more Mammon, enough at least for a down payment on a horse.

I was under no illusion that this was a long-term commitment. Sister Immaculata (maybe she was) came looking in the back garden, found me without difficulty behind a thicket of privet where I was lying in ambush waiting for the Indians.

"Pedro, you and Tomahawk wait for me here, I'll be back in a minute."

My imaginary friends never let me down.

"Come! Sister Conchita wants you in her office." Obviously I had not mastered the art of camouflage. "Take off that silly mask!" She held out her hand. I unmasked and disarmed myself but would not hand over any of my precious things. Ran upstairs to my room, wrapped the holster belt, guns and mask in a hand towel, hid them under my pillow then climbed the extra flight of stairs to the office at the top of the house.

I knocked on the door tentatively.

"Enter!" the Sister boomed as I prepared for the worst.

It was a small room, barely big enough to house a couple of filing cabinets, Sister C's battered leather-topped desk and a pair of matching chairs, upon which sat a man and a woman with their backs to me. On the wall behind the sister was a 'paint by numbers' scene depicting Jesus walking on a lakeshore with his cronies.

She coughed, and removed her glasses, letting them dangle on her chest suspended by what appeared to be a 'rosary' for which she had found a secondary utility. There was a strong smell of cologne.

"Come, stand next to me, I want you to meet Mr. and Mrs. Abercrombie."

Relieved that I was not about to be punished for some obscure transgression, smiling shyly, I went and stood next to her and looked at my feet. Mr. and Mrs. Abercrombie stood and introduced themselves, both shook my hand warmly, sat back down. I did my very best to avoid looking at them.

"Stand up straight!" I felt I was letting Sister C and the church down not behaving like one destined for sainthood, so standing erect like a Prussian Hussar I lifted my eyes to look at the couple in front of me.

Mr. 'A' was slim and tall, even seated he commanded respect; the kind, intelligent face looked me over. The well-tailored dark grey suit sat comfortably on his shoulders, in his lap was a black bowler hat, soft hands resting atop the dark wood handle of an upright furled umbrella. His wife was modestly dressed, wearing a navy blue, mid-length pleated dress, white blouse with a cameo-type brooch at her throat and a colourful silk headscarf around her neck.

Mrs. A asked me some simple questions, such as "How old are you? What is your favourite colour?" That type of thing. Sister C made some notes on a pad and chirped in from time to time praising me up somewhat, with no mention of my religious zealotry, particular eating habits or lack of personal hygiene. All traits strongly encouraged and admired by the clergy, especially the latter.

The interview was over (for that's what it was) and I was released.

I hurried back to the waiting Pedro and Tomahawk. Obviously they, unlike me, had mastered the art of camouflage as I was unable to locate them in the greenery. I strapped the guns on and as soon as the mask was in place and knotted I saw them clearly, the white steed grazing, Pedro wearing a large yellow sombrero outstandingly ill concealed in the privet.

There was something odd about this mask. Did it enable me to see things that were not there, concealed from ordinary eyes? Was there some hidden potential or was it just my imagination?

The words 'orphanage' and 'workhouse' do not conjure up comforting concepts, made all the more dreadful by Hollywood and Victorian literature. So perhaps 'children's home' would be more fitting for our residence. The months spent there were mostly happy and carefree for my siblings and I, nurtured in the bosom of Mother Church, entwined in the crotch of blind, hairy faith.

A ground-floor front room with bay windows had been converted into a small dining hall with the addition of three large, rectangular dining tables with ladder-back oak chairs to match.

Our meals were prepared in the adjoining kitchen by a lay cook named Deidre. That is as much as I knew about her. She said very little; when she did speak she sounded like Groucho Marx with a sinus infection. Her helper, Mrs. Bacon, recently arrived from Jamaica, more than made up for the cook's silence.

She was a large, jolly lady with an impenetrable accent, seemingly without a care in the world, knew her place in life, putting her faith in her creator and His worldly representatives.

We shared and revered Our Lord. He was always portrayed as a white man with a beard, serene and unflinching even as the Romans poked him with spears and drove spikes through his body.

Nevertheless, I was troubled. If He created us in His image why was she was so different?

When I asked the 'Father' about this glaring discrepancy he put my mind at rest.

"The Lord created all tings and in his wisdom he gave black skin to those that lived in Africa so that they could live there comfortably and have no need for the 'sun lotion' we white people have to smear on our bodies," he continued. "Have yer seen what the sun does to white people on the beach?"

I had to agree; the Lord was vengeful and jealous yet showed great consideration to the well-being of his creatures.

"Take the Chinese, they have the slanty eyes because there is a lot of wind in those places." It all made perfect sense.

Not many black people in Bexhill, apart from Mrs. Bacon and a couple of kids at school. All I knew was what I had seen on the screen at my local cinema back in Pest.

Black people were generally depicted as white-eyed savages with bones through their noses, often dancing around simmering cauldrons containing the stoic explorer, he secure in the knowledge that relief in the form of another white man wearing a pith helmet at the head of a posse of friendly savages with elongated necks and teeth filed to points would arrive before the water temperature exceeded that of a comfortably warm bath. At this time I had no reason to question this casual racism. Indeed, all one needed was to look around: reinforcement was everywhere. It was hard to avoid the perception that as a 'white' person I was cut from finer cloth.

Mrs. Bacon, endowed with cherubic patience, was assured of her place in Heaven, in expectation of which she cheerfully performed all the worst jobs in the kitchen.

She sang beautifully, just slightly off-key, as she washed and scrubbed. Happily peeling buckets of potatoes for hungry mouths.

Bowls of food were passed through a serving hatch and plated at table.

The fare was wholesome by the standards of the day, conforming rigidly to the diktats of the Church; certainly better and more regular than any Gita could provide.

It was 1957 and this being a Catholic institution, Friday was the day I dreaded most – there would be fish. Oily sardines or pilchards marinading in unsavoury juices on a bed of toast for breakfast and some kind of white fish for dinner.

No amount of cajoling or threats would or could induce me to allow the smallest particle of seafood to pass my lips. They (the sisters) even tried to force-feed me, holding my nose and trying to force my gob open. Clamped firmly shut, I managed to breathe through my teeth, immediately and dramatically spitting out any residue that got past my lips.

"You will not leave this table until you have a clean plate! Children all over the world are starving. You should be grateful for the food the Lord has provided for you," and so forth.

None of these words had any effect on me. Sister Conchita's patience was wearing thin and I was surely pushing all her buttons and ringing her bells with this weekly carry-on. I would not give in.

Sometimes I was able to offload a chunk of cod to the kids sitting near me.

My main collaborator was called Mick who looked like 'Plug' from *The Beano* with the addition of perpetual rivulets of snot oozing from his nostrils. He would and did eat anything but was unable to fill the deep void carved out of his life by the injustices he had suffered at the hands of the Church.

Halitosis was his only friend. Mick and Hal were one: his chum followed Mick everywhere. The six spoons of sugar he liked to use to sweeten his tea had already decayed his gnashers beyond recovery. He just plain refused to brush the few teeth he still had. The rotting stumps did not even benefit from the gentle abrading motion of his top lip.

Mick suffered from 'Stiffupper', a self-inflicted survival mechanism made chronic by being shunted between Irish 'homes' before ending up in Bexhill.

He told me, "I never knew my mum or dad... they had to give me to the Church. We had no food at home. Plenty of grub in the Church, though, lots of yummy bread and jam!"

Mick and truth were at best distant cousins. Most of what came out of his mouth was demonstrably false, yet the story about his parents somehow rang true to me.

Apparently, his mother, unable to cope with abandonment and the shame associated with a bastard child in profoundly Catholic Ireland left him at a convent gate. This, by many accounts, was not unusual. I tried to befriend him, but he remained distant unable to open up, to trust another human being. Whether he chose the solitary life or had learned to avoid intimacy having suffered the social death of a thousand cuts was impossible to know. By the time our paths crossed he was thoroughly institutionalised, a friendless loner with antisocial tendencies shunned even by the Sisters of No Mercy. I wonder what happened to him.

Alone in the dining room, I used my time to sculpt the mess on my plate into a fairly passable image of Jesus's head complete with halo.

Sister C bustled in. "Just eat some of it, be a good boy, please." Summoned by the bell to attend to her prayers, with a wag of her finger she left.

Sometimes, when Mrs. Bacon was busy rattling the pots and pans I would open a window and lob a lump into the rose bushes or pull the rubber plant out of its pot and bury a pilchard under the roots. It passed unnoticed that of the four once identical plants the one nearest to where I usually sat appeared... NO... was...larger and shinier, perhaps due to its proximity to the window and the benefit of more sunlight, hard to say really.

Akos and Margo soaked up the new language like sponges left out in a deluge.

They lost their mother tongue, it seemed, in a few weeks, and to this day know only English. I was a bit slower on the uptake and still retain a fair understanding of the Hungarian language with severely limited vocabulary and (no doubt) terrible grammar. The assimilation was well underway. I wholeheartedly threw myself into becoming if not quite English at the very least some kind of hybrid Brit. This transformation, I felt, had to be achieved in the shortest time possible.

CHAPTER 10

A NEW NAME

Choice is a luxury not often lavished upon a child.

The church had inadvertently given me a gift. My confirmation into the RCC was coming up and I needed a new name.

Rarely if ever in life are we given the opportunity to choose our own names concurrent with the wisdom to make sensible decisions. My first choice will clearly illustrate this point. To me it conjured up images of rapid, circular motion like a whirling dervish or perhaps Walt Disney's Taz on a rampage.

Where this notion came from remains a puzzle, must have heard someone being called Spiro and I liked the sound of it.

Unaware of the ties that bind and names that divide, how one may be pigeonholed into a particular camp or culture and the impact a simple label has on relationships, I wanted to take Cohen as my middle name. I offered Manny one of mine. I truly thought that exchanging names would be an easily achievable expression of our solidarity.

I could see no reason why he, like me, could not simply change his name.

This naive notion did not allow for the complexities of life in general and the significance of names in particular, an early tutorial in the innumerable little mysteries of life. I soon learned that names are more than just a handy way to tag a person but are, in many instances, clues to ethnicity.

Mess with them at your peril.

Manny knew all too well what it meant to be part of an oppressed minority. His parents barely escaped the pogroms, settled in an English seaside town, and in a valiant effort to assimilate sent their son to a Catholic school, yet the thought of changing a name was inconceivable.

It was hard for me to understand such stubborn entrenchment.

A new life needed a new name.

Strong objections were raised by Father O'Reilly, reinforced by a couple of hearty slaps on the thighs from Brother Luke for good measure. I felt the breath of the Holy Ghost inspired my private delusion and I continued to lobby for Spiro, alternatively whining and offering what I thought were well-reasoned arguments.

Emanuel Cohen was disinclined to adopt either of my birth names.

"You know that if I were to even suggest such a possibility my parents would have an apocalyptic fit!"

Of course he was right: Attila would have ill-suited the only obviously Jewish kid in a Catholic school. As if his Romanesque nose and alien beliefs did not attract enough scorn, the odd name would only bring him additional ridicule.

I was unaware that he was not only ineligible for the sacred rite I was about to undergo, but also doomed to eternal damnation (stigma is sticky) as an accidental member of the tribe that cruelly condemned Our Lord and Saviour.

This was what I was taught and in spite of ever-mounting evidence of their fallibility I still trusted my indoctrinators. Nothing came of my proposed name swap and we continued to be as thick as thieves. Manny and I, united in isolation, thrown together by circumstance, in a minority of two.

What saved us from burdening the full weight of being social outcasts was that we were both good at football. We stuck together, no matter the odds.

He and I were inseparable in collective segregation, blood brothers in reality.

Ready to take up for each other against the masters or the playground bullies, abuse, physical or mental was part of our daily regime.

The fact is I could not find any support for my wacky name choices in any quarter, so I dropped the idea.

The long-anticipated confirmation date was only a couple of weeks away and I needed to come up with viable names.

In a state of self-induced enchantment I knelt in the empty church waiting patiently for… something, any event really that I could conjure into divine intervention.

Squinting, praying hard, I concentrated on the Virgin Mary. Draped in her customary ultramarine robe, she was unmoved. Is it conceivable that the Virgin Mother of Jesus was so under-resourced that she did not have access to a change of livery?

Her unabashed gaze rested on my brow. Nestled in the corner grotto, her head was tilted to the left, delicate hands at prayer. I waited for a wink, a twitch of her little piggy or even a well-timed guttering candle. She remained statuesque.

No matter how hard I implored, those heavenly clouds failed to produce a drop of holy water.

The nave at St Richard's was lined with stained-glass windows at regular intervals depicting images of saints, mostly grumpy-looking, bearded geezers holding scrolls in their limp-wristed hands, or keys larger than a man could readily slip into the folds of his robe.

There were two, however, that I particularly admired. They were warriors.

The 'Father', emerging from the vestry, seeing me on my knees, came over.

I could smell him coming long before he sat down next to me. A pungent mixture of incense, stale sweat and altar wine followed him like a fetid shadow. I scratched my nose to mitigate the assault on the olfactory sensors.

"What is that man's name?" I pointed to a striking image depicting a saintly knight slaying a dragon, his head surrounded by a celestial halo, glorious in victory.

Impaled on the lance, the beast looked troubled, a hint of contrition in its double-glazed eyes. It appeared to be convulsing, thrashing wildly, blood oozing freely from the neck area and pooling at the feet of the white stallion.

Both horse and rider were untroubled by the encounter and appeared to be in deep serenity.

"That is St. George, the patron saint of England." Father O'Reilly went on to explain at length the legend of the aforementioned saint, but my head went to a different place and I heard nothing.

"What about that one?"

"Ah," said he, "that is the archangel St. Michael, enemy of Satan, angel of death, Defender of the Faith etc." He continued in this vein, happy for the opportunity to display his knowledge of these weighty matters.

That settled it for me, that was exactly how I saw myself, a saintly crusader in training.

"When I am confirmed I want to be called George Michael." I looked at the Father; he grunted, turned and walked towards the vestry. I took this as approval and that was that.

I was still young enough; surely there would be plenty of time for revision if the assumed names became a burden.

Had I been allowed to have my way, the childish and unwieldy combination of Spiro/Cohen would certainly have come back to haunt me in my teenage years.

I had no intention of joining the Jewish community, nor did I aspire to own a chip shop, so on reflection George Michael was, as luck would have it, the more practical option.

Over his shoulder he said, "Time for your lesson with Bro. Luke. Go now, hurry up, he's waiting, you know he gets angry if you're late!"

I stood up, rubbed my knees, rushed to be taught a lesson.

"You are three minutes late, hold out your hand!"

Two brutal swipes landed on the proffered left hand. I smiled evenly at his close-shaven, greasy face; a smear of dried spittle garnished the corners of his mean lips.

"One more for your defiance, hold it out, not that one, the other! Now let's get down to work."

The 'brother' was tasked to instruct me in the 'four pillars of the faith', followed by a lengthy session of catechism. These absolute truths were the root cause of my suffering.

The casual nature of the abuse I suffered at the whim of this man of God would lead me later to start questioning some of the more incredible teachings of the Church.

But for now I was fully in the grip of 'Mother Church', immersed up to my neck in her alphabet soup of shifting precepts.

Not the most patient of men, wholly unencumbered by basic human values or the virtue of forbearance, the Bro. made energetic use of the finely shaped, polished piece of mahogany salvaged from the backrest of a G Plan dining chair. Randomly applied to my hands and buttocks, this instrument of correction was never far from his reach.

He took obvious and immediate delight in its application whenever my parroted responses deviated from the text.

The so-called Sisters of Mercy, who were largely responsible for my welfare and had encouraged me in my fantasy of becoming a priest, pressured me in more subtle ways. Their methods of exacting punishment were insipid compared to Brother Luke and his novel, unexpectedly effective use of the then popular utilitarian furniture range, soon to be eclipsed by cheaper and better-designed Scandinavian imports.

"Why did Jesus not keep a journal?" Bro. Luke was incensed by my impertinence.

"How dare you question the Word of God? You are a miserable sinner and will burn in Hell if you keep asking such ignorant questions."

Despite mounting evidence of massive deception, I clung to my chosen faith. It seemed impossible that so many could be wrong. I continued my search for revelation.

In time, the only 'revelation' I experienced was that there was no real evidence of a divine being.

We are careening down the corniche. There is no one at the wheel.

Later, slowly, as the scales fell rattling from my eyes, the whole charade gradually became clear to me.

It was a big, fat lie.

The playground fights were, by modern standards, pretty tame affairs. The sight of a scuffed knee or blood from any part of the head or face would usually put an end to a scrap; peace and harmony regained, normality returned and the clock ticked on.

Play went on as usual, lessons being nothing more than interruptions until 3.30, when Manny and I would walk home together unless I felt compelled or was instructed to present myself for further indoctrination, choir practice or any other task befitting those, such as myself, seeking heavenly approval at almost any price.

Torn between sticking with Manny in case he was ambushed or furthering my nascent career as a priest, I chose to serve God on this particular occasion.

The next day, Manny was not in class.

After school I went round to his house. His mother opened the door and invited me in. Something was wrong; normally I would have been left waiting at the door.

She told me that on the way home last night he was attacked by some boys from the C of E school down the road and had taken a bit of a beating. They whacked him simply because they thought he was a Catholic. If they had an inkling that he was a Jew, well, it would have been worse for him. As much as they disliked Catholics, they hated Jews.

Bexhill General kept him in overnight; he had taken a bit of a crack on the back of his head when he went down. In the morning they gave the all-clear and he was discharged. My chosen religion dictated that I blame myself for not being there to help him. Another cloud rolled over my newfound faith.

The Lord works in mysterious ways.

CHAPTER 11

THE VISIT

Sister Conchita told me that my mother was driving down at the weekend and I was to make sure to scrub behind my ears, cut my nails and wear my 'best' clothes.

Akos and Margo were also prepared, bathed and dressed for the occasion.

"Driving? What is she driving?" Surely she cannot have learned to drive and made enough money to buy a car. Ever optimistic, my reasoning was that if she had a car she must be doing well and was coming down to take us home.

I should have been surprised, but by now was so used to unexpected events and had learned well that my welfare, if not survival, was predicated on the ability to adapt. Nothing surprised me anymore. Mentally, I readied myself to leave but made no preparations.

Excitedly guarded, nevertheless, the possibility that she may be coming to pick us up was wonderful news. I ran around to find Akos and Margo. Having second thoughts I did not tell them anything other than that Mama was coming for a visit.

Sunday morning after mass I returned to find A&M sitting together on his bed. They were both all spiffed up, looking good in their hand-me-down clothes. Hair brushed, shoes polished.

"Mama is coming to take us home!" I wish I had not said that out loud. I really wish I had kept my trap shut. In my excitement I had blurted out my wish, based on what? Nobody said anything about going home. I led them downstairs; we sat as assigned, waiting, waiting, A&M looking grim.

I took a deep breath. "Well, I am not sure about Mama coming to pick us up but we will at least get to see her and I feel sure we will go with her soon." This was exactly what I did not want. A&M started to weep, gently at first; then, as if trying to outdo each other, they really started wailing.

Looking foolish, hopping from foot to foot, did not make them feel any better but it bought me time to think of something, anything, to stop the awful noise they were making. I knelt in front of them, trying to hug them both, making 'there, there' noises.

Nothing I said or did had the desired effect.

"Listen, what's that noise?"

Swallowing their sobs, they pricked up their ears.

From the front of the house the throaty roar of a motorcycle rattled the windows.

Although told to wait until called for (moving from a particular spot without permission was a punishable offence) we could not resist climbing on chairs, peering out of the window to see what all the fuss was about.

My jaw sagged, stomach churned in a rebellious way.

A shiny new Triumph Bonneville sat on the drive. Gita had dismounted from the pillion of the throbbing machine. She jerkily raised the home-made perspex visor and removed her helmet. A tangle of shockingly bright red hair burst free. Victor stopped the motor and put the stand down.

Tucking the helmets under their arms they stood on either side of the Triumph.

Plastic overcoats not dissimilar to the one I had abandoned in the quagmire at the Austro/Hungarian border graced their bodies.

The design and manner of construction were familiar but the fabric was of superior quality and had all the characteristics of fine Moroccan leather.

Hurriedly adjusting the Medusa-like tangle on her head, she applied a slash of crimson to her lips. The helmet dangled from her arm like a handbag. A small crowd of little people gathered around the motorcycle, jabbering to no avail as she and Victor were constrained by language and could only grin inanely.

Akos started to cry again. "How can we all fit on that motorbike?"

I was at a loss for words.

Sister Conchita shooed the kids away and greeted the aliens warmly, ushering Gita into the sitting room. Victor stayed with the bike, wiping it down with a rag, wisely keeping out of the way.

We waited, sitting exactly where we were left by Sister Sandra.

The door opened and Gita rushed in. A&M jumped up and into her well-padded embrace. I stood aloof, took a good look at her.

She seemed a little plumper than the last time I saw her. Still attractive yet verging on the lardy side. Her face was well made up, eyes heavily defined.

A vividly vibrant purple and green polyester trouser suit adorned her heavy-footed frame.

In true Hungarian style her squeezes and kisses were unrestrained. She lunged at me as I recoiled slightly, embarrassed by the slobbery attention. This was an outward manifestation of my ongoing transformation from a soppy, simpering mother's boy to the serried ranks of the stiff upper-lipped.

Quiet desperation and stoicism encouraged by the Church, and much admired by the Brits. Mustn't grumble!

She cooed and fussed, stroking my head and nuzzling me like a dog. Indeed I felt like an abandoned pet unexpectedly reunited with its owner. If I had had a tail it would have been wagging.

It was obvious that this was just a visit. I hid my disappointment. A&M both cried, wanting to go with her. She soothed them with hugs and kisses, promising to return soon and we would all be together.

We enjoyed the short visit greatly; the exotic hair and mode of transport raised our stock in the eyes of the other kids and indeed the sisters.

They left as suddenly as they arrived. Donning their helms, the visors attached by rusty push studs were lowered and they roared off down the road. The upgraded plastic coats flapping, unlike the prototypes, in the wind.

The assembled 'goodbye committee' dispersed.

Life seemed to return to normal.

Some time before Christmas the Abercrombies arrived unexpectedly (to me at least) and I was told to pack some stuff for a few days away. Already pretty much institutionalised and used to unexpected turns nevertheless, I was reluctant to leave, and made a feeble protest not entirely out of self-interest, being concerned for A&M and their well-being when I, as head of the family, big brother and protector, was away.

There was little to be done, certainly a boy had no voice and future events were decided without reference to me.

Once the RCC steamroller moves, do not lie in the road.

I said goodbye to A&M. "Be back in a few days – hopefully," I added.

The Abercrombies were waiting in the hall below, looking up and smiling as I lugged my small cardboard suitcase down the stairs. Crammed with Lone Ranger gear, a change of underwear stuffed into the boots, leaving just enough room for my wash bag and a thick, knitted jumper, in case it got chilly. I made a point of bumping the case along the banisters all the way down, face a grim mask of resentful resignation. Their smiles slipped slightly but they both retained composure.

I was shown to their parked car out on the forecourt where the oil spots deposited by the Triumph were still clearly visible.

It suddenly occurred to me that I had never been in a car.

It looked brand new, clean, shiny, the polished chrome bumpers and trim gleaming in the afternoon sun. The significance of the dark blue paintwork and the make, Morris Oxford, would in due course be revealed.

Perhaps this new adventure would not be so bad after all.

The smell of the burgundy leather was wonderfully memorable and I still love that old car smell; there is something reassuring about it. I was allowed to sit in the split-bench front seat. There were no seat belts. It was an optional extra that they thought unnecessary; we lived in a time when smoking unfiltered cigarettes was not only manly, but also good for your lungs.

The car was a feeble attempt by British designers to emulate the current American offerings: deep-dished steering wheel, Cadillac-style fins, and as this was the de-luxe version it featured a heater, clock, manual screen washer, passenger sun visor (with mirror), over-riders, twin horns. A two-tone option was available and quite popular: for this very reason it was just a wee bit too flash for the Abercrombies.

To me it looked to be straight out of Dan Dare's garage, ready to fly into the stratosphere to see off the Mekons.

This was better than church!

As is the way with inquisitive boys I asked Mr. A many questions about the gauges, knobs, buttons and levers. He was a patient man but cranking the window up and down a dozen times in awe of the technology that allowed this to happen did test him.

Sharply, "Please stop that!" Mr. A had his limits.

While I was distracted riding the range, interring the fish dinners and practising to be a priest, the RCC and Mr. A had decided my future. I was to be put in their care and packed off to boarding school.

The journey from Bexhill to Lewes took about 45 minutes. Mrs. A asked,

"What kind of music do you like?"

"I don't know, what kind is there?" I was being probed, gently and efficiently in an effort to get to know who I was – hard for the class-conscious English to pigeonhole a foreigner, especially one that looked just like them. The fact that my stepfather was a dentist pleased them greatly and gave them hope that this sullen, pious boy may yet have promise.

Indeed fortune had smiled on me.

The Abercrombies lived in a modern, brick-built, centrally heated four-bedroom bungalow up on the cliffs overlooking the town, surrounded by a couple of acres of land, some laid to lawn and the rest a rambling wilderness, perfect terrain for the Lone Ranger. They also had an unheated outdoor pool which became a pond in the winter months, a dark green habitat for scary creatures. All manner of hungry monsters lurked just below the surface. Giant tentacles would curl around ankles, dragging the unwary down; schools of ravenous piranha ready to strip flesh to the bone waited in the depths.

I always gave it a wide berth in the off-season.

During the summer I learned to swim there coached by Mr. A, supervised by Mrs. A. They were a lovely, genteel couple and made every effort to put me at ease, welcoming me into their world. There were references to a son named Sanders (Alex was considered too common) who was away at school but for right now at least I was the focus of their attention.

The house was an oasis of good, solid, upper-middle-class Catholic sensibility in a town with a strong anti-papist sentiment. They chose to live in Lewes because of the town's proximity to Glyndebourne and were regular patrons.

The sitting room had a big, open fire, floor-to-ceiling bookshelves either side of the mantelpiece, quality furniture and a shiny, black baby grand with neat stacks of sheet music atop a side table. The earlier questions relating to music now made more sense. Mrs. A had been an opera singer and was an accomplished piano player, Mr. A could tickle the ivories a bit himself; at times they would sit together for a Brahms variation or a bit of Scott Joplin.

I knew nothing about music and, try as I might, could not muster any enthusiasm for opera. They endured with great patience hours of my percussive disharmony at the keyboard, pleading with their eyes for me to stop. Mr. A in particular developed a tick in his left eye yet they never said a word... a fine example of English reserve.

There was talk of piano lessons but it never came to anything.

For the first time in a long time I felt safe. Unlike back in Budapest, my privacy was respected. The Abercrombies would not dream of barging in without knocking.

I imagined that this must be what it's like living in a fancy hotel. I had a bedroom with en suite bathroom, a bed that you could get out the wrong side of, clean sheets and towels.

It was all very proper.

At breakfast we sat at a large, oval table with a crisp, white tablecloth.

The crockery all corresponding, the plated cutlery set according to convention, at centre table stood a silver rack in which wholewheat brown toast cooled, cut corner to corner geometrically aligned and thoughtfully placed next to the lidded butter dish and knife.

A mix of brown and white sugar lumps sat in a crystal bowl, the griffin-clawed sugar tongs laid alongside.

Tea was poured from a white ceramic teapot, coffee from a silver plate swan-necked coffee pot. The white linen napkins, ring bound to complement.

There were cheery "Good mornings!" Immediately followed by formalised enquiries as to the quality of the sleep we each enjoyed. The answers were stock; a true Englishman would never admit to a restless night.

In awe, still somewhat overwhelmed by events, I waited to sit down to breakfast with the Abercrombies.

Under normal circumstances I would not have hesitated to dive in (table manners not having been high on Gita's agenda) but I waited until they both sat, Mr. A helping to seat his wife. I waited for cues.

They reached for their napkins, unfurling and laying the linen on their laps. I did the same and waited for the next move. "Coffee or tea, darling?" Mrs. A asked her husband. "Coffee please," said he, glancing at the front page of *The Times* before putting it aside to enjoy on his commute to the city. He was too well bred to be reading a paper at breakfast. She turned to me.

I followed form: "Coffee please." As she poured, Mr. A used the tongs to transfer one brown lump to his coffee and stirred gently.

Breaking protocol I took six white lumps. Mrs. A glanced over her glasses at her husband as she first poured a dash of milk then the tea into her plain white teacup. They said nothing.

I had a lot to learn.

The breakfast banquet was not put on for my benefit but was a daily occurrence in the household. The 'Full Monty' on offer these days is a mere soupçon of the splendid feast consistently available at the Abercrombies'. Choice of cereal or porridge with warm milk, soft poached eggs, bacon, sausages, fried mushrooms and tomatoes, toast, honey, marmalade, coffee and tea, still one of my favourite meals.

Mr. A, as befitted an Oxford graduate and senior civil servant, wore the uniform: pinstripes, bowler hat, briefcase, rolled umbrella; weather forecasting in those pre-satellite days was a perilously unpredictable business. His equilibrium would have been deeply disturbed if his favourite umbrella was not readily to hand.

Mrs. A would drop him at the train station. He joined the bowler brigade bound for London Victoria. *The Times* enjoyed, crossword decrypted by the time his train pulled into the station. His place of work, the offices of the Admiralty in Whitehall, a brisk, 25-minute walk and part of his exercise routine on rainless days.

Sanders, their son, came home from school for the holidays and I felt he was a bit miffed at finding me sharing his space and his parents' attention.

In truth, we did not have much in common. The street urchin and the English public school toff were not a natural pairing. In spite of our obvious differences over time we became pretty good friends. When he found out that I was also a 'philatelist' but had left my stamps behind, he freely shared some of his with me, effectively seeding my new collection.

A Christmas tree was erected in the corner of the sitting room and over a period was dressed with baubles and lights. Below the branches colourfully wrapped boxes and packages of various shapes and sizes appeared over the following days.

Off to one side was a sturdy-looking wooden trunk with black metal gate hinges and handles at the sides, the latch at the front secured by a festive green ribbon.

Traditionally, opening the presents was a Christmas Eve activity at the Abercrombies' so after dinner on the 24th Mr. & Mrs. A sat back in their wingback easy chairs sipping port from lead crystal glasses while Sanders and I rummaged under the tree. Sanders's gifts were of the practical educational kind: books, classical records, Meccano (Erector) and chemistry sets. He was very happy and got what he largely expected.

Intended for me, I found nothing except an envelope with a printed index card inside with the numbers 0511 in bold type. To say that I was disappointed would not adequately describe the green demon of jealousy that rose in my throat. The parents looked on, enjoying the moment. They then pointed to the plaid rug draped over a boxlike object sitting against the wall. Pulling the rug aside revealed the wooden trunk.

George M. Decsy was stencilled on the top in black lettering. Another strange English custom perhaps?

The green ribbon through the latch had been replaced by a combination lock with four tumblers. Now it all made sense. Fumbling excitedly with the lock, the numbers aligned, click, the padlock opened.

I laid the lid of the trunk against the wall. The look of disappointment was impossible to hide; the items I could see were not at all as expected. Having seen Sanders open his gifts, I had expected similar treatment. The trunk appeared to hold nothing of interest for me; all that was visible was neatly stacked piles of clothes, in particular: several light grey shirts in cellophane packaging, long and short, dark grey trousers, socks (also grey), underwear – string vests, Y-fronts (soon to be grey), a blue blazer with a badge on the breast pocket, black lace-up shoes and a couple of two-tone blue, diagonally striped ties. What cruelty was this?

"Keep looking," said Mr. A smugly as the other two looked on, enjoying my by now obvious distress.

Digging deep past the layers of attire I did find 'real' presents. *Beano* and *Eagle* annuals (my favourites), a pencil case full of writing implements, and a red and cream plastic transistor radio with earpiece; this little marvel of technology would be the instrument that filled my ears and warmed my heart while the undernourished body lay shivering under the threadbare blankets at Mayfield College.

"Try the blazer for size," said Mrs. A. I put it on.

"It's too big."

"Perfect, she said, room to grow."

The emblem on the breast pocket (precision-stitched by Mrs. A) sported a baffling arrangement of letters. What was patently clear was that I was to be sent to boarding school.

I had no idea if Gita knew anything about what was planned for me. Even if she did, in the face of the all-powerful RCC, there was nothing to be done. As usual, I had no say in these momentous decisions about my life. I thought I was ready for anything but had not reckoned on the English boarding school system. The trunk and I would be delivered to Mayfield College where I boarded for almost two years.

CHAPTER 12

MAYFIELD COLLEGE

The Morris crunched up the gravel drive aptly named Little Trodgers Lane, stopping in front of the heavy wooden doors.

From the back seat I looked up at an imposing, red-brick Victorian building and a chill ran up my spine. Was this where the Count lived? What new hell was this?

Brother Gregory, the headmaster, was all smiles greeting the Abercrombies warmly.

Ignored in the back seat I sat and waited. Mr. A finally opened the door.

"This is George." He motioned for me to come out.

The Brother reached out to shake my hand.

He was a small man with piercing eyes and soft hands, wearing a black cassock with cloth-covered buttons. A stained, ivory-coloured collar encircled his vulture-like neck. Short cape over his shoulders, a large brass crucifix dangling mid-chest.

I could feel the animus behind the eyes. He did not like me. I definitely did not like him and was afraid of what he may do once the car disappeared down the drive.

My fears were well founded. After that first day the only 'human' connection I had with Bro. Gregory was when the business end of his bamboo cane came into contact with my arse.

Mr. A helped me carry the heavy box into the school. Bro. G led us into a large room full of trunks all precisely stencilled and padlocked. He pointed to a spot where it was to be left.

This was the moment I had been dreading. Mr. A stood erect, shook my hand, ruffled my hair. "See you in a few weeks." He slipped a 10-bob note into the top pocket of my new blazer, turned and left.

The welcoming smile slipped from the face of the Bro. He looked at me with undisguised contempt.

"How do you pronounce your name?"

"George," I replied evenly.

"No, you idiot, your surname!"

"Decsy like taxi." It was the best I could come up with.

"Follow me, Taxi," he barked. No more George until end of term, then!

Christian (first) names were only used when there happened to be a couple of Smiths or Joneses in the room.

I followed Bro. G in silence as he wheezed his way up the well-worn stone staircase, pausing every few steps to catch his breath.

What happened to the happy life when my rock was Uncle Joe? When my only concerns were how to be a good Communist who also played a decent game of football. Why was I cast into this nightmare where nothing made sense, where lard was brown and bread was white? Where we went out to the Inn up on the downs.

A faint wisp of incense lingered but was overwhelmed by the trail of tobacco mixed with boiled cabbage left in the wake of Bro. G. Was it possible to be scrubbed and ordained? So far the evidence was to the contrary.

In silence Bro. G showed me my locker and my assigned bed in the lower dormitory. Warehousing around 40 boys, the beds were so close that one could hold hands with the kid in the next 'pit'.

The thin, unsprung mattress on the iron-framed bed was cratered by the shuddering ejaculations of boys who had wanked themselves into a stupor since the school was founded.

A small, two-tier nightstand for pyjamas, towel, wash bag etc. stood between the beds and was to be shared with the boy adjacent.

This, to put it mildly, was disappointing. Having a large bedroom to myself in Lewes did nothing to prepare me for these new privations.

Another new boy sauntered up the row of beds, turned right towards the windows, making a beeline for the bed next to mine.

I sized him up as he swaggered towards me.

Dogtooth check sports jacket, cavalry twill trousers, knitted waistcoat, brown suedes, pastel paisley shirt and red tie. I watched him out of the corner of my eye, pretending to read the school paper.

With a curt nod in my direction he started to stow his belongings.

Monogrammed pyjamas, shiny new rugby boots, Parker pens in a fancy box and Basildon Bond writing paper were carefully arranged into his section of the nightstand.

I watched in silence as he wrapped a well-oiled cricket bat in a fluffy white towel and slipped it under the bed.

As I was going to sleep within farting distance of this twat I thought I'd better introduce myself.

"Hello, I'm George." I offered a hand.

He looked me over.

What he saw was a skinny kid sitting on the edge of his bed nervously swinging his legs.

The brand new school uniform with the blazer sleeves down to the knuckles instantly classified me.

Somewhat reluctantly he took my hand and gave it a limp shake.

"Simon Gibbins."

Judging by the quality of his kit he was well adjusted to the finer things in life. Testing the mattress for bounce, he sat down heavily. The solid steel cage that laughably passed for a bed topped by the thin horsehair mattress did nothing to cushion the jarring dislocation of his lower back.

"Bloody 'ard, innit?" I deliberately used the vernacular to see his reaction.

"This is bollocks, mate, when do the mattresses arrive?" Or words to that effect.

I started to like him better.

Over the next few days we both ran afoul of Bro. Francis.

Me, for reading a *Beano* during one of his interminably boring religious monologues, and Gibso for the meticulous attention he lavished on his hair.

"Vanity is not a virtue, Gibbins." Bro. F's face flushed a terracotta red; distorted with pious rage, he ranted on at length on the theme of the seven deadly sins, most of which Gibso and I were well acquainted with. Mother Church would in the fullness of time fill in the blanks.

We soon became firm pals and sat next to each other at the back of the class, sniggering at Bro. Francis and his ridiculously desperate efforts at indoctrination.

The more he singled us out for extra prep or a few angry whacks on the palms, the closer we became.

To keep young men busy (the Devil has work for idle hands!) the school had a full weekend of compulsory activities. On Saturdays there was rugby or cricket; we still played football at breaks in spite of the disapproval of the brothers.

There was a choice of three activities after mass on Sundays. Scouts had no appeal for me after the Little Drummers. Tying knots or whittling sticks for badges did nothing to further my martial aspirations.

I wanted my Brasso-stained finger on a trigger; marching around with guns, target practice, black polished boots and shiny brass buckles were much more to my liking.

We weren't quite old enough for the Army Cadets so Gibso and I had little choice but to join the 'Walkers'.

This motley crew populated by wankers and misfits suited us perfectly.

Walking and wanking was exactly what we did.

Our rambles often took us into Mayfield village where we regularly ran into a column doing the same from St. Leonards, an RC boarding school for girls. These encounters inflamed our collective imaginations and were almost as exciting as a visit to the village chip shop.

The stick-legged rank and file, caps in short trousers were captivated by the mere sight of a knee. Pubescent imaginations sparked by a wayward curl of blonde hair.

We were obsessed with sex: a well-thumbed copy of *Lady Chatterley's Lover* was so popular among the wanky walkers that you had to put your name on a waiting list!

It was also high contraband: being caught with such in one's possession would mean instant expulsion.

"They have three holes, you know."

"Who does?"

"Girls! My sister told me."

"Rubbish, what twaddle, she must be pulling your plonker." Ha-ha. "I wish she would pull mine."

This is what passed for conversation in the ranks of the 'Walkers'.

Gibso, never short of cash, indulged himself (and to a lesser extent me) at the tuck shop run by the prefects, a lucrative sideline and object lesson in exploitation.

The endless stream of parcels from his mother made sure that we were both well supplied with biscuits, home-baked cakes and, most importantly, high contraband in the form of comics.

What he did not have was a transistor radio.

"Let you use it for three sheets of paper and two Ginger Nuts…"

"How long?"

"Half an hour."

"Make it an hour."

"OK, done!"

I passed the instrument over… pretuned to Radio Luxembourg. Gibso soon had a stack of comics which he traded like the entrepreneur he would become. It would not be a huge step from DC Comics to the recreational drugs trade. Dealing in school contraband would be excellent training for a short but extremely lucrative foray into the nascent drug scene of the sixties and seventies.

Comics were a seminal influence in my life also.

So much so that I often had some difficulty staying grounded.

The ads in the back pages managed to prise a few shilling from my sticky palms.

The X-ray specs were too tempting to ignore. I sent off my postal order and waited with great anticipation. The ad graphically depicted a skinny nerd (not unlike me) ogling a shapely woman of indeterminate age. Strangely, seeing through the dress was well within the scope of this techno marvel but the knickers were impenetrable.

The days passed. Just as I was ready to give up on becoming a schoolboy voyeur the small package arrived.

Eager to test the limits of my new powers, I went over to the infirmary.

We called her Sister Betty. The word 'matronly' aptly describes her looks and occupation.

"I had a nosebleed earlier and…"

She cut me off. "Sit down, Taxi. I'll be back in a tick."

I slipped the glasses on and waited.

She bustled back into the room. "Now then, let's have a look, say AHHH!"

Screwing up my face, squinting hard to see through her sister's uniform only resulted in one of the lenses falling out, clattering on the linoleum floor.

Despite the abject failure of this device the attempt to enhance my powers would not stop there.

I sent away for the Hypno-Coin.

The Invisibility Helmet.

A tripod-mounted Machine Gun.

A Nuclear Submarine.

Charles Atlas's 32-page illustrated booklet.

And a couple of green rocks convincingly labelled Kryptonite.

It took me a while to recover from Chronic Optimism.

One corner of the dorm was partitioned off.

Into the roughly 18-square-foot space was crammed a bed, a desk, two chairs, and a small bookshelf.

A lurid picture of JC with an anatomically incorrect yet searingly radiant heart hung on the north wall, a depiction of St. Francis Xavier on the opposite.

This is where Bother Francis slept, held prayer sessions and private tutoring.

Happily, I was not rewarded for my good behaviour and diligent study by being one of the select few.

Not only was he my form master, which put me in the firing line for dark sarcasm and whacks with a yardstick, but also supervised my dorm where he continued to abuse me. I would suffer regular beatings for talking after lights out or some other, what were to me at least, minor transgressions.

The 'slipper' was his chosen tool of punishment. More like a sandal of the type favoured by the Nazarene, the coiled-rope sole would leave a jolly nautical impression (Flemish coil) on the cheeks. The leather-strapped upper a reliably no-slip grip for the hard-working Bro.

He seemed to take a good measure of pleasure from these encounters. I hated him passionately and thought about how to wreak revenge on this sadist, a word that, as yet, had no meaning for me.

Owen was by any measure a very handsome boy. Wavy, blond hair, baby blue eyes, you get the picture! He was not in my form so I had little contact with him, but even to my innocent eyes he, over time, displayed personality changes that we talked about in the dorm.

It all started when he was summoned to Bro Francis's room right at the beginning of term.

"What did he want?" He was two beds away from me so technically a neighbour. I had no qualms about asking.

"Oh, er, we prayed together and he showed me some photos."

"Of what?"

"Of Jesus and his mates walking around Lake Galilee… talking and swimming together."

"You mean pictures of Jesus, drawings, paintings?"

"No, they were photos."

I had more questions but we were interrupted.

"What are you two gabbing on about?" Gibso came back from the bathroom, a cheeky tartan dressing gown over his stripey pyjamas, a large, brown leather wash bag dangling from his limp wrist. Not quite the image I wanted for my gang of extortionists.

As a diversion I asked, "How do you manage to get those creases in your pyjamas, mate?"

"Well... I just fold them and put 'em under my mattress." Pulling up a corner he showed his other pair in situ.

Strange boy.

So it went.

It seemed there was a steady stream of boys selected for prayer and study sessions but I was never included.

As far as the Bro was concerned, I was better employed as a whipping boy.

"Taxi, see me outside my cubicle!" Not only was he incapable of pronouncing my name but also seemed to delight in every opportunity to punish and humiliate me. These pre-lights-out beatings were held in full view of my dorm.

"Bend over, touch your toes!"

I reached a little lower. After the three customary whacks I stood up and looked at him evenly. Wrong move.

"Did I tell you to stand?" His face flushed crimson, angry spittle spewed from his rage-contorted mouth. "Who told you to stand? Insubordinate brat, you must do as I tell you. Bend over! I will teach you respect even if I have to beat it into you!" Three more vigorous whacks followed. "Now go to bed!" He stood and watched me walk back to my bed before turning the lights off.

I did not cry; in fact, I made a point of not even rubbing the point of contact until safely under the covers.

Years later, I ran into my nemesis in the street right outside Clapham Mansions. He spotted me first and came over beaming, shaking my hand warmly, asking about my welfare.

"So nice to see you again, George." The cunt was even using my first name!

I had long fantasised about this meeting but instead of beating him to a bloody pulp I was so stunned to run into him virtually at my front door that I was instantly back in short trousers. Pavlov would be pleased.

He walked away in the direction of Clapham South tube station, a satisfied smirk on his mush.

He still had me.

As he disappeared into the morning commute anger overcame fear and I ran after him.

Perhaps it was lucky for both of us that I could not find him.

Gibso and I fell into the school routine.

Mealtimes were a good example of how the system worked.

The refectory table was long enough to seat about twenty boys on benches either side.

A large thug improbably named Lovely was Head of House. He and his enforcers dispensed favours, deciding which of us could line up for seconds. Varying degrees of punishment were meted out for unspecified transgressions. New boys to Plunkett House received a lot of unwarranted attention.

Every meal started with prayers led by Bro. Gregory, delivered from a raised lectern.

In silence we lined up for the nasty slop that passed for food in this house of learning.

While seated, proper posture was positively reinforced by the prospect of a vicious punch to the small of the back administered by a designated prefect. Often, it seemed to me, deliberately timed just as a globulous spoonful of porridge was raised to the gaping maw.

This humiliation was a great source of entertainment for the senior boys.

In spite of suffering at the hands of prefects and masters a modicum of expensive boarding school education forever stays lodged in my head.

Coming from a Communist country, where it was a matter of principle if not fact that we were all equal, to a society riddled with distinctions, some so subtle that it was nigh on impossible not to run aground on the craggy shores of the British class system, I quickly learned to nuance speech patterns and mannerisms. Between school and under the influence of the Abercrombies I became a bit of a snob.

A tendency I have not been able to completely expunge.

In due course Simon and I enlisted a third recruit to our little gang of misfits. Chris's father was the landlord of a seaside pub which in the eyes of many of the other boys made him "common". He was perfect for us. Chris's lumbering size made him ideal for the role of 'enforcer'. We took him on as our muscle.

The gang was now complete. To strike fear into the hearts of our classmates, we decided to call ourselves 'The Boys'.

The name may not have had the desired effect, but we did command a certain level of respect due mainly to Chris's size.

"You better hand over that Wagon Wheel if you don't want to get hurt!"

He was straight to the point. Simon and I shared the fruits of his minor extortion.

There were the school bounds and the unknown beyond referred to in hushed tones as Out of Bounds. A low, barbed- wire fence separated the two.

The other side was heavily wooded with a slow, meandering stream running into a small, shallow lake. As far as we were concerned this was the Enchanted Forest and we explored the area whenever the opportunity arose.

One Sunday after we had trudged our way to the village and back we went OOB.

Wandering deeper into the woods to the other side of the lake we came across something that was irresistible to boys.

A large, rotten tree trunk leaned over the lake, looking as if it was ready to fall.

"Let's push it over." Without much ado, Gibso and Chris joined me on the trunk and we started to jump, edging further out over the water.

Not much thought was given to the likely outcome of this escapade.

Just as the trunk with the three of us on top of it came splashing down a voice bellowed from the woods. "Oi... what do you think you're doing?" Wide-eyed, up to our knees in muddy water, we froze on the spot.

I had run into him before but never got a good look at him nor knew his name. We referred to him as Farmer Giles. The quintessential angry farmer, worked like a dog sunrise to way past sunset for what was, when you totted it all up, less than a living wage.

To him, we were spoilt little public schoolboys with silver spoons so firmly lodged that we would never know an honest day's work.

He marched towards the lake cradling his shotgun, shouting for us to stand still.

What a good wheeze!

"Let's go!"

We ran laughing and squelching our way back to school pleased to have gotten (not so) clean away.

A change of clothes and the incident was forgotten.

Alas, not by Farmer G.

That evening after prayers before supper, with the whole school present, Bro. Gregory roundly condemned the arboreal vandalism and invited the perpetrators to own up.

"Come, come! You know who you are. The Lord sees all and there is nowhere to hide!"

It was hard to deny his logic. I glanced over to the other two sitting opposite and slowly rose from the bench.

They followed suit.

"You three boys outside my study before lights out!"

This could mean only one thing, six of the 'best' in pyjamas.

I could already feel the bite of the bamboo on the cheeks.

My first thought was escape.

The Boys got together for an emergency meeting, quickly deciding that we should make a run for it. But where should we go?

At times the Abercrombies had taken me to Brighton and let me loose with a pocketful of coins in the Pier arcade. Somehow I persuaded the other two that we should go there, describing the town in fantastically glowing terms, playing hard on the prospect of finding girls hanging around the arcades. I told them about a group of 'greasers' I had seen taking turns kissing a skinny girl in a tight, red turtleneck sweater behind the fortune teller's booth. She seemed to be enjoying the attention and did nothing to discourage the activity. This last bit of information was enough to launch us on another brainless escapade put into comic effect.

To avoid raising suspicion we left the school grounds one at a time and regrouped at the chip shop in the village. Gibso bought us all a meat pie and we shared a portion of chips before setting off in a southerly direction.

For several hours we walked in silence following a compass course, the only useful thing we left school with. I was starting to have my doubts, somewhat baffled as to why we were out here as I knew that as surely as the swish is followed by the thwack we were only postponing the inevitable.

I said nothing but was probably not alone in questioning the wisdom of our hasty departure. As night closed in and the temperature fell we approached the outskirts of a small town.

"Let's stop for a while, get some rest," Chris pleaded as the new black Oxfords had blistered the skin on his Achilles tendon. It was decided we bed down for the night in the well-constructed wooden bus shelter on the edge of town. Using telephone books from the nearby booth as pillows, we fell into a fitful sleep.

Was it morning already? I must have slept right through the night.

Blinking awake, a bright light was shining in my face. It was not the rising sun.

"Hello, boys, what's going on 'ere, then?"

The torch was attached to a towering blue giant.

The other two looked to me and without hesitation I launched into an elaborate web of lies.

"We were out on a school walk and somehow got separated and got lost blah blah…" He was having none of it.

The brown leather-gloved hand reached out, grabbed my left ear, applying enough torque to elicit squeaking noises from my chill lips.

"Don't play games with me, sonny, you need to come up with a better story."

The sergeant, a lumbering giant of a man, heaved himself out of the Wolseley. He ambled over to take a look at us huddled in the corner of the shelter.

"Give him another quarter turn, Barry," he said to the younger copper.

It may yield questionable results but I can attest that torture does work. I was ready to confess to any number of crimes or sign any document shoved under my nose. "OW OW…. please stop."

The constable released his grip. "I will tell you everything." Touching my ear I checked for permanent damage but it had sprung back to its original configuration.

"Get in the car, we are going for a little ride, no talking!" The sergeant held the back door open and we scooted onto the lush leather bench seat. For a second I thought they would take us to Brighton, but according to my compass we were going north.

The journey gave us plenty of time to contemplate the fate that awaited us.

Before daybreak the car crunched to a gravelly stop in front of the school door.

The sergeant rolled himself out of the car, dawdled over to the heavy arched wooden doors, lifted the large, cast-iron knocker and repeatedly brought it down with considerable force.

He took a step back, clasped his hands behind his back, and raised his heels in the classic 'Allo–Allo …what's going on 'ere, then?' stance.

Nothing. He went at it again.

This time a light came on and the door opened. It was Bro. Gregory blinking in his nightshirt, an angry scowl on his sallow face.

"I think these belong to you." Sarge opened the door. "Out!"

We stood by the car, sheepishly hanging our heads, staring at the floor.

Looking up at Sarge and down on us, Bro. G turned and gave Gibso a sharp cuff around the ear. "Get to bed right now! I will deal with you in the morning." He tried to slap me and Chris but, forewarned, we managed to duck by him unscathed.

Not sure about the other two but I could not sleep pondering the doom that the rising sun would herald.

We got up at 6.30 with the rest of the dorm, dressed and sat on our beds as instructed. The rest of the boys went off to breakfast.

Cassock flapping menacingly, the indignant Bro. G swept into the dorm, Francis hard on his heels.

"You three are a disgrace to the school." We stood resigned to our fate.

"This hooligan behaviour is not what we expect from Catholic boys. And you... Dixie or whatever your name is, are probably the instigator of this travesty. It will be a miracle if this 'incident' does not feature in the local paper. In your pyjamas and at my door in five minutes!"

Just enough time to slip on an extra pair of underpants.

We lined up outside his study.

Gibso went first. The thwacks were clearly audible through the door, as were his cries.

"Bend over, boy!"

He must have straightened to ease his pain. All this was torture to Chris and me. He went next. Gibso came out crying and avoided my gaze.

"Dixie, in here! Touch your toes." As I bent down to examine the intricate Moroccan beadwork on my slippers, I promised myself that this would never happen again.

Bro. G was breathing hard, red-faced from his previous exertions, but managed to get up a good head of steam to make sure I got his point.

Standing back a few steps he made a run at me, the cane coming down precisely across both cheeks. It took a microsecond before the flesh sent the pain message up the spine to the brain which in turn triggered the tears. It was the fourth kiss of the cane which opened the sluice gates. Silent tears rolled down my cheeks. I clenched my jaw, not a peep escaped my lips.

This cruel bastard was not getting the full measure.

I am convinced that my silence left him grinding his teeth in frustration behind his thin, mean lips. Silent defiance was my only mode of attack.

He would have liked to hear me wail in pain and rail at the sheer injustice of the process. Knowing this made it easier to bear the humiliation.

I also knew well that at the time this kind of punishment was routine in many schools both public and state, and that the attention I received was by no means out of the ordinary. It was thought by many to be an essential part of a character- building exercise. I am unable to draw any such conclusion but perhaps can say that if educators want to teach respect they must first show restraint. I am happy to know that these somewhat barbaric methods are no longer practised or permitted in civilised societies.

CHAPTER 13

REUNITED

Gita and Victor settled into their digs in The Bush, the sad, dingy room almost spacious now that we were away in the 'country', the gas stove out on the landing positively under utilised, the bathroom up a flight on another floor now more of a convenience for the clench-cheeked tenants.

After some months of rejections, partly on the grounds of insolvency, with a large helping of prejudice thrown in, Gita somehow managed to convince the landlords of a small Edwardian mansion block in Clapham that she was a good risk. I think the RCC may have had a hand in the deal.

The Irish, along with other minorities, were now well established, so it was the turn of the highly visible West Indians to bear the full brunt of bigotry. Although not treated nearly as badly as the West Indians, in general, Eastern Blockers were not welcomed with open arms.

At some point my mother also managed to satisfy the Church that she had the prerequisite furnishings and the flat was properly kitted out to raise a Catholic family.

Was she in fact capable of doing a decent job of parenting?

They sent someone around from the local parish to see if the accommodations were suitable for raising children and to make sure that she was not living in sin (Victor), running a brothel or engaged in some other activity deemed immoral by the Church of Rome.

Interestingly Gita had considered taking up the oldest profession as a new career path by becoming a 'Madam' but was dissuaded by her friend. Marta had abandoned her old line of work, which, as far as I could see, involved slapping large gobs of Nivea cream on the faces of gullible women. With the backing of her thuggish husband she set herself up in the 'escort' business. The shopfront in the Edgware Road masquerading as a model agency seemed to be doing very well.

"You need connections, Gita," she said. "Negotiation skills and a working knowledge of the English language are also necessary." She made no mention of her minder. Gita had none of the above and her accent would be impenetrable to the average punter so this scheme was quickly abandoned.

The RC had done their due diligence.

A&M were allowed to go and live with her in Clapham.

I was enjoying the holidays in Lewes, the hooligan slowly replaced by a more genteel persona carefully honed and refined by the Abercrombies, and at the other end of the spectrum, beaten into me by the Brothers of St. Xavier.

I was quite happy and content enough to send away for stamps sold by the pound and made what I thought were well- negotiated trades with Sanders. Summer days were idled away swimming in the pool, exploring the grounds and becoming an avid reader of science fiction. I immersed myself in the genre, dreaming of fantastic alternative civilisations.

The writings of Isaac Asimov, J.G. Ballard et al. fired my imagination. Behind my locked bedroom door safe in the bosom of my new family I travelled light-footed through space and time.

Television was considered to be the work of the Devil in the Abercrombie household so without regular reinforcement the Lone Ranger fetish was being displaced by an ever-growing interest in girls.

At the end of summer break it was decided that I should be allowed to visit my family in Clapham for a few days before returning to Lewes and school.

I packed a few things for a short visit, and Mr. A drove me to the station and put me on the train; my mother was to meet me under the big clock at Victoria station.

True to form she was late; I stood under the clock in my best long trousers, cap and blazer anxiously looking around for her.

Breathlessly she arrived. "Sorry, darlink, I get wrong train." She had to speak English to me as I stubbornly refused to acknowledge the Hungarian language, a symptom of my need to assimilate and, hopefully, finally to belong somewhere. It seems my whole life has been spent seeking a place, a time, a philosophy, a group to belong to. I've never quite felt fully comfortable or at 'home' anywhere. In this surely I am not alone.

In her eagerness to squeeze the breath out of me her hat fell to the ground. I bent to pick it up.

"I like your hat, did you make it?" "Yes, darlink I 'ave one in every colour. But this yellow is my best one."

We took the tube back to Clapham South and I never returned to Lewes or to school.

"When you go back to school?"

"Not for a long time, Mama."

I told Gita my education was complete and I did not need to go back to school.

Ever.

This lie fitted well with my pledge never to endure another thrashing. The feeling of liberation was exhilarating. No more slipper, no more caning, no more bad food, no more Latin; for a short time I would live in the happy doldrums of life.

Gita's understanding of how the education system worked in a country where she struggled to find foodstuff to her liking and deal with the ordinary things in life was scant at best, and it took little to convince her that I was now fully educated and ready to go to work.

"Delighted, darlink," to have me home, seeing the potential to add to the household coffers, she was easily swayed. Within a few days Victor had got me a job as a commis waiter at Cunningham's in Curzon Street (I lied about my age) where he was now head waiter.

No idea how all this went down with the RCC. I never went back to school or saw the kind and generous Abercrombies again. I know I disappointed them and let myself down badly; from time to time I still feel a twinge of guilt.

The big city and the bright lights had me.

A&M were sent off to local primary schools and had their own troubles. As we know, children can be cruel little bastards. They were routinely taunted, subjected to casual prejudice, even downright abuse. The physical scars may have healed but the psychological damage remains.

Floundering at first they adapted quickly, learned to keep their heads down, swim with the shoal.

The third-floor apartment was, compared to the Flat in the Bush, positively palatial, comprising three bedrooms, a bathroom and a huge living room which could be divided by folding wood-panel doors. There was an old-fashioned kitchen at the end of the long, L-shaped corridor. The small back windows overlooked the well-tended communal garden, in the centre of which was a rather sad, old mulberry tree.

The back kitchen wall was equally divided into three small recesses, a scullery with a 'butler' sink (rubbish chute on the side wall), larder in the middle and a gas stove in the third. A hand-cranked service elevator accessible through the side kitchen window was used to wind up heavy shopping and buckets full of coal from the individual storage bins at ground level. The quantity of coal needed for the open fires in every room plus the range in the kitchen would have fed the voracious firebox of the Flying Scotsman. It was expensive and messy so Gita made do with a couple of paraffin stoves and a three-bar electric heater, pressed into service only when there was frost on the inside of the window panes; even then, rarely were we allowed all three elements as they would eat up the money in the meter at an alarming rate. So, instead of hoisting fuel for the fires we used the lift to raise breeze-block-sized slabs of lard and yellow cake in quantities to withstand a short siege.

On 'special' occasions, my mother arranged dinner parties for the whole family. A paper tablecloth was laid and candles in saucers arranged to add a touch of sophistication. Her efforts to normalise the fact that there was no money to feed the meter, or indeed the family, fooled nobody, yet she persisted.

"Isn't this lovely? It reminds me of those days when your father took me to dinner at fancy restaurants." She smiled at me. I took a huge bite of yellow cake.

Always a hearty eater but a terrible cook ("Lardy Lardy" was her mantra, lumps of bacon fat, deep-fried in the rendered pig product was a staple), when there was no money for her cholesterol-laden Hungarian health food we would fall back on 'yellow cake' and Nescafé for dinner.

The concoction masquerading as cake came in one flavour and two sizes, industrial and commercial. Both roughly the size of Estonia (albeit shaped differently), often needing the large wheelie trolley to shift a week's supply.

Regular forays to nearby Balham Market were organised.

The stall specialised in baked goods and did a roaring trade. We joined the long lines of the needy.

Nutritional value was an alien concept to us and, although entirely free of natural ingredients, we loved this by-product of the nuclear-refining process and ate pounds of the stuff.

It filled us up and that was that.

At some point we acquired a TV. Probably I should credit Victor for the convenience of having the world at our fingertips. The unreliable screen in the corner became indispensable to our lives. The monochrome images became our teachers.

This marvel of technology was our new window on the world. Instead of going out to the pictures regularly, where we could in effect stay as long as we liked for the price of a cheese sandwich, we became couch potatoes long before it became fashionable to admit that one only watched the news or *Panorama* for a bit of weighty content.

"Shall we go to the pictures or stay at home and watch *Naked City* or *Dragnet*?" asked Gita in her Zsa Zsa accent. This was a tough choice.

Even now, I can clearly recall the taste of yellow cake and instant coffee mingling in my mouth as I settled in to watch the wrestling, which had become a weekly ritual.

That bastard Mick McManus somehow always managed to win by illegally punching his opponent while the referee was distracted by arguing with a spectator!

We hated him as much as we despised Jackie Pallo, even though they were arch-rivals. Gita was particularly fond of Big Daddy and his nemesis Giant Haystacks, perhaps because they were big and bouncy like her.

"You are big, silly idiota!" she shouted at the TV. The referee was unmoved by her abuse.

Chain-smoking her preferred brand (Player's No.6), Gita teetered on the edge of the sofa.

By now, I was having serious doubts about the antics in the ring but she remained convinced.

"It's on the telly." Ergo, it must be real.

I still resented Victor's presence and remained wary yet somehow I knew that he was stumbling through the rubble of his own life and at times I felt compassion for this flawed fellow human being.

Yet, over time, the relationship with Victor went from poor to hostile. I resented his presence in my family and the power he had over me at the restaurant.

He was a mean drunk.

When I caught him taking swigs from the open bottles behind the bar, he would resort to a bit of verbal abuse.

"Stop watching me, you useless little shit, worthless excuse for a Magyar boy! Get down to the kitchen, chef will give you a bowl to bring up."

A creamy knob of butter melted gently atop the green peas.

On the long climb from the basement kitchen I gobbled a couple of spoonfuls, carefully rearranging the remainder. This was not just because I was hungry, it was an act of defiance.

My hours at work were limited so I would leave much earlier than him. On the journey home I planned my revenge.

He often came home well after midnight. Deep into his cups, the share of the night's tips clinking in the pockets of his penguin suit trousers.

At times, while he lay in a drunken stupor I riffled his pockets. Feeling entitled I decide to tax him and regularly helped myself to modest sums to supplement my meagre wages.

He always went out of his way to treat me well in front of Gita, which only fuelled my resentment. He made some progress with A&M but knowing what I knew about him from work and his past, I feared and hated him in equal measure.

When he first entered that train carriage and our lives back in Budapest he gave Gita, and me, the impression that he was a good person, a regular bloke caught up like the rest of the nation in the tumultuous events of the day.

He was friendly, polite, charming even, but as time went by life and booze got the better of him. Gone were the homely pipes, replaced by roll-ups or cheap fags, early optimism turned to bitter resentment. The clean-shaven, humorous, ambitious, dapper Dr. Jekyll had turned into Mr. Hyde, his outsize hands readily used on Gita, me and to a lesser extent, Akos.

Unable to cuss in English, when roused he spewed forth a colourful stream of Hungarian abuse calling Gita, her mother and several female generations back all pox-ridden whores, and suggesting that my mother craved to be fucked in the arse by a donkey.

Frustrated at every turn, his ambitions and dreams slowly crushed under the weight of Gita's demands, the many unsuccessful business ventures drained his energy and resources. His fondness for alcohol was not matched by his capacity to maintain equilibrium or humanity; what was once a proud and industrious man had become a gutted, hollow human being.

There was much fighting, mainly about money. Victor was fond of throwing crockery around the kitchen which often resulted in blood, sweat, tears and a visit from the local bobbies.

This was not only a huge embarrassment, but also a frightening reminder of the dreaded midnight knock on the door back in the Old Country.

To my knowledge Gita never filed a formal complaint as Victor turned on the charm and always managed to wheedle his way back in, managing somehow to stick around for years. Sometimes living in or after a particularly bloody incident, Gita, threatening him with the ultimate deterrent, Interpol, got rid of him, at least for a while.

In spite of the beatings we all endured at Victor's hands, especially Gita, I now have a soft spot for him, remembering the good times, too – he bought our first refrigerator, another marvel! It was tiny by modern standards, delivered by the men from the LEB wearing khaki-coloured coats of the type favoured by shop stewards at the Ford plant in Dagenham. Two pints of milk, a dozen eggs, butter and a chunk of cheese just about filled the shelves. Maybe room for a small brick of Neapolitan ice cream crammed into the freezer compartment next to the peas.

When Victor had a good day, managing to divert some of the tips which were supposed to go into a tronc to be equally shared by all the waiters, he would bring some special treats home. Frozen cheesecake in the icebox or some cherry pie would appear on the bottom shelf.

When sober, Victor could tell a good story, even better when he had a couple of drinks in him.

Among his many tales he claimed to have been a captain in the Hungarian Army as well as working for the Romanian secret police, playing a covert yet significant role in the uprising. I knew these stories were a pack of lies but said nothing. He of course had no reason to remember me from our first encounter back in Budapest. I knew well the difference between a regular Army uniform and that worn by the ÁVH.

As he drank his tales grew taller; by the fourth shot of whisky his eyes crossed so that it was a hard to tell who he was ranting at, the veins at his temple bulged, arms flailed like windmills. Often this was the prelude to a bit of domestic violence and we would tiptoe around him as Gita stroked his ego, tried to soothe his troubled mind.

If she managed to calm him and put him to bed the evening ended without violence.

Often her efforts to ease his pain would only ratchet up the volume; he would start with the vile name-calling. Then, inevitably, it would end with a full-scale assault on the crockery. If that did not satisfy his rage he would turn on my mother, slapping and at times punching her to the ground. Raging, he loomed over her; she curled up into a defensive ball.

Jumping on his back in an effort to stop the onslaught I did what I could to defend her. He just shrugged me off, throwing me to the floor next to my mother.

One of these days, Victor, one of these days the worm will turn.

Some of his previous life was spent in the 'restaurant' business, having part-owned one in Budapest, so he knew enough about the game to wheedle his way into his present job, at least until, nipping at the whisky a little too early in the day, he tripped and dropped the Lobster Thermidor on the table before falling into the lap of the man with a bib tucked under his chin. He was fired and, as I came with him, I went with him.

By now, I had learned enough about 'waitering' that I was able to blag my way into a proper job with my own tables at a German restaurant called Schmidt's in Charlotte Street.

My mother nagged Victor until he gave up searching for a restaurant gig and started to look around for other means of gainful employment.

Seemingly overnight he became a painter/decorator. Given a few lurching hours of training with a mate, another Hungarian drunk, he practised his craft on the walls of our flat with limited success. Going by the results I would hesitate to hire him, especially if your tastes ran to wallpaper patterned at regular intervals.

One day he showed up wearing a yarmulke.

I asked him about this sudden conversion. He laughingly explained that he was touting for painting jobs in Golders Green and as long as he pretended to be one of the chosen people, walked lightly among the circumcised, he could confound his customers by being circumspect about the ways of the Jews, claiming his parents were to blame for his total lack of knowledge of all things related to Judaism (and kept his knob hidden!) the punters would just take him for another ignorant schmuck.

Truth is elusive, comedy divine.

Still, he managed to earn, learn and provide; my mother continued to put up with him and he with her.

A shiny red telephone was wired in and displayed on a small table in the hall. A powerful symbol of our upward mobility.

More ornamental than functional, the dial tone rarely heard due to a chronic dearth of readies.

The television, now with two channels, was serious competition to the pictures. We all loved the cinema but it meant leaving the comforts of home.

The 'box' was much more conveniently located in-house, a short walk to the kitchen/bathroom, sprawling on the sofa much comfier than cinema seats; above all, it cost next to nothing.

Gita never bothered with the TV licence, calculating the odds of getting caught to be slim at best. Detection devices were crude and reliably inaccurate when it came to densely packed urban dwellings. The only way to get fined was if they came round and caught you red-handed. This would never happen as we only answered the door in response to a private code.

In constant fear of the meter reader, the milkman and the rent collector, she had me draught a letter to The Queen asking for financial assistance. Her list of grievances were long, our deprivations laid out in graphic terms.

I went along with this exercise in grovelling mendicancy, thinking that I would never send it.

"Did you put letter in box for Queen?"

"Yes," I lied. It was getting a bit shabby, slightly sticky from sharing my pocket with a half-eaten toffee apple for a few days.

In the end I thought. 'Fuck it', and dropped it in a letter box.

In due course a response arrived from the Palace written by HM's secretary telling us, more specifically Gita, in short, to bugger off and get a job.

A visit to the cinema was a special event requiring a lot of planning. If it was worthwhile getting off the sofa then we would make a day of it.

Gita treated the outing as an indoor picnic.

A trip to 'Westbury', the deli around the corner, would have to be made to pick up a few items.

A typical menu would consist of Hungarian salami (the Italian was considered inferior), Black Forest ham, sharp, mature Cheddar, green peppers, tomatoes, whole pickled gherkins in a jar and fresh, crusty bread, butter, and a jumbo-sized thermos of weak coffee, enough food to keep us going all day.

I often wondered what the cleaners thought about the mess we must have left, breadcrumbs, slippery gherkins, pepper seeds, a blunt knife on squidgy tomatoes. She managed to assemble fairly passable sandwiches on wax paper laid out on her lap. All this while distracted by the cinematic magic of Bela Lugosi morphing into a bat and flying out of the unglazed castle window. A stranger's hand on her thigh was an additional distraction.

On one particular visit to a cinema in Praed Street (if I remember correctly) we sat like coconuts at the fair waiting for the wooden ball to arrive; in the middle of the theatre at a sparsely attended presentation of some back-to-back Dracula marathon, having munched our way through several pounds of salami with all the trimmings, we settled in for the third tour of Dracula's castle.

Gita asked me to change seats with her – we swapped seats.

Presently, I felt a hand on my right leg and understood why she put me there. Unfortunately, the man on my right was an equal opportunity groper and we ended up moving, en masse, to another row, leaving our errant gherkins, tomato seeds and salami skins.

My mother could not abandon the notion that had we ended up in America she would have become another Zsa Zsa Gabor.

"If we had gone to Merka I was also movie star like her." Blaming the dearth of diamond-encrusted necklaces and exotic furs on her impatience in Austria, she convinced herself and anyone else willing to listen that had she got on the flight to America she would, by now, be hobnobbing with Hollywood's finest.

In truth, apart from the accent Zsa Zsa and Gita did not have much in common. Both collectors of sorts, my mother hoarded junk like Zsa Zsa accumulated husbands.

When Victor, having committed another minor atrocity, was banished, she, unlike Zsa Zsa, attracted alternative suitors without visible means of support or realistic prospects, unfailingly hooking up with men having the humanitarian instincts of Bulgarian bear baiters.

The fact that she lived in Clapham instead of Hollywood also somewhat set her apart.

On workdays I rode the Black Line between Warren Street and Clapham.

Coming through the ticket barrier at Clapham South I walked outside the station and into the following scene:

A group of noisy, excited men were huddled over a small table. The action and prospect of something for nothing invariably drew me in. There was some kind of card game involving money. It looked simple.

I stood and watched for some minutes. The dealer sat on a milk crate behind a small folding table. There were three cards in play, queen of hearts and a couple of random black cards. The dealer showed all three then moved them around rapidly. All the punters (or more accurately, mugs) had to do was 'find the lady'. Convinced that I had a winning strategy I reached for my wallet, kept an eagle eye on the red queen and confidently put my pound down. This was easy, in a blink of an eye I had doubled my money.

The man standing behind me made encouraging noises. Going for the big one I pulled a fiver out, waiting for the shuffle to stop. Anticipating an easy win, I put my hard-earned cash on the card I was certain was the winner.

The dealer flipped the card over next to the one I had bet on showing the red queen. My fiver was swept up along with other monies, and when a fellow mug started making a fuss someone from around the corner shouted, "Copper!": man, cards, and table vanished into the sunset.

The reluctant refugee had a lot to learn.

At age 14 my faltering career as a waiter came to an abrupt end when I picked up a copy of the *Evening Standard*.

Under the jobs section I saw, Wanted: Trainee Film Editor/ Messenger blah blah. I applied and to my surprise got the job. The starting wage was 4 pounds 1 shilling + Luncheon Vouchers. Not what one would term generous but the word 'film' sounded seductive and I was told the prospects of promotion were good.

I loved the cinema; this, I thought, may be a way into the glamorous world of movies.

The dazzlingly playful lights of the West End and the beguilingly sleazy attractions of Soho were a big part of the attraction, too.

From Clapham, the grubby red carriages used to carry me to Tottenham Court Road, a short walk from Wardour Street and Film House where the Warner-Pathé offices and editing suites were located.

The daily commute home would often involve a meandering diversion through an alley connecting Wardour and Dean Streets.

The amusingly named St Anne's Court had more than its fair share of beatnik-infested cafés, porn shops, brothels and strip clubs. I did a lot of window-shopping, stopping to admire the glossy black and white photos of the lovely ladies posed seductively for my delight.

One Friday night, emboldened by my unopened wage packet, engorged with lust and cash, I walked down the narrow stairs to a sub-basement suggestively lit by a low-watt red bulb.

The grubby window, to the left of the door, seemed to have been purposefully ignored by the window cleaner. Perhaps a visual clue as to what may have been on offer. Taking a deep breath, I rang the bell.

A grumpy-looking man with a badly reset nose and ears resembling an albino floret of broccoli showed me to a booth saying nothing, turned and went through what in the gloom seemed to be a curtain made of multi-coloured glass beads. The interior was kitted out like a dimly lit Wimpy Bar.

I started to have doubts; perhaps this was not such a good idea. The street was just steps away.

Too late, with a jangle, from behind the beads a moderately fetching, slightly overweight middle-aged lady emerged and headed straight for my booth. Smiling, she sat next to me, blocking the means of escape.

"Hello, sweetie. I'm Deidre," she chirped in a friendly way. "What's your name?" Adding without pause, "Aren't you a bit young to be 'ere?"

My impulse was to respond with, "What's a nice girl like you doing in a place like this?" – but I told her my name was Spiro.

I looked around and indeed I was by far the youngest person in the room.

The whole place smelled of stale cigarettes and sweaty palms. Commingled with this assault on the nose were the most pungently aromatic products the manufacturers of budget cosmetics could blend.

Deidre, resplendent in a shiny electric blue 'Suzi Wong'-style dress, hem high above the knee; the slits on both sides revealed an indecent amount of creamy thigh.

Dragons in pursuit of each other's tails scampered around her hefty breasts.

Puffed with the cream of love. In the grip of mysterious urges it was easy to lie.

"I'm 22!" I said with conviction.

Why would she not believe me?

On the restless edge of fashion, wearing my bespoke Burton's charcoal-grey shadow stripe work suit (not sure why I make this distinction as it was the only one I owned), tapered trousers (without turn-ups or pleats), three-button box jacket with two vents (by my request), ticket pocket, white shirt, skinny black tie (knitted), black leather side-lace winkle-pickers, I looked good in spite of the lustrous shine on the arse and elbows.

Perhaps the bum fluff on my chin and cheeks aglow with an internal radiance a couple of shades lighter than the lamp in the window put me in the youthful-looking category but I saw no reason for her to question my maturity.

"Champagne! Pour moi, what will you 'ave, darlin'?"

The grumpy man returned with something fizzy for her which looked more like soda water from a siphon than a grape product from France and a bottle of the sweet brown bubbly for me.

I took a sip, she downed hers in two gulps and ordered another.

It arrived along with a piece of paper on a plastic plate, the numbers, writ large in pencil, 'Two pounds 10 shillings'. From behind the curtain the distinctive sound of a SodaStream discharging could clearly be heard.

The symptoms were immediate; breathing became shallow, the room started to swirl.

Suddenly ashen-faced, colour drained from my cheeks and as I fumbled for my wage packet she ordered another.

If I had knowledge of these things 1 would have to say that clinically I was in shock.

To steady my nerves, I shakily reached for my cigarettes, opened a fresh packet of 10. Folding the flap back suggestively I offered one to Deidre, just like I had seen in the movies. "Ta very much... what kind of name is Spiro anyway?"

I may have been the only person buying Strand, the preferred smoke of losers, the tag line suggesting that this particular brand of cigarette was a viable substitute for a girlfriend.

Never was the slogan "you're never alone with a Strand" more inappropriate.

Two pounds 10 shillings! It was not a mistake and the third glass of 'champagne' was on its way.

Fuck! Even in my stunned state it was obvious that her drinks were a quid a pop and if I stayed any longer I would not be able to buy a ticket home or give my mother the 30 shillings she was expecting.

"Big Spender" played on the jukebox as I squirmed in my Y-fronts, the blood further retreating from the extremities ready to fight or fly.

Dick Tracy or James Bond would have known what to do but then of course if they had patronised this kind of joint they probably would have adequate funds to indulge their fantasies.

Exposed as the naïve fool that I was, trying wretchedly to find a way out of this predicament without embarrassing myself further, feet firmly planted on the blocks, I prepared to make a dash for the door. Could I make it back to the street uninjured?

From behind the beads grumpy now looked menacingly ready to enforce the contract I had unwittingly entered into when I sat in the booth.

In a mumbled whisper I told Deidre that I had no more money; she reached out, took my hand, lowered her head conspiratorially, peering compassionately through lashes that made no attempt at deception, leaned and whispered in my ear.

"Never mind, darlin'. Finish your drink, I'll just sit with you for a bit." She started filing her nails, asking me about my job, where I lived, what I did in my spare time.

In the inside pocket of my jacket, neatly folded, was my old Lone Ranger mask, I thought about putting it on to 'see' if there was a way out of this little jam, If I put it on now I would probably get a good pummelling from the grumpy geezer and be thrown out as the wrong kind of deviant. The mask stayed in my pocket.

From behind the curtain grumpy read her signal and troubled us no further.

We sat and chatted; rather, she talked and I listened, relaxing somewhat as she proudly told me she had two sons, both at Cambridge, one reading Chemical Engineering, the other Theology and Religious Studies.

My assumptions (once again) had been shown to be informed by ignorance.

I did not reveal my true age or name.

Out of small talk, nails filed to stiletto-like points, she started to apply a radiant red polish.

I was somewhat relieved that they would not be digging into my back yet curious as I had heard such things enhance the 'experience' though I was unsure which of us would benefit most.

We sat. The rasp of file on nail was replaced by the silent application of varnish. Was this my cue? Mustering reserves of dignity I was not entitled to I thanked her deeply, rose and left much poorer, but a little wiser.

Hope belongs to youth.

CHAPTER 14

THE ROAD TRIP

Clapham, London 1989

Blinking to focus I raised my head. A middle-aged badger with slightly bloodshot eyes was staring back at me. Starting at the temples, the grey follicles were marching steadily north, a poignant reminder.

Squeezing the red-striped toothpaste onto the bristles of the electric toothbrush, I inhaled deeply. Minty molecules rose to fill my nostrils.

The house lay still as I trod lightly down the stairs. I walked past Jessie still dozing on her cushion next to the fireplace.

It was still dark outside. I sat on the back garden wall and took a few deep lungfuls of morning air.

Was I doing the right thing? What if I was unable to find him? He may have become demented or died for all I knew. There were many uncertainties yet I felt driven to find out about this man, the love of my mother's life.

My semi-detached life dwelt in a terraced house on a lovely, quiet street. Now that Mrs. Best, the last remaining old person on the street had died, it was completely populated by younger couples, some starting families, others with kids already riding their bicycles. We lived well, comfortably some would say. My little business was thriving, we had two nice cars, a new kitchen and bathroom, even built a conservatory on the back of the house where I had my drums set up.

So why did I suddenly have this powerful urge to seek out a man of whom I knew only what Gita had told me? I strongly suspect there is no definitive answer.

Going back into the house I crouched down to let Jessie lick my face while I tweaked her nose before going upstairs to wake the family.

The first rays of the sun loomed over the rooftops.

Lazy morning mist rose to the warming glow as I gently prodded Phoebe and went to rouse Petra.

She looked so angelic, sleeping in her little girls' room, lots of books on her small painted bookshelf made festive by the addition of stickers and drawings. Already she was showing a talent for the graphic arts. Her favourite stuffed animals scattered at the foot of the bed awaited her morning eyes.

Hanging by a nylon filament a wooden seagull with weighted wings soared gently on her breath. I stroked her face.

Sharply she said, "Why are you waking me up so early, Daddy? Do we have to get up already?" She was liable to be a bit grumpy when woken.

"We have a lot to do, get up!" Then I stumbled downstairs to put the kettle on and load the toaster.

We had been together for about ten years, Phoebe and I, mostly content, at times even happy.

I will concede that I had not been the most consistent of partners, and seen in the rear-view mirror of life it must have been difficult to live with me, always at odds with the world, trying to find a clear path to an unknown destination. Our cherished child Petra papered over the cracks for a while but as time went by, I became ever more self-absorbed and distant.

A silent accord was reached between Phoebe and me. We would shield Petra from our discontent, and in a vaguely optimistic way I thought this trip would reset our relationship.

While the sleepy-eyed neighbours were slapping their 'snooze' buttons there was much activity in our house.

Phoebe and Petra were back and forth to the car with a continuous stream of packages and baggage which I crammed into the hatchback with total indifference to future accessibility or the slightest nod in the direction of good organisation.

The suspension on the fire engine red Ford Sierra 4X4 (with a/c, remote locking and multifunction alarm) sagged noticeably as the scruffy-looking holdalls were moulded into shapes beyond the imagination of the designers.

There was more denim in the back of our car than at a Status Quo gig.

Every available inch was jammed with the blue stuff cut and stitched into shapes the Eastern Blockers were known to covet.

In hope of confusing overly diligent Customs agents, the large number of jeans and other products were cunningly distributed among our personal items.

Softer packages containing our travel essentials suitable for an extended continental holiday, pillows and blankets etc. took up half the back seat, leaving just enough space for Petra to make a cosy nest for herself and her stuffed animals.

One of the 'significant' items in my kit was the recently purchased electric toothbrush.

I knew no one who had invested with such reckless abandon in personal dental hygiene. Although cumbersome by modern standards it was considered 'cutting-edge' at the time. Not to be confused with one of your newfangled NiCad, cordless, induction-charged machines now readily available at 'Poundland' for about a tenner. Oh no! This baby had spring- loaded external metal contacts on the base as well as on the handle which were cunningly designed to work intermittently, and after a couple of weeks were already showing a flush of oxidisation.

The handle had to be thick enough to accommodate the heavy battery and the effort to lift the thing and keep the brush in gentle contact with teeth for the recommended two minutes would, if the operator was careless, result in overdeveloped biceps on the favoured side.

When abroad, it was by no means certain that it would function at all due to voltage and socket adaptability issues.

The reason that I had bothered to include this potentially unreliable and relatively bulky item was that in the event I was given the opportunity to exhibit this marvel of Western technology and demonstrate its effectiveness I knew the Magyars would be suitably impressed and I could, for a brief moment, wrap myself in the smug blanket of superiority.

There were two other items that I never travelled without, the red neckerchief of the Young Pioneers and my Lone Ranger mask.

The kerchief served as a link, a reminder of the past.

The mask? Not sure, really. Did it have some special properties or was it just a fillip to my imagination?

"Have we got everything?" I asked, leaning heavily on the tailgate until it clicked.

The 'Red Hotel' was ready to roll.

Petra had named the car on our last family holiday to the Côte d'Azur.

Unable to find a place to stay that we could afford, I simply parked the car on the promenade right by the beach. Exhausted by our frolics in the sun we all slept well. The local Gendarmerie in Juan-les-Pins paid us no heed.

As the sun cleared the mist and the street started to show signs of life I shifted into first, pulled away from the kerb, turning right onto Nightingale Lane, passing Clapham Common to our left heading for the South Circular towards the A2, then to Dover and the ferry.

The 'Chunnel' project was still being wrangled over by the parties concerned. How the Brits and the French managed to co-operate long enough to complete this engineering marvel is a wonder in itself. Anyway, we preferred to go by boat – even in heavy seas!

The ferryman paid, we drove up the ramp onto the tired-looking British Rail ferry sloshing around in the relative calm of Dover Harbour.

Parking the car on D deck, we found seating on one of the lower decks amidships in a largely futile effort to minimise the motion and to mitigate disturbance to the delicate components of the inner ear.

The rain stopped as the ramp was lowered and I drove the Hôtel Rouge onto French soil.

For obvious reasons, uniforms have always raised an unnatural fear in me. In this instance I need not have worried as we were waved through unmolested by both Customs and Immigration.

Besides, how can an official wearing a cape and a pillbox hat be taken seriously?

We had driven through Calais many times but had never stopped.

On this occasion all three of us were in urgent need of the facilities as the toilets on the ferry were awash and unusable. Compared to the stench on the boat, the French pissoirs were like a breath of fresh air.

The plan was simple as these things go – five days should give us plenty of time to get through Western Europe. I was now truly on my way, yet the closer we got, the more I questioned the wisdom of the whole thing. I had preconceived a joyous reunion; surely he must have wondered about me. Did he even know that I was a reluctant refugee? On the other hand, what if he was dead or so demented that my arrival meant nothing to him? How would he react to me? How would I be when I stood in front of him? I was conflicted, racked by doubt and a little bit afraid of what lay ahead.

There was a void at my core which might only be filled by undertaking this journey with P&P at my side; the presentation of my family was an important part of indicating to my father (and the world) that I am a 'normal' family man steadfastly plodding towards the artificially aerated, tepid jacuzzi occupied by the bourgeoisie (to which, I am ashamed to admit, I aspired), ready and eager to immerse myself.

If I need to roll one trouser leg up and perfect my funny handshake, then so be it!

The need to belong to something somewhere was powerful. Nevertheless, bubbles of anxiety insistently rose to the surface – was I destined to walk alone?

Leaving Calais behind we headed into the French countryside.

Our spirits lifted by the brightening day, a hint of lavender in the air and the open road ahead.

Pointing the car in a north-easterly direction we drove down the tree-lined secondary roads, windows wide open, air unconditioned.

Phoebe turned on the stereo and fiddled with the tuning. We joined in the chorus of 'Yellow Submarine' with scant regard for the veracity of our claim.

Our intended lunch stop was Dunkirk, less than an hour's drive away.

The bulk of the BEF were evacuated from those beaches and wharves back in 1940s, the Allies suffering a massive defeat which was, by the clever use of propaganda, turned into the "miracle of Dunkirk". Churchill cautioned against exuberant optimism, stating that: "We must be very careful not to assign to this deliverance the attributes of victory, wars are not won by evacuations." WC was held in high regard and indeed was a charismatic war leader, talented in many ways, historian, painter, writer, orator, the list is long, not to mention his parliamentary career spanning 56 years, so it is easy to overlook his many shortcomings.

I include this digression to inform the reader that at the time I was a keen student of military history and wanted to put myself on that infamous beach to evoke the spirit of Operation Dynamo.

"I thought you were eager to get to meet your father? Why the hell are we piddling around?" Phoebe looked at me quizzically.

'Anxious' might be a better word to describe my feelings. I looked for any semi-viable reason to dawdle. It seemed that the closer I got, the more fearful I became.

I was desperately clinging onto Gita's version of events. Somehow, I knew the truth would be painful.

We found a restaurant overlooking the battleship-grey waters of the English Channel or La Manche, as the French would have it. The sun high overhead in the now cloudless sky made it warm enough for us to sit on the terrace.

A waiter approached, menus in hand.

"Good moaning, I am very 'appy to grit you!" How did this Frenchman know we were Brits? Was it that obvious?

"Merci, mon brave homme," was my witty retort. He looked at me with a hint of a sneer on his fleshy lips, and continued. "Today our 'Plat du Jour' is." He pointed to the English translation on the five-page menu. Phoebe and I went for the set lunch and Petra (always willing to try new things) insisted on Moules Marinière even after I pointed out that it was not a pizza.

To our amazement she demolished the huge plate of molluscs; silently I was pleased that she could stomach the nasty-looking filter-feeders when I could not.

Like many kids of her age she could probably live on pizza, maybe a token bit of green stuff on the side to lend a bit of contrast.

It was also reliably available even in remote areas.

On the African Savanna or deep in the jungles of South America there was always a franchise near you.

Roaming anthropologists hacking through pristine rainforests searching for lost tribes or missionaries looking to save the 'savages' from eternal damnation would routinely stumble upon a Pizza Hut or Chicken Shack nestling in a sun-drenched clearing.

The natives had forgotten how to hunt and now relied on fast food for their survival.

What were once happy, healthy tribesmen were now fat, grumpy consumers. Such was the power of Little Caesar and the Colonel of Kentucky. The blow darts and arrowheads dipped in curare were ineffectual in preventing the corporations from ploughing these fresh fields of commerce. Fat tribesmen in plaid shorts and wife-beater tee shirts now roamed the forest in search of pizza and fried chicken. No need to seek out the poison dart frog when marinara sauce was readily available.

Such is progress.

Our planned route meandered somewhat through France as we all enjoyed the lovely countryside and I at least was eager to bend the ears of the natives with my smattering of the language.

I was force-fed Latin and French at Mayfield College and often wondered if the time spent on Latin, a 'dead language', may have been put to better use: carpentry or welding perhaps.

Dexter, sinister, resplendent centurions marching their cohorts up and down hills may be significant knowledge for scholars, doctors, churchmen and the lovers of cryptic crosswords in the posh papers but knowing how to join metal and shape wood are skills I still have not mastered. The claim that "Le chat noir est sous la table" does not go far when haggling with a French mechanic. Phoebe, on the other hand, having paid much more attention in school, was able to chit-chat freely.

Rather than head straight for the Belgian border we spent the afternoon cruising down tree-lined avenues enjoying the 'foreignness', the settlements sensibly spaced and sized for people, arranged by pedestrians for pedestrians. Mopeds and bicycles were everywhere. The tendency to street anarchy freely exercised. Traffic lights and signage were invisible to the riders of these two-wheeled contraptions.

The Hôtel Rouge glided effortlessly down the avenues and through charming towns and villages populated by well-entrenched stereotypes.

Road workers in blue overalls, berets, the ubiquitous yellow Gitanes dangled from raspy lips as they leaned on shovels or directed traffic around large holes in the road. They differed only in detail from their British counterparts.

The fact that the historic city of Lille was occupied by the Germans in WW1 was of little interest to P&P but for me there were many good reasons to include this slight diversion.

La Grand Place was top of the list and it was en route to Vimy where there was an extensive trench line I was eager to visit.

"What a cute car!" I had stopped next to a Citroën 2CV in the municipal car park. Petra jumped out to walk around and peer in the windows.

"That's what I want when I grow up." Indeed it was quirkily charming and so very French. This particular model had a sunroof made out of the same fabric as the deckchairs in our back garden and like a l'oignon could be peeled all the way back to the boot, exposing the seats made of tubular steel covered with the same material. The flat, two-spoke steering wheel appeared to be made from the same stock. The whole of the interior including the dash and steering wheel was spray- painted creamy yellow, like the colour of a bottle of Gold Top milk. There were rudimentary designs of flowers spread across the bodywork. The contrasting colours added to the pleasing ensemble. This was a sign of times to come. What if the flower power 'hippy' thingy had its genesis in Northern France rather than Haight-Ashbury?

Now there is a thought to contend with.

The car was so basic it could have been designed by a child. No need for a garage, just put it back in the Dinky box for the night.

My daughter knew a thing of beauty when she saw it. The venerable 2CV, in spite of widespread derision from the motoring press, exceeded all expectations. A surprising commercial success, demand was so strong that at one point there was a five-year waiting list and used cars were selling for more than those bouncing fresh out the factory gate.

Following a leisurely stroll and refreshments in La Grand Place, admiring the medieval square lined with historic buildings, we set out for Vimy.

The town itself is unremarkable but the Battle of Vimy Ridge was fought on this site, and close to the Canadian War Memorial there are well-preserved trenches and fortifications that I was interested in seeing, an enthusiasm not shared by Phoebe or Petra.

"Just a quick look around, won't take long." To sweeten the diversion I told them I had a treat lined up when we got to Vienna. While they strolled around the Memorial I went down the trenches.

The utter insanity of WW1 has always troubled me, millions killed to satisfy the inflated egos of a handful of leaders deluded by the scourge of nationalism. Here, in this field, Canadians shipped from new world ports came to die. Just in this tiny corner of the killing fields there were over ten thousand Allied casualties and an unknown (probably higher) number on the German side.

Such futility is hard to comprehend.

Walking in the Canadian trenches in a trance-like state I put myself in the boots of a young soldier fresh off a Manitoba farm wondering how the fuck he ended up in this hell-hole; perhaps he volunteered because his buddies signed up or he was persuaded by the crude propaganda designed to appeal to his sense of loyalty to the 'Old Country', to go halfway around the world, fight on a foreign field in a conflict he did not fully understand with nothing to gain and everything to lose.

Feeling like I had depressed myself for long enough I walked back down to rejoin P&P at the memorial and we headed back into town. Almost too late to find us digs for the night but we did eventually manage to secure a room at the Hôtel Rafael.

The small lobby was reminiscent of the one in the Pink Panther movie starring Peter Sellers (one of my faves) where the classic "Does your dog bite?" scene was shot.

Our room at the top of the building was less than salubrious. The 'fleur-de-lis'-patterned wallpaper was faded and peeling at the joins. There was a strong smell of mothballs. The furniture and fittings appeared not to have been replaced or indeed much moved since the Germans had been billeted there during the war. The en suite was more en corridor and was shared by any number of guests.

Still, we were happy to have a room for the night and not to have to resort to the Hôtel Rouge.

Petra was asleep and we laid her on the sofa, covering her little body with a double-folded blanket. Exhausted by the events of our first day on the road we, too, were soon fast asleep. Rising early, energised and ready to continue our adventure, we left the Hôtel Rafael in search of breakfast.

At the Café de la Gare I ordered coffee, croissants and pain au chocolate. While we waited for the waiter (grumpy in spite of himself) to bring our food I flattened a crumpled leaflet Petra found under our hotel bed from which we learned that back in 1802 the Emperor Napoleon had ordered the roadsides planted with plane trees so that while his armies marched on their stomachs they also benefited from shade over their heads.

This thoughtful gesture was much appreciated by the Wehrmacht in 1940.

Only about 35 miles to the Belgian border, anxious to get some miles behind us, we checked out, leaving Vimy and the ghosts of 'The Ridge' behind.

The frisson of leaving France was immediately dampened as we approached the Belgian border. The immigration and Customs officials in their sombre uniforms emblazoned with intimidating insignia had the expected effect of casting a shadow, albeit briefly, on our happy cocoon. A generic fear of uniformed authority and the vague feeling that I must be guilty of some unspecified transgression rose in my throat.

"Vat ist der purposs ov your visit?" asked the uniform, smiling in a welcoming way.

On edge for a moment I thought about trying to explain but verbal ejaculation dribbled out. "Holiday."

Surely this young border guard posed no threat and was just like the rest of us clowns, preoccupied by the mundane and trivial.

Phoebe handed over our documents. His hooded eyelids widened slightly, pupils visibly dilated as he saw the light blue 'travel document' covertly sandwiched betwixt Her Majesty's royal blue passports. This demanded his full attention.

The muscles at the corners of his mouth relaxed, allowing gravity to do its work. His expression became stern as he put on his "don't fuck with me, I/we mean business" face and opened a large, black ledger, running his fingers down the columns, then shuffled some papers to give himself time to ponder his next move.

In flowing script on the inside cover of a true blue, two-window British passport is a request to let pass without hindrance and to render assistance to HM's subjects should they encounter difficulties abroad. Failing which, the threat of a flotilla of gunboats showing up on your shores is strongly implied.

My pale imitation offered no such assurance; in fact, it all but disowned the bearer, warning in a bold font that should the holder find him/herself in some kind of foreign difficulty you are on your own, Jack! Do not come awhinging to HM government as you will not get a sympathetic hearing.

The guard examined my document closely and picked up the phone, presumably to call for backup. My breathing became increasingly shallow and erratic.

Palms began to leak as I strove to maintain an air of nonchalance.

A squad of menacingly attired and heavily armed gendarmes did not surround our car and I was not dragged away to some internment camp for the stateless.

Back in 1972 I had applied for British citizenship and after many months of waiting, I received a curt letter from the Home Office, aptly based in Lunar House, Croydon, informing me that my application had not been successful. No explanation was given.

I should have been a pretty solid candidate: never out of work, paying taxes like a good drone. I could only surmise that the couple of juvenile interactions with the local bobbies had queered my pitch.

Dashing off a letter to the Chief Constable asking for a detailed account of my 'criminal' activities of record was less than helpful. In due course another short but very formal letter arrived telling me that it was not policy to convey that information – even to the perpetrator.

So, here I sat in fearful agitation waiting for the inevitable grilling prior to the return of my document.

Judging by the thickness and weight of gold braid on his cap, shoulders and sleeves, a much higher-ranking older man with a kind face joined his subordinate in the booth.

He had a large bar of dark chocolate (with nuts) in his hand and residue between his teeth. Examining my document carefully, a short exchange followed as they held up the photo page, peering down at me.

Apparently the likeness was close enough and all was in order.

The official stamp came down hard on the visa page.

Snapping off a few squares of chocolate, the senior officer offered them to us on the foil wrapper. We accepted gratefully and rolled into Belgium.

A collective sigh of relief wafted through the car as we munched on the squares, agreeing that even the French (given a choice) would prefer Belgian chocolate.

As the miles passed by the girls settled into a contented reverie.

The Kingdom of Belgium is difficult to define: Poirot, Mercator, lace and chocolate come to mind. If England is a nation of shopkeepers then Belgium is a nation of gardeners. They are to be seen countrywide bent over, diligently prodding the dirt with their hoes.

We were happy to leave the Kingdom and lay siege to the German frontier.

Directed by a sharply featured and uniformed German policeman to join the line of cars, we waited to complete the inevitable border formalities which would be conducted with customary efficiency, alas without chocolate or welcoming smiles.

My travel document was scanned briefly but did not raise the expected additional scrutiny and was returned without a murmur.

The culinary delights of the fatherland have always been high on my list of 'proper' foods: the wursts, schnitzels and cabbages sour and sweet, steaming bowls of Sauerbraten and potatoes cooked in variously interesting ways.

Apart from sampling the rib-sticking food, the other major attraction was the German speed limit, or rather the lack of one. I wanted to push the car to see what it could do.

We did both, as well as sampling a variety of beers, strudels and gateaux rich in substances normally associated with clogging of the arteries.

I managed to crank 129 mph out of the car but even at that terrifying speed (at least for the girls!) the Porsches and BMWs still passed us at an alarming rate.

It was time for a stop; easing into the slow lane (if there is such a thing in Germany!) we slipped up the next exit ramp at random. The top offered a left or right option; the left sign indicated 8k to Bad Soden, and the other 5k to Sheitzenburg.

Which would you pick?

It was a serendipitous choice. Bad Soden looked not unlike a fair-sized German provincial town organised and laid out haphazardly, indicating it was a burg of some maturity.

As a bonus the unmistakable sound of 'oompah' music wafted in on the late-afternoon breeze, mingled with the mouth- watering aroma of roasting meat no doubt carefully basted by cheery, rosy-cheeked, buxom wenches.

The image on the St. Pauli Girl beer label came to mind. An insipid brew much loved by tourists, avoided by the natives in droves who preferred brands with more body and proper German-sounding names like Löwenbräu and Bittedrinken.

The town seemed to be full of people and parking the 'Roten Hotel' was almost impossible: had to backtrack a half-mile or so to find a space.

We walked towards the centre of town, drawn by the music and the delicious smell of Wurst on the Barbie.

The town was abuzz with what seemed to be a medieval festival.

This unexpected diversion had promise.

Mingled within the crowd were grown men wearing Lederhosen, white knee socks and silly hats with a clutch of feathers attached to one side or t'other.

Dressed in complementary fashion, the Damen wore the dirndl, which consist of a bodice, blouse, full skirt and apron. They were uniformly well rounded, robustly built, with superior upper body strength giving them the ability to lug around eight steins of beer with easy grace.

The plaza at the centre of town was the site of what can only be described as a 'circus' without elephants. We strode into the scene trying to take it all in.

There displayed was the 'Bearded Lady'; granted, she did have a heavy 4 o'clock shadow but the obviously blatant application of additional clumps only cheapened the effect.

The 'Strong Man' made heavy work of lifting unlikely loads accompanied by much grunting and grimacing. Ingeniously, when 'Samson' (as we immediately named him) hoisted the classic two black iron balls connected by a pole, it sagged dramatically.

A convincing demonstration of German engineering, leaving the credulous with the impression that there were some Newtons involved.

Could anything be taken for granted? Certainly not here, not today!

The ageing contortionist put a brave face on it as he creakily manipulated himself into a fairly passable pretzel. Random acts of juggling were to be seen everywhere.

A small band of dwarves colourfully attired as jesters passed through the crowd.

We had walked into a bizarro fest. So much going on that it was hard to focus – an unintended result, maybe, which pickpockets were happy to take advantage of.

"Keep a good eye on your bag, Phoebe." I shifted my wallet from back to front pocket.

It seemed like a good opportunity. I put the mask on; what with all the weird stuff going on it would be unremarkable and would go unnoticed except by my family. Phoebe looked at Petra and there was a synchronised rolling of the eyes.

"Your dad is wearing that stupid mask again."

They had no idea what this tatty, old mask was capable of and for years had put up with my disconcerting ways, adding this behaviour to my long list of quirks.

Amazing what you can get away with as a 'displaced' person.

And there he was! Although looking much older and somewhat stooped the resemblance to AH was striking. Adolf was conducting the band. At least that is how it seemed to me; logic would dictate it could not be him, nevertheless, the likeness was uncanny.

The moustache black, without a sign of greying, tight-fitting Lederhosen plainly outlining the testicle containing the seeds of a new master race, white woolly knee socks snug in a pair of shiny black boots with a hint of alpine design. Not a stranger to vanity or hair dye, the straight, dark forelock described a diagonal across his forehead. No hat.

The image would be recognisable to anyone who had paid any attention to 1930s news footage of AH strolling around the grounds of the 'Berghof', soaking up the sun and the adulation of cronies and sycophants. Or anyone who had ever watched the 'grey channel' as (much later) my dearly beloved young son Danzig would call the History Channel.

In case you are wondering, he was not named after the heavy metal band Danzig, rather after the old name of the city of Gdańsk (ceded to Poland by Germany then back to Poland), home of the Solidarity movement founded and fronted by Lech Wałęsa, the man who lit the fuse and was largely responsible for the beginning of the end of the Soviet Union and its domination of Eastern Europe, a true hero of the people.

I nudged Phoebe. Slightly hysterically I indicated in the direction of the bandleader. At this time he was facing the music (or not if he really was AH!) with his back to the audience. Wielding the baton with gusto he truly did have the affectation and mannerisms of AH at a Nuremberg rally.

Phoebe looked at me quizzically: "What?"

"Do you see him?"

"Who?"

"Hitler, right there, conducting the band!"

"The whole band kind of look like him." I had not noticed but on closer scrutiny indeed each member of the band had at least a slight resemblance to the leader; not quite the genuine article but an extended family group of AH doppelgängers.

"Wait until he turns around!"

With a splash of cymbals the 'ooompah' came to a crescendo. AH spun on his heels to loud cheers and shouts of "Heil!" Taking a bow, did he just extend his right arm at 45 degrees or was he just acknowledging the audience? Snappily he lowered his arm and seemed to look right at me, nodding curtly as if to say, "I told you so."

The memory continued to haunt me. I was unable to shake the image of the Corporal.

The whole experience was starting to bother me and I wondered if I was becoming slightly unhinged. I thought about dumping the mask but could not bring myself to do it. Folding it carefully, I put it back in my pocket.

If it was a look-alike, then it was a breach not only of good taste but blew a hole just below the waterline of the popular notion that the Deutsche Volk had been bamboozled by the Corporal.

Obviously AH still had some fans, at least in this neck of the Schloss!

Somewhat stunned by the surreal events in Bad Soden, bellies full of Bavarian brews and stuffed like sausages with sausages, we dawdled our way back to the car.

"Did that really happen?" Phoebe said to nobody in particular, looked at me quizzically.

As I am a 'nobody', but harboured delusions of adequacy, I answered dryly, "They say travel broadens the mind but mine has been flattened and twisted like a six-lane Möbius strip!"

I was prone to making pompous, trite, obscure statements.

"What is a Möbius strip?" asked Petra.

Unable to forgo the opportunity to display my intellectual superiority to a six-year-old I demonstrated the principle using the car's seat belt, explaining that it is a surface with only one side and one boundary component so that if an insect were to walk along the length of this strip, it would return to its starting point having traversed the entire length of the strip (on both sides) without ever crossing an edge.

"What is it for?" asked Petra.

It was a good practical question, and as I had no answer I slipped the car into first and made a big show of being a thoughtful and courteous driver as we headed back to the autobahn, bound for the Austrian border.

Vienna plays an important role in European culture. A city full of intrigue, grand architecture, museums and galleries, steeped in history, cursed by geography.

As we approached our hotel near the centre of the city on this bright and crisp morning I could not help but notice how unhappy the Austrians seemed to be, conservatively dressed in drab colours, heads downcast, avoiding eye contact with us and each other. They went about their lives seemingly unable to find joy or satisfaction in a life many would consider privileged.

Perhaps they were still mourning the loss of the empire or being 'good' Catholics were doomed to suffer having surely sinned in some fundamental way and had no right to happiness.

The burden of original sin sits heavy on pious shoulders.

Are the wretched Austrians not aware that the soul is scrubbed and all is forgiven once the penitent mumbles a few Our Fathers or Hail Marys?

Must have been a great racket back in the old days when indulgences were sold and the Pope commanded the masses.

The Germans, contrary to expectation, were a much jollier bunch, which was odd for a nation with a large Protestant minority denied the salve of absolution.

Unknown to the family I had made reservations at what I considered to be a pretty swanky hotel in Vienna. I chose this particular venue for our short stay because it was centrally located and had an indoor rooftop pool which I knew we would all enjoy.

I strived to keep us on the 'go': distraction was the name of the game.

Anything really to delay the big event. At quiet times, I tried to imagine his visage. The face was in constant flux, the features would not settle in my mind. I squinted at the old, grainy photo that I carried in my wallet but could not sharpen the image. Do I resemble him in any way? Will he see himself in my face?

I gave Phoebe the address of the hotel and asked her to navigate. The maps we had were old so after a number of wrong turns and a great deal of cussing on my part we eventually drove up the curved driveway, stopping at the entrance. A rather paunchy uniformed doorman with a feather in his cap (what is it with the feathers?) greeted us from the top of the short stairway.

He made me think of Hermann Göring dressed as Der Jägermeister, the portly foppish yet nimble head of the Luftwaffe. A fully paid-up member of the silly hat club, his wide-brimmed felt bonnet boasted more feathers than Robin Hood's quiver.

HG was a peacock and loved the trappings of power (especially the dressing-up bit). Like Kenneth of Barbie he had an outfit for every occasion, so while hunting on one of his country estates (kindly donated by a wealthy Jewish patriarch in exchange for an exit visa) he would always be nattily and appropriately attired for the occasion.

The doorman (as befitted his title) opened what he thought was the passenger's door and was confused momentarily by the steering wheel, quickly recovering from this slight jarring of the psyche to waddle around the front of the car to open Phoebe's door.

She exited gracefully. I handed the keys to the doorman who in turn passed them to a 'varlet' – we walked into the lobby followed by the bellboy laden down with our scrappy mishmash of holdalls I optimistically referred to as luggage.

Although the façade was a bit baroque the interior was all slick glass and marble.

The check-in procedure should have been easy but my faux passport caused the (by now) expected interrogation. A small clutch of hotel workers lined up to feast their eyes on that rare commodity. The proffered Amex card confirmed my liquidity and normal service was resumed.

The big surprise for Phoebe and Petra would be the fully climate-controlled rooftop swimming pool. I was keeping this significant detail from them, but in my excitement I let slip some reference to 'a pool' which was immediately pounced on by Petra – "So Daddy, is there a pool? Where is it? There is nowhere to put a pool here in the middle of the city!"

The 'bellboy', a slight, stooped man in his fifties, uniform trousers at odds with his white socks, showed us to our suite.

In a futile effort to maximise his potential he resolutely demonstrated the correct operation of the curtains, TV and telephone, pointing out the light fixtures and coat hangers while amiably chatting away in Austrian German. We nodded and grunted at approximately appropriate times. I slapped a 5-Schilling note in his outstretched hand and escorted him to the door, both of us talking at each other like the aliens we were. Gently pushing him out into the corridor, thanking him deeply with unmistakable hand signals and pats on the back.

I took a quick tour of our new digs.

Pretty nice, two rooms – a dedicated bedroom, the other a sitting room with a sofa bed for Petra. Yet, yet there was something odd about the whole arrangement. The main bathroom was hotel-appropriate: toilet, shower, bath, sink. The second toilet area off the sitting room contained a bidet and a sink – who says the Austrians don't have a sense of humour?

The elevator had a dedicated button right at the top of the panel with a figure depicting a 'diver' of indeterminate gender plunging into squiggly lines. Petra pushed the button, doors closed and we began our ascent to the roof.

What a delight! A good-size pool covered by a cast-iron and plate-glass structure reminiscent of the Crystal Palace in SE London. The pool itself was ultramodern, in keeping with the rest of the hotel, a mix of old and new, pleasing to the eye with good utility.

There was no one else in the area; nevertheless, in the manner of German tourists in Ibiza, we commandeered three loungers, carefully arranging our stuff to ward off encroachers, before plunging into the warm, clear water.

Our private frolic was interrupted by the arrival of a short, round gentleman looking not unlike Nikita Khrushchev (without the mole) and his companion, a much younger woman in her early thirties.

'Escort service' flashed through my head. Leggy with short, wavy, blonde hair, even Slavic features, pale, almost ivory skin with a fuchsia-pink slash of a mouth.

Mr. K, befitting his appearance, greeted us loudly in Russian, his booming voice reverberating around the enclosure.

Demonstrating my multilingualism I repeated his words back at him. He responded in his native tongue with a long sentence ending in what seemed like a question.

"I'm sorry – I do not speak Russian," said I in my poshest English voice.

"Iz OK! I speak de English perfekt," responded Mr. K. "Are you on de 'oliday?"

His companion, languid with disdain, viewed us with suspicion verging on contempt, the kind of look you get when you know she would have been happy never to have set eyes on us.

Mr. K seemed amiable enough and we chit-chatted a little before we both realised that there was nowhere to hide. He introduced his wife Natasha; she nodded coolly in our direction, flipping the pages of a glossy magazine absently, a flicker of a smile creasing her radioactive lips.

I introduced my family and admitted to being on a holiday without revealing the core reason or destination. Loudly, as if he suspected I was hard of hearing, he explained that he and his wife were returning from some agricultural conference in Leipzig and had stopped off in Vienna for a bit of R&R.

Wearing dark blue Speedos more appropriate to the Black Sea resort town of Sochi (not renowned for its palm-fringed, white, sandy beaches dotted with tiki bars) than a fancy hotel in Vienna, he continued in some detail about his trip, demanding the attention that I grudgingly gave. I imagined him in an ill- fitting blue-grey suit standing on the podium in Red Square, absently waving his Panama hat (a gift from Fidel?) at the precisely aligned columns of marching troops.

The image would have been complete if he had whipped off his flip-flop and started bashing it on the bar!

The sledgehammers were ready to go to work. Unknown to me and my new Soviet friend Reagan would simply ask Gorbachev to "tear down this wall" and soon thereafter the wall came tumbling down. In the meantime, Mr. K continued to harangue at length, feeling the urge to educate me on the USSR's agricultural policy, yields and quotas etc, huge advances in horticultural sciences, its ramifications on East/West relations.

The USSR effectively dissolved itself in 1991.

If his five-year plan was to drive us away from the pool area, he was way ahead of schedule, succeeding admirably, at least, in that respect. We picked up our stuff and returned to our suite to prepare ourselves for a night on the town.

Apart from history and 'culture' what has Vienna got for the tourist with limited time and resources? "How about Prater Park?" This suggestion got popular approval so we got directions from the front desk and headed out.

Prater is a large park in Vienna's Leopoldstadt district. One of the main attractions is the wooden Ferris wheel, believed to be the oldest in the world. The nightly light display is also rumoured to be worth seeing.

A few minutes of leisurely strolling while window-shopping took us to the park.

I am not particularly fond of 'tourist traps' but Petra was excited and Phoebe was happy to go. The big wheel was the big draw: for its age and method of construction it was impressive. P&P lined up for the ride. I declined and sat on a bench nearby.

A shaby, older gentleman sat down next to me, panting as if he had just outrun a fat gendarme.

I sized him up without making eye contact.

He had beautifully asymmetric features; a contemporary reference would be Stephen Fry, a discouragingly clever bastard. I feel great kinship with this flawed genius (his mother was a Hungarian Jew) and our views on important matters correspond neatly.

Well dressed (for a tramp), I thought, as befitting a prosperous city that took care of its less fortunate citizens.

Catching his breath, he said, "How are you enjoying my beautiful city?" Surprised by his perfect English, it took me a second to figure out how he knew where I was from, the *Frommer's Guide to Austria* in my hand may have given him a clue.

I would have called him Mr. Tramp but he took the trouble to introduce himself.

Klaus-Peter Drumpf had been a high-flying lawyer and had got involved in some kind of Ponzi scheme leading to his disbarment, disgrace and divorce, the details of which I could not quite grasp. Why he would reveal his life in such detail to me, an imperfect stranger, I do not know.

"Have you heard of Donald Trump?"

"Is he a friend of Hugh Hefner?" I thought I read somewhere that he attended one of Hugh's parties at the Playboy Mansion.

"No, wait! I remember now, he is some kind of rich businessman from New York married to a woman from Russia."

"You are half-right, my friend." Klaus-Peter pivoted towards me, tapping his handsome antler-topped cane on the leg of the bench.

"Indeed he is a property developer but his wife Ivana is from Czechoslovakia. He and I were business partners."

I had no reason to doubt this statement and could only nod feebly. Should I be impressed or horrified? Klaus-Peter was convincing. Knowing very little about Trump, his family history or his business practices, I listened in silence. KP ran through a summary of his dealings with his partner and it was plain he felt that he had been left holding the bag for Donald.

I took it all on face value.

While P&P rode the Prater Ferris I listened with interest to Klaus-Peter. It was a tragic story of rapid descent from a position of power and influence to the soup kitchen and street life. He hinted that the fiend of avarice had been unseated by alcohol and street drugs. Speaking in a monotone, showing no emotion, he told me how his partner, friends and family had abandoned him at the nadir of his life. I detected no bitterness in him, only resignation and acceptance reflected in his gentle eyes. We came from different worlds yet for a brief moment we were one.

He from a place where everything was possible, and I from a place where butter was an extravagance. Capitalism had lavished riches upon K-P, but when life put a few potholes in the road, he stumbled. His words affected me on a fundamental human level. This chance encounter touched a raw nerve and was profoundly moving to me. Sitting right there on that bench in Prater I struggled to keep from crying.

Who can say they have never been dragged through the mud and dumped in the shite?

Klaus-Peter laid a hand on my shoulder and comforted me, softly telling me that all was well and as it should be. Feeling foolish, dabbing my eyes, I quickly regained my composure.

My expectation was that at some point he would ask me for money and I had been prepared to help him in some small way.

In the end he asked for nothing other than someone to talk to, a sympathetic ear, and I was happy to oblige. With the help of his cane Herr Drumpf stood up, bid me good luck and walked away in the direction of life.

The next day we would be in Hungary.

Bags were repacked.

The 'bellboy', referring to previous experience, knowing that I was a light tipper, did not show so we lugged our luggage down to the lobby and checked out.

The 'Rot Gesthaus' was waiting out front.

This was the last leg – one more frontier to cross and we would be in Hungary.

Can I call that land home? In short, 'no' is the answer, it is where I was born but most of my life has been spent in England and if you knew nothing about me you would take me for a regular Brit. I have become expert at finding common ground and fitting in wherever I happen to find myself. When asked where I'm from, as I often am, I say London.

Yet there was a need, a yearning to discover something of my roots. As far as my ghostly father was concerned, I knew I was dawdling, equal parts curious and afraid. What does the word 'father' mean, or 'home' for that matter?

These are abstract terms to me. I live in the world and have many fathers.

Was I merely the fruit of that tree he shook vigorously back in 1945? Did he cast his pregnant lover aside like an old shoe? Did Gita end the relationship? Or were there factors beyond their control that caused the separation? These were some of the questions I needed answers to.

Is 'home' where you were conceived and have abandoned to memory?

Is 'home' the land that accepts you freely, nurtures and educates?

Our mother made her choice and we could do nothing to affect the outcome. Would it be reasonable to expect a parent to consult their children in matters of life and death?

The newborn is a hostage to geography. If you are born into a Christian community, you will join the ranks of the faithful. The madrasa will have the child nodding like a demented robot. The cracks in the Wailing Wall will be grouted with prayer notes left by children dressed exactly like their forefathers.

The child has no choice: swallow the faith pill and conform, or risk rejection.

Apostasy is treated with various degrees of harshness from informal shunning through excommunication onto death in some of the more extreme religions.

To a lesser extent, patriotism and adherence to unshakeable tenets based on inherited beliefs or tradition are enforced by threat of either divine retribution, peer pressure, coercion, ostracism, denouncement etc.

What compels our parents, teachers, tribe, clan or country to infect young minds, perverting their humanity? That is the big question that needs to be asked.

Is this the work of the Devil?

The newly minted are doomed by the ones that love them by passing on their prejudices and superstitions, greasing the axle of ignorance.

Is this the work of the Devil?

We repeat the errors of our forefathers and learn nothing from history. How can we break this cycle?

People die for faith and country without understanding what/why we/they are sacrificing or being sacrificed for.

Is this the work of the Devil?

If I believed such nonsense it would be easy to lay the blame for all our troubles at the cloven hoof of the 'horned one'! Truly, we can only blame ourselves.

CHAPTER 15

THE FINAL FRONTIER

Aglow with excitement, tempered somewhat by a nagging apprehension. Would I meet him today? I knew that if I found Laci he would be very happy to see me; not so sure about the 'father', though. No turning back; there was only one way to go.

I pointed the car east. We had about 50 miles to the Hungarian frontier.

The border crossing routine held less anxiety for me now as I had a secret weapon: I could understand well enough and speak a little of the lingo. And I had Petra, my beautiful, charming daughter; her childish innocence and gentle smile had proven to melt the coldest border guard's heart.

There were two cars ahead of me. On either side of the barrier were tangles of barbed wire, a graphic reminder of my previous journey 33 years ago in the opposite direction.

Phoebe handed over the passports to another fresh-faced, blue-eyed 'boy' barely out of school.

He opened my 'book' and noted my place of birth: Budapest, Hungary. Wished me a 'good day' in Hungarian, appeared pleased when I had the appropriate response.

"Yu 'ave a bootifully dauta!" he said, practising his English, smiling toothily.

Obviously sarf London had replaced Russian as the compulsory second language in state schools. This was good news.

Visas examined and passports stamped we were released. In my eagerness to get away I stalled the car, attracting unwanted attention from well-armed lethargic border guards. I restarted the engine, and drove away smoothly.

We needed food, having had nothing but a couple of boiled sweets since early breakfast. I pulled into a roadside eatery.

Hungarian food never fails to disappoint. Lumps of unidentifiable meat drowned in goo, as was on offer here or at fancier restaurants high in pretence (one of the three 'P's to avoid; the others are pedantry and pomposity), the same meal could be had with flowers and a tablecloth at more than twice the price.

Served with clumpy rice or soggy potatoes, the generous portion sizes distracted from the poor quality of the nosh. This meaty concoction steeped in mysterious juices was widely believed to be able to loosen the most chronically impacted bowels.

Sadly, these establishments are everywhere. I avoid them whenever possible.

Today was not one of those days.

The cosy little restaurant across the street looked inviting; glancing at the menu board outside, it was in four languages: Hungarian, German, Russian and English.

This meant that there would be something mind-numbingly boring to eat for the average tourist. Perfecto!

The 'greeter' (who we found out later was the owner) scuttled out and was cloyingly obsequious. He unleashed a frightful grin. The perfectly aligned gleaming uppers sited over a yellowing tangle of aged enamel hinted at a work in progress.

Eagerly pouncing on the opportunity to transfer much-needed tourist money from my pocket to his, he showered me with broad-spectrum compliments, finally settling on Petra, going on about how lovely she was. I dared not disappoint him; we entered the dimly lit cellar.

Downstairs it was a fairly large space, looking as if it could have once been used as a taproom. We were ushered to and seated in an arched alcove.

"Velcome, velcome!" The owner hovered, producing three menus open at the English page. Filled our water glasses. Moved off.

The set lunch offered:

Peas soup with smoked substances.

Stick-cooked chicken with potatoes and vegetables.

Cake of the house.

The waiter came over ready to take our order. Dressed in traditional garb... at least convincing enough for the punters. Pencil poised.

"Vat yoo vant eat?"

I responded in English. "Vat do you recommend?"

He naturally assumed that I did not speak Magyar and as the owner passed our alcove the waiter mutters over his shoulder, roughly translated, "Look at this idiot, he is wearing a 'Kis Dobos' badge." I had pinned this symbol of the Young Communist to my jacket when approaching the border and had completely forgotten about it.

I ordered two lunches and a pizza for Petra.

The 'peas' soup was orange in colour and contained nothing resembling a pea; the smoked substances were another enigma. Still, it tasted good.

The entrée or main was chicken chunks on a wooden skewer with chips and a mêlée of unidentifiable vegetables cooked to slop known locally as lecsó, the Hungarian ratatouille.

The cake of the house was Black Forest gateaux with a dollop of ice cream on top.

While waiting for the waiter to return with my change a tipsy Gypsy violinist appeared as if on a tight schedule. The bill settlement was cunningly delayed until the fiddler had a go at a bit of extortion. Emoting sadly behind his thick handlebar moustache (made popular by Kaiser Wilhelm II), he laid into his fiddle imploring with cheerless eyes, mournful notes flying off his bow.

He had no idea the damage both emotional and aural that he was causing. As was my custom I tipped him lightly, hoping to send him on his way; undeterred he continued until I palmed a couple of extra coins into his pocket.

The address I was given as a possible starting point in the quest was out in a little village in the area known as the Puszta, the great Hungarian Plain. The land is devoid of geographical features, the sky only pierced by the occasional church spire.

The Plain is best known for its horsemen know as 'csikós', the Hungarian cowboys famous for their horseback tricks, descendants of the fierce nomadic tribes who first settled in these fertile lands who are now largely reduced to performing circus stunts for tourists.

Phoebe and I bent over a map spread out on the bonnet of the car.

I felt like Rommel planning a fighting retreat with the Desert Rats breathing down my neck, but it was only Petra chewing gum and panting noisily. The map was faded with age and heavily creased with use, the names of towns mostly unpronounceable, and the village we were seeking was nowhere to be found.

This was what we city folks refer to back 'home' as the 'sticks', even though in this case it was mostly grassland.

I knew we were close, at a crossroads with no idea which way to go.

Trusting to luck I turned left.

Dirt roads took us to a village which was just a collection of charmless buildings plonked down on the plain. Cunningly arranged, no doubt to confuse tax collectors and roaming commissars, there were no street signs or numbers.

They know where they live and have no use for indicators.

I was forced to stop and ask for directions.

A wizened old man with serious curvature of the spine pushing a perambulator was the only person to be seen. The pram was piled neatly with stacks of apples and plums separated by a piece of cardboard.

"Excuse me, sir!" I ventured politely. He ignored me and kept pushing. Dogs started to bark as if sensing the presence of outsiders. I got out of the car with the address on a scrap of paper and fronted him.

Louder, "Excuse me, sir!" The dogs also turned up the volume.

He was so crooked that he had to raise one leg and swivel sideways to look at me.

Holding up the scrap of paper I asked him in halting Hungarian to please point me in the right direction. He mumbled at me unintelligibly for some seconds, revealing a mouth totally bereft of teeth.

I wondered how he tackled the apples.

Glancing at the top line on my bit of paper he pointed to a neat, freshly painted house with a well-tended garden. There was a small lorry parked to one side under an awning made of reeds. All he needed was the name. Without further ado he bent himself to his task and went about his business, pushing the battered pram squeakily down the road. By sheer luck we managed to stumble not only on the right village, but also almost on the house itself.

I parked in front of the truck and got out to knock.

The door opened a crack and when my eyes adjusted to the gloom I could make out a lady around fifty – hard to gauge as the rough country life had taken its toll – dressed in a full skirt, white embroidered blouse with bell sleeves, her head covered by a traditional scarf.

As best I could I told her who I was: the door opened wider as her smile grew broader. Flinging the door wide open, she lunged at me. I struggled to breathe as this woman clasped me to her bosom, raining kisses on my head and face. I assumed that this must be my 'aunt', Mrs. Dombi.

Stunned by such an unexpected display of emotion, I rocked back on my heels and she fell on top of me. There was much tittering from the car.

We untangled ourselves and stood up grinning at each other, brushing the powdery dirt off our clothes as we sized each other up.

She had heard that we were on our way, from whom or how was not readily apparent.

Her husband appeared from a shed at the bottom of the garden, coming to see what all the fuss was about.

"Welcome, welcome, please come in." He seemed a little unsteady on his feet and there was the unmistakable aroma of alcohol on his breath. I waved to the girls to join us. Phoebe and Petra were also greeted warmly and we went inside.

More greetings and hugs were followed by insistent invitations to stay.

I had not wanted to trouble them, but could not refuse their kind hospitality. I talked to the girls and they were fine with this unexpected diversion. They agreed it would be churlish not to stay for a night.

The modest house was neat and clean. My mother claimed this lovely lady Eva to be my aunt but I had never heard her name mentioned until a few days ago. She bore no physical resemblance to Gita and, unlike my mother's, her place was squeaky clean and well ordered. Somewhat of a domestic diva putting me in mind of the likes of Martha Stewart. Denied the benefit of corporate wealth and ready access to single-use gadgetry cunningly crafted by Ronco (which inevitably would join the charred wooden spoons and rusty egg slicers consigned to the back of the bottom drawer), she managed to keep her house in showroom condition.

Without children, she devoted her energies to domestic duties and keeping her husband out of jail. Meagre resources were trumped by imagination, ingenuity and sheer creativity; the interior of the house was a showroom for the Arts and Crafts movement.

She provided us with wonderful, tasty meals and a comfortable place to sleep.

The girls shared the spare room. With the addition of goose down quilt and pillows the large sofa in the living room was made into a comfortable bed for me.

It came as no surprise that her husband Jeno was a feckless drunk. Our arrival only served as an excuse for him to uncork the plum brandy, once again pouring a generous shot for himself with a little taster for Phoebe and me.

With much drunken gesticulation it eventually became apparent that he made his living by hauling stuff around in the small lorry parked outside.

From livestock to scrap metal he moved and traded anything, ducking and diving like a Magyar 'Del Boy'. A 'man and a van', 'off his trolley in a lorry'. When his services were in demand or there was some petty larceny afoot he would leave before dawn, having partially sobered up from the night before, returning at the end of his day unable to walk a straight line, his driving skills somehow unimpaired.

Mrs. Dombi clucked and fussed but was resigned to her fate and just got on with it.

On day two we explored the village. This took about 45 minutes. To describe it as bleak would be generous. Granted, there was a central square with a small church and a couple of down-at-heel café/bars. The waiters stood idle and the priest prayed alone.

Indeed, Mrs. Dombi came up with an address for me – the last known for my father.

Itching to get going yet we felt obliged to stay a second night to keep our host happy.

She and the girls were enjoying each other in spite of the language difficulty, busying themselves baking and making, preparing food and laughing at the folly of men.

I sat with Jeno in the living room, indulging in the very folly the ladies found so amusing.

We drank 'pálinka', the Hungarian moonshine which he distilled in his shed at the bottom of the garden. I had no idea that this was common practice countrywide and, although illegal, the police did not bother to pursue the bootleggers if small quantities were involved and consumed in-house. It smelled like rubbing alcohol with a hint of unidentifiable fruit, could have been plum or apricot; after the first shot it really didn't matter. I kept up with Jeno as far as I could, a safe distance from the table centrepiece, a candelabra worthy of Liberace in which flickering candles of various shapes, colours and sizes had been whittled down to fit the receptacles. The table arranged with her best china and flatware all matching, Mrs. Dombi had pulled out all the stops.

Three shots was my limit.

Jeno drank steadily without noticeable effect.

I, on the other hand, seemingly in the time it took Jeno to refill his glass, had become a pixilated clown. My eyes refused to focus. Words slurred past my lips. The distillate also shifted my politics alarmingly to the right. I listened to his litany of woes and found myself in ready agreement with his 'line 'em up and shoot 'em' political perspective. This was the last refuge of those lacking ideas or solutions and pitifully, for tonight at least, I was one of them.

What drives men/women to seek solace/answers in a bottle or some form of chemistry?

For me, it may be summed up in one word. That word is 'fear'. I know this is simplistic and one may argue that there are many factors at play here; granted, we are complex beings, our electrochemical processes mysterious and our psyche bewildering.

I think for me it is the fear of failure, of not reaching one's potential due to some real or perceived failing or inadequacy.

Safe in my zip-up pocket, snuggled next to the mask, was my father's last known address. We packed up our stuff and said our goodbyes to Mrs. Dombi – Jeno came reeking out of their bedroom and said his bleary-eyed farewell, before shuffling back to his bed. Thanking Mrs. D for her kind hospitality, we drove away in a cloud of dust.

Our destination was the Hotel Gellért in Buda where I had reservations.

Situated on the west bank of the Danube, at the foot of Gellért Hill, overlooked by the Citadella (a popular tourist attraction), built around 1850 by the Habsburgs to keep an eye on the revolting Magyars.

I drove down my old street heading west towards Elisabeth Bridge and Buda.

Since the last time I was here in 1956 traffic had increased significantly. Instead of APCs and tanks cluttering up the city, Trabants and Ladas clogged the streets.

It seemed that beige was the most popular colour; most of the buyers, given a choice, would probably go for any other, red, or electric blue perhaps. However, as far as the factory was concerned you were privileged to be allowed to own a car. Any deviation from the standard colour required a further demonstration of gratitude, in the form of cash.

The cars were churned out in impressively disorderly fashion, customer choice and satisfaction not figuring prominently in the master plan or high on the list of management priorities.

Hotel Gellért was an Art Nouveau extravaganza. No need for a rooftop swimming pool here as it was attached to the famous Gellért Spa and Baths which had an outdoor pool with a wave machine built in 1927 still in daily operation, largely unmodified to this day.

Before the forced march across the border, I had spent many happy hours wave jumping in this very pool.

As I recall, every hour a bell would ring and the wave-generating machine would be turned on for ten minutes or so. This would be the signal for the oldies to leave the turbulent shallow end and for kids to frolic in the artificial surf.

What happy times those were for me, oblivious that I was living in a Soviet satellite state teeming with discontents, seething with anger, blissfully unaware of the storm clouds gathering in the eastern sky.

The hotel had seen better days. Staff and management did their best vacuuming the faded and worn carpets, polishing the metal fittings and making the furniture smell nice. Travel guides described it as having 'charm and character', a handy euphemism for an establishment engaged in a heroic struggle to keep its 3-star rating.

The bellboy insisted on calling me "My lord" so reluctantly I overtipped him on the basis that that is what a Peer of the Realm or a deity would do.

We had a nice, roomy room, high ceiling, big windows overlooking the car park, with an extra bed wheeled in for Petra.

It was getting close to dinner time. Unpacking hurriedly, we returned to the front desk looking for a restaurant. While walking through the lobby holding Petra's hand I was accosted by several young, well-proportioned and heavily made-up ladies. In between taking black tea and nibbling small cakes they complimented me on having the good sense and genes to produce a pleasant-looking child. This strangely perverted notion is commonly held among the Magyars. In a largely paternalistic society women, it seems, contributed little to the external appearance or IQ of their progeny.

Phoebe, being a bit smarter and a keen observer of humanity, declared these charming, friendly ladies to be hookers.

Of course she was right; around seven each evening the night shift began to filter in and the trolling for prospects began. International trade and investment from abroad was starting to ramp up and the hotel was full of foreign reps and dealmakers. Natural prey for the lobby ladies.

The next day, while waiting for the ladies to get ready, gazing out of our window on this beautiful sunny morning I noticed three men circling the 'Red Hotel' warily, as one would an alien craft unsure of the space visitor's intentions.

I called out for P&P to come and see. "Watch this!" I pushed the remote unlock on the fob. The clunk of the doors unlocking, the tap on the horn with the flash of all four indicators and headlights stopped the three in their tracks. We laughed and ducked below the sill. The three men were joined by two others, forming a committee to discuss the event. Surrounding the alien craft they continued to circle warily, edging closer, arms outstretched as if expecting to make contact with a 'force field'. When the moment seemed right I pushed the lock and arm button. They recoiled, alert for encounters of the fourth kind, perhaps a 'tractor beam' snatching one up as a specimen destined for internal probing with extraterrestrial implements.

For some reason this struck me as hilarious and my laughter infected the girls.

The committee below reconvened by the driver's door for further analysis and discussion. I then locked/unlocked the car randomly; this childish mischief threw their well-reasoned theories into disarray.

Eventually they got bored, gave up and left. Strange how this incident brought us closer together as a family; shared laughter is indeed a panacea.

Ah, the power of Western technology, good for a laugh.

Tantalisingly close to my personal goal, many questions starting with 'what if' once again rose. After 34 years, what if I waited one more day?

Until the news of his illness I had not given much thought to my biological father; he was nothing more than a grainy photo, a second-hand memory.

I mused that I may well have been the unwitting gooseberry on their romantic encounters, snug in the belly of the beast. So this newfound desire to be in his physical presence was puzzling to me. I was hoping that the meeting, if it actually happened, would provide all the answers. I was very uneasy about the whole affair.

In the meantime, I found another diversion.

I decided to knock on Laci's door before my father's. Excited about seeing my childhood friend we headed towards our old building at 82 Rákóczi út. Even if he did not live in the same corner flat maybe someone knew of his whereabouts.

We grew up together and were inseparable in boyhood; I played with him almost every day. He taught me chess, I taught him how to spit great distances. He taught me the value of friendship, I instructed him in the intimate details of female anatomy (as I knew it). His teachings had lasting value, mine were soon exposed as the product of an overactive imagination. Seemed like a fair exchange at the time.

Also, I was curious to see if the plastic wallet in the tin box under the stairs was still there after all these years; even without monetary value it would be a nice souvenir and a tangible vestige of an interrupted life.

Driving around looking for a space to park in the square I stopped in front of the church and was momentarily transported. Standing to attention in my crisp, white shirt and short trousers, lined up with the rest of the Little Drummers waiting for Gomba to shuffle through the creaky church doors. The memories come flooding back. Nothing much had changed except that there were no symbols of Communism to be seen.

The cross was back on the top of the spire.

"Are you OK?" asked Phoebe.

"Yes, I'm fine, just having a bit of a flashback." She pushed me for more.

I told her about the Little Drummers and what went on in the square.

As the words formed on my lips, tears welled up in my eyes and I mourned in silent remembrance for my old life. A confused, desperate little boy behind a man's eyes.

The square was just a couple of blocks from my building in Rákóczi út.

I asked the girls to please wait in the park and enjoy the leafy shade, swings and slide while I went to see if Laci was around or indeed still lived in the building.

Rounding the corner I was again overcome with emotion as I approached the big, wooden doors, the crazed brown paint exactly as I remembered it. Stepping through this dark portal was like entering the twilight zone; a noticeably cooler shadow loomed over me, a shiver ran up my spine and for a brief moment I was unable to move.

Memories jostled one another as I recalled a panorama of unconnected images.

Two Gypsy women squatting in the doorway, modestly hidden by their multilayered skirts as they peed on a pile of builders' sand, chatting cheerfully, unabashed by the disapproving looks of passers-by.

Street musicians of varying quality and entertainment value would strike up in the courtyard; a regular feature was a man cranking a music box of some kind, partnered by a monkey dressed like an Ottoman Turk, complete with a red fez and curly-toed slippers. The ape sitting on the 'musician's' shoulder was trained to collect the newspaper-wrapped coins thrown from the walkways by those that enjoyed this momentary diversion. Others not swayed by the mechanical melody aimed their missiles at the entertainer, he and his simian sidekick taking avoiding action whenever necessary.

The string quartet that played Bartók and Mozart on battered instruments with great flair and emotion, the balconies lined with appreciative listeners.

Standing in the middle of the courtyard I looked up and turned, slowly drinking in the moment, letting the random memories bubble up.

For a moment I was lost to this world.

The slamming of a door snapped me back.

It was time to dig up the cache under the stairs.

As I got closer it was plain to see that things had changed.

The soft dirt that had yielded easily to my childish excavations was now replaced by sharp-angled concrete. It would have been fun to have witnessed the discovery and reaction to the note I included with the cash. I had the local posse in mind in case by chance one of them unwittingly stumbled onto the hidden loot. I had not anticipated that the old, wooden stairs would be replaced.

There is no way to know whether the incantation had any effect but when I slipped the note into the wallet there was a part of me that believed Gypsy hexes were particularly potent. In childhood my mother certainly did nothing to dispel the power of the Roma, often threatening to sell me to the next caravan that happened to clatter by. I lived in fear of that possibility and had great respect for the power of their curses.

The first-floor corner flat bore the name Dvorák Lászlo under the doorbell; Laci is the diminutive of Lászlo.

He still lived there.

I pushed the bell and waited nervously – nothing, then a second time with insistence.

How could there be no one home? My emotional state and high expectation overcoming rationality, he was probably at work. I'll come back later, I thought. As I turned to leave there was the sound of a latch being thrown.

Laci opened the door.

It took me a moment to realise that this boy standing before me could not be my old friend. He looked just like him, but unless the Commies had discovered the elixir of youth and conspired to keep it from their enemies, this boy was not him.

Laci Junior (he had his father's name) stood and listened as I explained who I was and what I wanted. Surprisingly he knew of me and I enrolled him in a bit of subterfuge; swearing him to secrecy, I told him that I would come back later in the day, after Laci Senior got home from work.

"If you see his car outside the building then he is home." That sounded reasonable. "What car does he drive?"

"He has a Trabant." Now there was a surprise.

"What colour is it?" Another surprise!

Back in the park P&P listened to my story patiently and with shared enthusiasm, even though this quest of mine had little to do with their idea of a continental holiday.

We walked to Gundel's Patisserie to sample their well-renowned, artery-clogging cakes accompanied by delicious espresso. The marble-topped tables were waited on by lovely ladies who at first glance appeared to be dressed like French maids from a West End farce.

We lingered over coffee and creamy pastries, each bite stiffening the blood. To kill time I suggested a stroll to Városliget (City Park) where the giant bronze of Uncle Joe had stood.

"This is where my hero fell." They looked at me blankly.

"I was here dancing on Stalin's chest, scratched my name on his arse and picked up a piece of his nose."

"Where is it? Do you still have it?" asked Petra.

"I don't know what happened to it, probably left behind like a lot of good stuff."

I was thinking about my carefree Communist youth and the plastic wallet.

Around 6.30 pm seemed like a good time to catch Laci home from work. I left P&P at the park again and walked towards my old building.

There were several Trabis parked out front, all of them beige. One of them had to be his. I walked up the marble steps, rang the bell.

Laci Junior opened the door. Index finger on lips, I made the universally understood sign for silence.

He grinned and called out, "Someone to see you, Papa!"

Laci came to the door, looked at me, back at his son, then back at me. His eyes seemed to bulge slightly and a shadow passed over his brow. Squinting, as if unable to believe his eyes for a long second. He took a half-step back and wobbled on his feet. Relishing this moment, I stood grinning inches from his face. Then, as if a light bulb came on in his head he lunged at me.

We fell into each other's arms speechless with joy, awash in tears.

How exquisite it was to be reunited with my dear friend after all these years. He had aged (as had I), yet the even features, blond hair and blue eyes so beguiling to old women and young girls were as I remembered them.

His wife Anya came to the door and we all jabbered excitedly. Wiping away tears I remembered the girls in the park.

"Please bring them up, we want to meet them!"

I hurried down to fetch them.

Introductions and hugs all round. Laci Jr. (who was about 10) took Petra to play in his bedroom. Grinning broadly, not knowing where to start, the four of us sat looking at one another. After a moment of awkward silence Laci's wife Anya took Phoebe by the hand and led her to the kitchen. As Laci and I sat beaming at each other, they set about preparing dinner, another activity in which language was no barrier.

In halting Hungarian and fluent English (which he understood well enough) I told Laci my story and listened to his.

"When my parents finally let me out of the flat I went looking for you. As you know there was total mayhem, no one answered your door and I had an awful feeling that I would never see you again." His eyes welled up as he recalled the moment. Shifting uneasily in his chair, he continued. "People were afraid to look over the ramparts. Those that still had doors shut themselves away, venturing out only when in dire need of supplies. After the purges and ÁVH round-ups things started to return to 'normal'. If your neighbour vanished you kept your mouth shut. We lived in constant fear."

Taking a good gulp of wine, hand slightly atremble, he smiled in a boyish way. "We just had to carry on, what else could be done? I did miss you, my dear friend."

Our lives had taken totally different paths yet the warmth and love between us was undiminished.

We were interrupted by a voice from the kitchen. "Would you two please lay the table?" A real, home-cooked Hungarian dinner of Paprika Chicken with dumplings, red cabbage flavoured with caraway seeds and honey, parsley potatoes with melted butter washed down with a couple of bottles of Bull's Blood was the feast laid before us that night. We chatted and drank the wine, a robust red which my forefathers would guzzle before manning the battlements to pour hot oil on the Turks.

The many invaders had left their mark: the Romans, most notably plumbing, baths and roads; the Mongols not too much, terror and fear only leave scars; the Turks, many things, predominately minarets and mosques (most now rebadged as churches, the houses of worship experiencing a resurgence as the grip of Communism loosened, fear of the regime edged out by dread of eternal damnation).

The need for a powerful supervisor was deeply embedded.

The last invaders, the Turks, had captured and held large tracts of Magyar territory, even setting up a Pasha in Buda, the Ottoman tide ebbing and flooding over the centuries until the Habsburgs finally ousted them in the early 18th century.

We drank the Bull's Blood and toasted our ancestors: the wine flowed and stories were told. It seemed, in direct proportion to the amount consumed, the tales became taller, the tragedies deeper, and the older we got, the better we used to be.

After dinner over a glass of sweet Tokaji we recalled happier childhood moments. I had no idea that Laci held me in such high regard, seeing me as a 'man of action' (I found this hard to digest!), himself as a stay-at-home plodder.

As a demonstration of my bravado (at least in Laci's eyes) he told the story of an older kid who frequented the park where we used to play football and generally do what in England is known as 'mucking about'. This kid terrorised us and the other denizens of the park to the degree that our games of footie were played with less than full attention, one eye constantly on the lookout for this bully.

We were all shit-scared of him.

This is what happened, as told by Laci.

"We were going to the park looking for a game, your father and I." He looked at Petra to make sure he had everybody's full attention. "Walking towards the slides by the sandpit we spot our tormentor, easy, as he is bigger and taller than the other kids. Even at a distance you can tell that he was indulging in a bit of casual violence."

Laci looked at me: I was amazed that he remembered this event so vividly.

"Your papa tells me to keep walking and get ready to run... we approach steadily, he (the bully) sees us, totally at ease, comfortable in the knowledge that he has nothing to fear, watches quizzically as we approach. When about 10 metres away your papa does a little shuffle, changes his stride, I think nothing of it; what I did not know was that he was 'measuring his steps'. When he came within striking distance like a coiled cobra, he struck without warning, landing a well-aimed, mightily effective punch right on the nose of the bully. Then he shouts, 'RUN!' We bolt like rabbits." Laci did a little running motion with his arms.

"At a safe distance we stopped and looked back. The bully has picked himself up and was now on his knees, blood pouring through his fingers as he cupped his broken nose, howling!"

Wide-eyed, Laci sat back, looking at me for confirmation.

I nodded in agreement. It was a true account. He did not need to know that on that day terror gripped my throat, and if you paid close attention you would have heard the distinctive sound of castanets emanating from an area roughly halfway between the feet and pubis.

I had to get home, the punch had dislocated my wrist and like the wimp I really was I needed my mama! It was a reckless act, but it worked.

We never saw him in our 'hood' again.

Lacikam – literally 'my Laci' – had, according to him, a much more 'normal' life, if there is such a thing. After regular school he attended a technical college to study electrical engineering and had been employed by a state-owned factory all his working life.

Commuting to work on the crowded tram, he was smitten by a beautiful young woman who routinely travelled in the same carriage to her place of work.

"He courted me for months, I ran out of excuses not to go out with him." Anya topped up our glasses. "He was a handsome man and persistent, wore me down until I agreed to marry." She smiled wistfully. Phoebe and I just grinned, not able to discern the feeling behind her words. Was this a fond memory or a regretful one?

They inherited the corner flat after the death of his parents; his father died after a short illness, mother followed within weeks. Almost immediately Anya became pregnant with Laci Jr., their only child.

The conversation got onto the subject of cars and I told them about my little caper in the hotel car park.

Laci and junior got a bit animated about my car and wanted to see it. We walked down to the square where the Red Hotel was parked.

"Do you remember this place?"

"Of course, this is where we used to listen to Gomba spewing his bullshit."

Laci and I exchanged knowing looks.

The small, leafy park surrounding the church looked neglected.

"Do you remember, Laci, how clean this used to be? There was not even a cigarette butt on the ground! Now look at it…"

We walked through the park to the other side of the square and there it was all red and shiny. He and junior stood wide-mouthed, eyes feasting on the seductively curvy lines of the Red Hotel. I popped the doors so that they could climb in and be awed by the technology of the capitalists.

"She is beautiful." Father and son laid their hands on the shiny machine as if it were an object worthy of adulation.

"What car do you have, Laci?" I already knew the answer.

He looked a little agitated, paused, stared off into space. "I have a Trabant."

I smiled smugly.

Laci through gritted teeth: "Do you have any idea what it took me to get that car? Eh-eh?"

I think he may have been a little annoyed with me.

As we walked through the park back to our building he told me how it worked:

The prospective buyer contacted the factory (there were no showrooms) and arranged to pay a sizeable deposit. This put your name on a waiting list where your money languished, accruing no interest, devalued by inflation, sometimes for years. Then as time passed and your order was finally being cobbled together, the distributor contacted the would-be owner who may, by now, be suffering from dementia and have little use for motorised transportation, being incapable of finding his slippers and had all but forgotten about the dream of joining the traffic jam.

A letter would arrive out of the blue; a phone call would have been easier but the request for the instrument and landline was in process, having been only ordered as recently as five years ago.

Formally and with great ceremony 'the letter' would demand the purchaser be at the distribution centre at a given date and time.

The fortunate few, the chosen ones (those that were still alive and in reasonable control of their faculties), were permitted to pay their balances in cash, the price adjusted for years of inflation, handed a receipt, some document indicating that the car was not stolen and the keys to motoring bliss.

Finally and most importantly, a grid reference denoting the parking space that their very own, less than shiny new car was occupying. This item was crucial as the uniformly beige and precisely parked rows of Trabants were impossible to distinguish. Granted there were a few red ones dotted about the parking lot.

The effects of sun, rain and a steady breeze had taken their toll and the red pigment was already reverting to its natural colour, beige.

This process was comfortably taken for granted by all concerned.

The 'Trabant' was built in the DDR supposedly as a rival to the Volkswagen, one of the bestselling cars in the world, which, unlike the 'Trabi', benefited from good design and solid German engineering unfettered by Communist ideology, and was churned out by the millions across the border in West Germany. The Communist version of the People's Car was designed by committee, with liberal use of recycled materials, not because they were ahead of the curve in that respect, far from it; in fact the two-stroke engine in the early versions was probably responsible for putting a large number of holes in the ozone layer. The DDR had their own version of the KGB, the much feared and hated Stasi operating on a similar basis to the Hungarian ÁVH, both rewarding informers, spreading fear, suspicion and mistrust among the population. Oppression did nothing to bolster enthusiasm in the quality control department. The 'Trabi' was totally unencumbered by 'extras'; if you wanted to 'sassy' up your drive with a rear-view mirror, a set of rubber mats or wallow in the luxury of a heater, you were on your own, comrade! There was a thriving black market in these premium items, a baby step towards free market capitalism. I am told it was wise to remove your wipers before leaving the car parked as it was highly likely that when you returned they would be gone, along with any other external items that may be readily removable, such as mud-flaps!

No wonder everyone gawked at the Red Hotel whenever we stopped at a light. We were positively mobbed by the curious Magyars when parked, the gleaming paintwork lovingly admired.

Junior was pushing Petra ever higher on the swings. Phoebe sat on a nearby bench watching her daughter giggling with mischief. Laci and I walked over to the front of the church and faced the steps leading up to the big, wooden doors. We stood in silence. I laid my arm on his shoulder and pulled his earlobe gently.

"My dear friend, I hate to say this to you, but I miss those days. You know, the marching around, Gomba and his quirky ideas, the naïve certainty of our lives and the football. How comfortable were our lives, it all seemed so easy to us. There was this awful structure to our lives, we trusted our parents and listened to our leaders. Ah, the sweet simplicity of it all."

He nodded. "You know, Ati, I think most people remember their childhood as a time of carefree wonder, but I can tell you that your mother did the right thing, brave beyond doubt." Maybe the right word would be reckless, I thought, but said nothing.

He continued, "After you left without a word it took a while for me to realise that you were gone, just like that, poof! I never expected to see you again and I am overjoyed to have you standing here with me in this square and welcome you and your family as my guests."

I echoed his sentiments and suggested he, Anya and junior should come and visit us in London.

I waved at Phoebe, pointing to my watch. It was time to go. Laci and I made arrangements for all of us to drive down to Lake Balaton after I had concluded the main purpose of my visit.

We strolled back to his flat, said our goodbyes to Anya; hugs and kisses all round.

Laci and I locked eyes for a moment before I turned to go. "See you in a few days, my old dear friend." I resisted the urge to correct him.

We walked back to the parked car in silence. On the drive back to our hotel Petra said, "I like your friend, he is very nice."

"Yes, he is, darling, I did not realise how much I missed him."

It was Saturday night and the lobby was lively. On the corner stage there was a set-up for a band, the lobby ladies were plying their trade, drinks were flowing and negotiations underway.

Large men in dark suits unobtrusively patrolled the floor alert for signs of trouble.

The intoxicatingly heady cocktail of wine, women and the absence of adult supervision would turn accountants and lawyers into werewolves.

Physically tired and emotionally drained, we went up to our room. The band kicked off at 9 and I needed a short nap if I was going to catch some of their set. The girls were fast asleep when I awoke at 9.30, splashed some water on my face, brushed my teeth with the electric toothbrush (still working) and went down to the lobby.

Now I have seen a lot of second-rate bands and indeed have been in a few myself, but this was truly pushing the boundaries of mediocrity. The frontman and rhythm guitar had a passing resemblance to Elvis without the benefit of the King's lush head of hair and sans the sequinned jumpsuit.

The 'band' were called 'The Tartars'. It said so on the bass drum and they did have a lot of sauce inflicting their 'music' on a captive audience. The bass guitarist affected the look of a young Paul McCartney with the collarless jacket and mop-like haircut. His instrument hung so low that he could barely reach the 'G' string. The 'lead' played a cheap imitation of a Sunburst Fender Strat and looked like he would be more at home with a fiddle under his chin down at the local csárda.

The drummer (unlike me) could keep metronomic time and had studied the rudiments well but was totally wooden and uninspired. The sum of these parts gave me an excuse for an early night.

Tomorrow was my father's day.

CHAPTER 16

THE MEETING

I had the address and good directions. The city map was on Phoebe's knee, she navigated me to the location. My stomach was churning.

Slowing down I cruised past the building, went around the block then returned and parked across the street. Looking up at the small, five-storey apartment building I nervously gripped the steering wheel. It was not too late, I could just drive away. "Just go, it will be fine." Phoebe patted my knee by way of encouragement.

I turned at the entrance and looked back at the girls before walking through the door.

The lobby was gloomy, had a dusty, neglected feel to it. There was an old-fashioned elevator with metal cross-hatch sliding doors, next to which was a glass-fronted board displaying the names of the tenants. There it was, Strohmeyer Janos, no. 8, fourth floor. Unlike some of the other names the lettering was faded and looked undisturbed.

A palpable fear gripped me. What would I find? How would I be received? Should I even be here? Racked with doubt I returned to the car.

"You must not give up, this is what you came for, there is nothing to fear." Phoebe and Petra both coaxed and chastised me gently. I returned to stand in front of the name board again. The elevator descended to the lobby and ground to a stop. It was empty.

Taking this as a good omen I opened the double doors, entered and pressed number four. Taking a deep breath I composed myself as the lift shuddered to a stop. Noting the freshly polished brass nameplate on the door, I spun the mechanical bell.

Presently the door was opened warily by a small, sprightly woman dressed as if she was about to leave, hat, coat, deeply veined hand resting on a wicker shopping basket with black rubber wheels.

We were both taken aback slightly.

In halting Hungarian: "I kiss your hand" (a formal greeting). "Does Strohmeyer Janos live here?"

For some seconds her face was impassive, then she spoke.

"Have you come to measure the windows?"

"No, are you Mrs. Strohmeyer?"

"Yes, who are you?"

I asked her again, "Does Mr. Strohmeyer live here?"

She narrowed her eyes. "Yes he does. Who are you and what do you want?"

I didn't know what to say, so just blurted out: "Your husband is my father!"

She squeezed her eyes shut as if to dispel a bad dream.

When she opened them I was still there.

"What are you talking about? It is not possible!"

"Please give me a moment to explain."

Visibly shaken, she listened to my story.

"I cannot allow you to come here and upset him, he has been very sick. Wheelchair, doctor, routine." These were some of the words I heard.

I was unable to absorb what she was telling me. Perhaps I had misunderstood her due to my poor Hungarian. I repeated myself, thinking maybe she had not understood what I had told her or had mistaken me for somebody else.

The set of her jaw indicated that there was no mistake.

Mumbling under her breath, she started to swing the door. Unbidden, my right foot stepped over the threshold as she tried to shut the door. Totally flummoxed, we stood stupefied for a long second.

For the first time she looked at me directly, searched my face. Seeing the anguish that must have reflected in my eyes, she said, "Come back tomorrow at 11."

I retrieved my foot. She shut the door.

For a moment I stood bewildered before taking the stairs down and walked back to the car. Hiding my emotions I told the girls that all was well and that I had to return the next day when they would be prepared and ready to receive me.

Thinking…What now? Why should I, a total stranger to my father's wife and likely a painful reminder of past mistakes, expect a joyful 'Hollywood'-style reunion? What right did I have to presume a fairy-tale outcome?

It was certainly not how I imagined the unfolding of this moment.

Deflated and disturbed I resorted to food as a distraction.

"Let's go and get some lunch." I moved the car to a side street nearby and parked. In silence, we strolled somewhat aimlessly for a while. I think P&P sensed my distress and left me to my thoughts. We walked towards another culinary disaster.

The following day at the appointed time I presented myself at the Strohmeyers' flat; my father's wife let me in and led me silently to a small room near the front door.

"Coffee?" I nodded. She left the room, heading, presumably, for the kitchen.

I sat nervously. The sound of a radio from an adjacent room, a mixture of news and classical music, filtered through the wall. I waited.

Mrs. S returned with a tray set with fine china cups with dainty handles, coffee pot, sugar, spoons and vanilla wafers; seemed like they didn't have a lot of people dropping by. I thought she may have been enjoying this opportunity to give her best china an airing. In awkward silence she poured coffee; I sat and waited for her to speak.

"I think it will be all right for you to see him… but you MUST NOT tell him who you are, I don't want to get him upset."

She must have given it some consideration the previous night. "Take this." In her hand was a tailor's tape measure. She looked at me intensely; I leaned forward to be sure I missed nothing.

"Your father has sat in that wheelchair for the last 15 years listening to the radio, rarely leaving the flat. His welfare and comfort are my priorities. You will go next door and pretend that you are the man we have been expecting to measure the windows for new curtains. Do you understand what I am asking from you?"

Taking the tape measure from her outstretched hand I nodded, drained my cup, and stood ready to do her bidding. She opened the door to the sitting room, indicated for me to enter, turned and walked away.

Stepping into the room, from the corner of my eye I saw a man sitting in a wingback armchair, a plain, dark green blanket covering his legs. My nerves were shredded but I remained, at least on the surface, icy-calm.

Intent on the radio, he paid me scant attention.

I avoided looking at him, but took a quick scan of the room. It was a good-sized space sparsely populated by chunky turned furniture more appropriate to a country manor than a flat in Budapest. The curtains were tatty, held back by grubby, frayed rope straps hanging at the side of the two large windows. I went to work.

Dragging a heavy ottoman over to the window, I started taking random measurements.

I could feel his eyes boring into my back but there was no reaction from him. No doubt he was wondering what the world was coming to – people walking into your flat without so much as a "Good morning!" standing on your Turkish heirloom with their smelly socks.

The news segment finished and they started playing Beethoven's 5th which I felt was appropriately dramatic for the occasion. Fussing with the curtains I continued to take inappropriate measurements. Altering my vantage point ostensibly to effect a more precise measure, I again glanced around the room. There was a tapestry on the wall above his head depicting a mounted knight in shining armour impaling a winged dragon with a lance. The image jarred me back to Bexhill-on-Sea and Father O'Reilly. Seemed like a few lifetimes ago.

He sat intent on the music. A wheelchair was parked in a corner.

As the music rose to dramatic heights he shut his eyes and raised his head. I took the opportunity to look him over. Serene, composed, youthful, angular features, good skin tone. Perhaps in his late-sixties, early seventies, lush head of white hair, alert in a detached way and immobile.

Having exhausted the measuring charade I stepped down from the ottoman and briefly locked eyes with him. There was no sign of recognition.

I rejoined Mrs. S in the small room next door. She was fidgety, rattling the cups on the tray as she tidied up.

Was this it? Had I come all this way to merely look at him, and he not knowing who I am? Hard to live with that possibility, yet out of respect I felt obliged to follow Ingrid's wishes.

Mrs. S, Ingrid, was not being unkind, just cautious and protective of her husband. Standing at the threshold I turned to face her. Wistfully she confirmed what I already suspected. The wartime affair that meant so much to Gita, this man who was the love of her life, saw her as no more than a dalliance, a diversion from the horrors of war. And yes, he may have loved her, who knows? I was prepared, so I thought, to hear this but coming from her lips in a 'matter-of-fact' way was another blow to my already bruised psyche.

Gita would never hear of this.

"I have loved your father since the day I met him, but I must tell you that your mother is fortunate to have escaped this wretched regime and the burden of the last 15 years caring for that wonderful man sitting in that room." She lowered her voice. "Go home and tell your mother I would gladly trade places with her."

I had nothing to say: this was an unexpected revelation and all I could do was stand and blink like an idiot.

Starting to weep gently she searched my face. She dabbed her eyes and sighed, "We deserve a better world, Ati."

It was very sad, and as her tears flowed I took her in my arms and hugged her frail body, gently stroking the back of her head. The radio in the next room masked her stifled sobs.

I felt as if I'd turned up for the Isle of Man TT in my leathers wearing flip-flops, totally unprepared for the emotional hornets' nest that I had stirred up.

"Come back tomorrow at the same time." She wiped her eyes and, smiling weakly, shut the door. I took the stairs back to the street.

Walking back to the park I was confused, disappointed and deflated. Seeing me approach, Petra ran at me arms outstretched and jumped, wrapping her little body around mine. The clouds lifted and the sun shone once more. That child is so precious to me, a mere look could brighten my day.

"Let's DO something, Daddy!" On a whim I suggested driving out to Lake Balaton. I had been a bit selfish and realised I had left them sitting around in various parks waiting for me for hours. Phoebe resumed her role as navigator and we headed out of the city.

Hungary is a small country and outside Budapest the traffic was light; in a couple of hours we were shoreside. Why not kill two stones with a diet, as they say. Maybe I could find the villa that used to belong to Julius. I had a rough idea of its whereabouts.

A leisurely drive took us to the likely location. I felt sure we were close but due to the hilly nature of this bit of the lakeside all the lanes looked similar. Not wanting to give up having come this far, I persisted for a couple of hours, even asking what I took to be locals – but no joy. We gave up and headed down to a café next to a small marina.

I asked the dockmaster about renting a sailboat. Would be fun to have Laci et al on a daysail.

We sat under the shade of a Heineken umbrella and sampled a local beer. A platter of Hungarian tapas, peppery sausages, cheese, salami and gherkins were unceremoniously dumped on our table.

Back at the hotel the working girls nodded and smiled at us as we made our way through the lobby; we had become family. There was a cordoned-off area in the corner guarded by a large man in a suit standing in front of a small, unlit sign which said, 'Casino'. How come I had not seen this before?

The girls headed off to the elevator and I to the gambling house. I wasn't too sure about the dress code but I felt I was suitably attired. A long-sleeve white shirt and chinos were deemed suitable and I was granted access. In the tunnel leading to the casino there was a slight downward incline and a sharp dog-leg to the left; the heavy swing-doors were opened by another man in a dark suit. Indeed I must be a "Lord" with all these people scraping and bowing.

Surveying the room, affecting the air of a rich boy coming home, I walked over to the blackjack tables.

Leaving P&P at the playground I walked back to my father's building, foregoing the clunky elevator and bounding up the stairs with a newfound lightness in my heart.

Ingrid, transformed, opened the door. Gone was the severe silver grey bun; her locks flowed and she was wearing a flowery summer dress. There was a hint of colour in her cheeks. The scarlet lips would do 'Rosie the Riveter' justice. I could see why my father was so smitten by her back in 1945.

The smell of coffee brewing and the soft sound of the radio permeated the apartment. Taking my hand, she led me into the small room and we sat, our knees almost touching. She looked at me intensely. A decision had been made.

"Now you will meet your father." Without letting go of my hand she walked me into the big room like the child I had suddenly become, leaving me standing in front of him.

I stared at the floor for a moment then raised my head to look at this man, my father.

Sitting regally in his chair, intent on the Strauss waltz swirling from the radio, he looked wistful, perhaps back to the time when the legs would do his bidding and he could swish Gita or Ingrid around the dance floor.

Suddenly he was aware and looked my way. I stood in front of him like a condemned man.

"Window man, have you the curtains already?" he asked in a voice one may adopt when talking to tradesmen.

I think I must have got down on one knee as our eyes were level when I said, "Papa – I am your son."

He blinked a couple of times as if activating dormant synapses.

"I knew it!" he cried. "If you were a real window man, then you would have measured the drop as well as the width." He laughed, exposing teeth the colour of American cheese.

I stood up, taking his age-mottled hand, and kissed his forehead. He tilted his head up and we looked at each other, a teardrop traced its way down his cheek. Seeing him weep, I could not hold back my tears. I covered my face with both hands and sobbed uncontrollably. Were these tears for what was or might have been? I do not know, it just seemed right that we bare our raw feelings.

Some minutes passed before we regained composure and as we wiped away our tears Ingrid returned with a tray of little open sandwiches, cakes and coffee… So distracted that for the moment I forgot about P&P. I told Janos that they were in the park. "Go get them, quickly." Ingrid went back to the kitchen to prepare more nibbles and I practically ran back to the park. Phoebe was studying the city map while Petra kicked a ball around with some local kids, reinforcing my belief that games, especially football, have no gender or language barriers. It seems to come naturally. How hard can it be to kick a ball around the grass? "Come on, let's go! Come meet my dad!" As the words tumbled out of my mouth I could scarcely believe what I just said.

It started to rain; we ran but were pretty well soaked by the time we got to the Strohmeyers' front door. Ingrid was all smiles and 'welcomes', ushering us in, finding towels to mop our heads and faces. Straightened up and drip-dried, they went off to the kitchen and I to the sitting room where my father sat quietly; while I was in the park Ingrid must have washed his face, combed his hair and changed his shirt. He looked newly energised, animated. Pulling up the ottoman, I sat directly in front of him.

"What happened with you and Gita?" I looked up into his cloudy eyes and saw my future. I could feel him now; for a brief moment we were one. Finally, he shrugged: my suspicions were confirmed.

"The war, you know, it was a very bad time, we got separated. I looked for her for many days, she just disappeared, no one had seen or heard from her. I feared the worst. The Russians were still rampaging through the city, no one was safe anywhere. During a lull in the fighting, a friend invited me to his house for coffee. That was when I met Ingrid." He paused for a couple of wheezy breaths. "I was a bit of a 'ladies' man' and easily seduced." He looked at me evenly, trying to gauge my reaction. "May I have a glass of water?"

I brought one from the kitchen. He took a few sips and continued.

"In the space of a few days the last of the resistance was neutralised and the Russians settled into their occupation. Budapest was in total chaos. My beautiful city was in ruins, unrecognisable to me. As soon as it felt safe I decided to go to my factory to see what it looked like, assess the damage, try and contact my workers. Just take the first steps to get it up and running." I had heard about this from Gita and already knew that my father owned a small factory making wood products, parquet flooring, panelling etc.

"It was a long walk, maybe 5/6 km. No public transport was running. From a distance the structure looked intact, just a few pockmarks from small arms fire. As I got closer an armed man came out of the building and watched me approach. This 'commissar' stopped me from entering my own building! Can you imagine?"

He had my full attention. All this was new to me. I was sure Gita knew nothing of this either.

He continued. "I tried to walk past him, but he pushed me to the ground. Through his legs, I could see leather-coated thugs ransacking my office. The Reds took everything. I was never allowed back into the building." He continued, eyes wide, palms upturned. "They would not even let me go inside to pick up my hat and coat. I could see them over the thieving swine's shoulder hanging on the hatstand just as I had left them weeks ago!" He looked at the floor. "Everything, including Gita, was taken from me."

Lowering his voice, he said, "Those Communist scum told me that everything now belonged to the 'people' and if I knew what was good for me, leave and don't come back. All those years of work, my livelihood gone." His voice trailed to a whisper. Looking away, he took a deep breath, composed himself.

"It was dangerous to remain. I was warned by a friend, a 'Party' member, that they suspected me of being 'an enemy of the people' and that I should disappear before I became one of the 'disappeared'. For my safety I left the city and stayed with relatives in the countryside. I did not know that your mother was pregnant and I never saw her again."

"Did you love her?" I was looking for a simple answer to a complex question and before he could answer me the ladies returned from the kitchen with food and drinks. I know he did not have a one-word answer and was relieved, as I suspected the long answer may not have been to my liking. I cannot judge this man, nor would I want to. Knowing what I did about my mother, it is entirely possible that she can be loved and despised within the space of a few minutes. It was a fruitless line of enquiry and I left it at that.

I was happy to be there and get a glimpse of this man and his life. He was pleased to see me and meet my little family, so pleased in fact that he asked me for a cigarette although he had not smoked for over fifteen years, since his unspecified illness struck him down. Ingrid forbade the cigarette, Janos insisted and eventually prevailed. Now there were three of us puffing away, me, Janos and Phoebe. Ingrid threw open the windows I had recently become so well acquainted with to let that wonderful, fresh, post-rain breeze waft in. I felt my mission was complete and left that small flat in Budapest at peace that day knowing that I would never see my father again.

On the very day we got back to London. My mother called.

"Georgie, did you find your father?"

"I did, Mum."

She could barely contain her excitement. "Well, tell me, what happened, did he talk about me?"

"Yes, he told me he loved you very much and did not understand how you two were parted by the war, it was a terrible time for him. He lost you and everything else in his life."

She listened in silence, but I could tell that she was choking back tears.

"He is exactly as you remember him, handsome, funny, charming. A lovely man, I am proud to call him my father."

I hung up the phone and looked in the mirror.

My father was looking back at me.

Janos Strohmeyer died peacefully in his sleep two months after our return to England.

"Hey, Kev, I want to come round later to pick Jessie up." I left the message on his machine. The events of the last three weeks were rattling around in my head and I needed to get back to my normal and that included having beloved Jesso at my side.

Meeting my father in the final days of his life led me to examine my own. There was no putting the genie back in the bottle, I had to make some drastic changes and seek my destiny. A desperate urge to abandon what I had and, as snug as it may have looked from the outside, life was killing me.

It was a dreadful thing but I had to leave. It was extremely painful to wrench myself away from the settled life. My main concern and the cause of most of my distress was leaving Petra. I still feel the guilt of that separation. Phoebe and I agreed to part on relatively friendly terms and I ran away to sea.

Two lives ended. One began.

EPILOGUE

It is revealing that this memoir is much more about my mother than my father. In spite of her many failings and often questionable decisions, my mother was a constant in my life and that of my siblings. We may have gone hungry at times but none of us were ever deprived of her unconditional love. There is a human tendency, a deeply rooted need, to find the embrace of one's parents. I have struggled greatly to find the 'right' conclusion to this memoir. What have I learned? Did it bring me comfort or just open old wounds? In truth, a measure of both.

Putting these words on paper has had some effect. If nothing else I do have a better understanding of who I am and why. By nature I remain an optimist and am fully aware of my situation and place in the greater scheme of things.

Yet somehow I expected this voyage to bring a minor epiphany or at least sharper clarity… alas, it has not. The waters are murky; roiling the bottom has not helped me to see where the monsters live. My personal experience and journey have shown me that, although the urge to reach out to an absent parent may be strong, one needs to be prepared to accept that it will not necessarily bring the expected closure.

So…"Wherever you go, there you jolly well are!" With apologies to Confucius!

Questions/Comments: thereluctantrefugee.com
thereluctantrefugee@gmail.com

THE RELUCTANT REFUGEE